Governing Borderless Threats

'Non-traditional' security problems like pandemic diseases, climate change and terrorism now pervade the global agenda. Many argue that sovereign state-based governance is no longer adequate, demanding and constructing new approaches to manage border-spanning threats. Drawing on critical literature in political science, political geography and political economy, this is the first book that systematically explains the outcomes of these efforts. It shows that transboundary security challenges are primarily governed not through supranational organisations, but by transforming state apparatuses and integrating them into multilevel, regional or global regulatory governance networks. The socio-political contestation shaping this process determines the form, content and operation of transnational security governance regimes. Using three in-depth case studies – environmental degradation, pandemic disease and transnational crime – this innovative book integrates global governance and international security studies and identifies the political and normative implications of non-traditional security governance, providing insights for scholars and policymakers alike.

SHAHAR HAMEIRI is Senior Lecturer in international politics and Research Fellow at the Asia Research Centre in the School of Management and Governance at Murdoch University, Western Australia. He is the author of *Regulating Statehood: State Building and the Transformation of the Global Order* (2010).

LEE JONES is Senior Lecturer in the School of Politics and International Relations at Queen Mary, University of London, and Research Associate at the Asia Research Centre at Murdoch University, Western Australia. He is the author of *ASEAN, Sovereignty and Intervention in Southeast Asia* (2012).

Governing Borderless Threats

Non-Traditional Security and the Politics of State Transformation

SHAHAR HAMEIRI AND LEE JONES

CAMBRIDGE
UNIVERSITY PRESS

CAMBRIDGE
UNIVERSITY PRESS

University Printing House, Cambridge CB2 8BS, United Kingdom

Cambridge University Press is part of the University of Cambridge.

It furthers the University's mission by disseminating knowledge in the pursuit of
education, learning and research at the highest international levels of excellence.

www.cambridge.org
Information on this title: www.cambridge.org/9781107110885

© Shahar Hameiri and Lee Jones 2015

First published 2015

A catalogue record for this publication is available from the British Library

Library of Congress Cataloguing in Publication data
Hameiri, Shahar.
Governing borderless threats : non-traditional security and the politics of state
transformation / Shahar Hameiri and Lee Jones.
    pages   cm
Includes bibliographical references and index.
ISBN 978-1-107-11088-5 (hardback)
1. Security, International – Social aspects.   2. Borderlands – Social aspects.
3. International cooperation.   4. Globalization.   I. Jones, Lee, 1981–   II. Title.
JZ5588.H35   2015
355′.033 – dc23   2015002192

ISBN 978-1-107-11088-5 Hardback

From Shahar Hameiri:
To my family

From Lee Jones:
To Allan Patience

Contents

Figures

Acknowledgements

We are extremely grateful for all the support – financial, intellectual, practical and personal – that has enabled us to write this book.

The research would simply have been impossible without extensive financial support from several bodies. The main funder was the Australian Research Council, through a Discovery Project grant for 'Securitisation and the Governance of Non-Traditional Security in Southeast Asia and the Southwest Pacific' (DP110100425). The research on Myanmar was funded by a United Kingdom Economic and Social Research Council grant for a project entitled 'How Do Economic Sanctions (Not) Work?' (RES-061–25–0500). We are also most grateful for financial support from the Association of Southeast Asian Studies in the United Kingdom, the Westfield Trust, Murdoch University's Strategic Research Fund and the School of Politics and International Relations at Queen Mary, University of London. Lee is also very grateful to the National University of Singapore and Stanford University for hosting him as the Lee Kong Chian Distinguished Fellow on Southeast Asia in 2014–15.

The project benefited enormously from some truly outstanding research assistance. We are particularly grateful for Dr Kelly Gerard's sterling work, which probably advanced the research by a full year. We were also very fortunate to be supported by Audriane Sani and Yodim Kusuma in Indonesia, Kyaw Thu Mya Han and Zaw Nay Aung in Myanmar, Mackenzie Tariobed in Vanuatu and Melissa Johnston in Australia. We also gratefully acknowledge the help of Khin Maung Nyo and Mathew Sheader in Yangon, and the willingness of our many interviewees – 125 in seven different countries – to take the time to speak with us. Tamara Dent and Sia Kozlowski provided excellent administrative support at Murdoch University's Asia Research Centre. Ingebjørg Helland Scarpello and Ashlee Jones were first-rate copy–editors, while Adam Sandor prepared the index.

x   *Acknowledgements*

We are both deeply indebted to our colleagues at the Asia Research Centre, Murdoch University and at Queen Mary's School of Politics and International Relations for their generous intellectual and professional support, which is hugely important for early-career scholars like us. They are outstanding models of collegiality who embody the finest aspects of academia. For specific comments and suggestions on our work we thank Stephen Gill, Sophie Harman, Kanishka Jayasuriya, Bryan Mabee, Tom Pegram, Jason Sharman, Fredrik Söderbaum, Garry Rodan, Phil Cerny, David Williams, Jeffrey Wilson and the anonymous reviewers of our previous articles. Three of Cambridge University Press's four reviewers also provided excellent comments on the manuscript that helped improve the final version. We are grateful to the Press's editor, John Haslam, for his consistent support, and to his colleagues who brought the manuscript to press.

Finally, we would like to pay tribute to our families and friends. Eschewing 'armchair research' to discover how things really work on the ground requires extended and repeated absences to conduct fieldwork, creating real challenges. Shahar would like to especially thank his amazing wife, Meggan, for her tremendous support during his time away in caring for their three young children, the youngest of whom was born while research for this project was in full swing. Without her, this book would not have eventuated. We thank all our loved ones for the companionship and moral support that make our work possible, and our lives pleasurable.

Introduction

In recent decades, non-traditional security (NTS) issues have moved from the periphery to the centre of the global security agenda. Problems such as transboundary pollution, epidemic diseases, transnational crime and terrorism, which are seen to have been intensified by economic globalisation, increasingly concern leading states (White House 2010; UK Government 2010; Australian Government PMC 2013), international organisations (UN 2004; EU 2003; NATO 2010), non-governmental groups and ordinary citizens. The latest United States (US) National Security Strategy proclaims: 'globalization has . . . intensified the dangers we face – from international terrorism and the spread of deadly technologies, to economic upheavals and a changing climate' (White House 2010: i). Similarly, the United Nations (UN) High Level Panel on Threats, Challenges and Change announced a 'new security consensus':

The United Nations was created in 1945 above all else 'to save succeeding generations from the scourge of war'. . . . [But] the biggest security threats we face now, and in the decades ahead, go far beyond States waging aggressive war. They extend to poverty, infectious disease and environmental degradation; war and violence within States; the spread and possible use of nuclear, radiological, chemical and biological weapons; terrorism; and transnational organized crime. The threats are from non-State actors as well as States, and to human security as well as State security (UN 2004: 1).

The identification of these transnational issues as 'security threats' suggests a certain logic to dealing with them. As the Copenhagen School approach to security studies argues, traditionally, to 'securitise' an issue means identifying it as a threat to some cherished referent object, raising it to the top of, or even above, the political agenda and mobilising extraordinary measures and resources to combat the problem (Buzan et al. 1998). Yet, in practice, NTS issues are addressed through a baffling variety of means which often do not resemble emergency measures and are frequently ineffective. The clearest example is the

1

effort to tackle climate change. Despite increasingly apocalyptic projections of global warming trends and their implications for international security, action has been limited, uneven and heavily contested (Rothe 2011). Responses range from total inaction to market-based 'cap and trade' emissions reduction schemes, carbon taxes and many more. Meanwhile, the implementation and efficacy of each policy is challenged at every step from multiple directions. The discursive presentation of climate change as a security problem is widely accepted (McDonald 2013). What is contested, however, is what kind of a security threat climate change is and what needs to be done about it; that is, its governance. Similarly, a comparison of approaches towards counter-terrorism and natural disaster management in Europe and Southeast Asia found that, despite being designed to tackle identical threats, the governance systems adopted varied widely, with no sign of convergence in sight (Pennisi di Floristella 2013).

Why should security governance take such myriad forms and produce such divergent outcomes? The answer, in a nutshell, is that both the definition of security and the manner in which security problems are governed are highly contested. The existing literature on new security issues largely focuses on conflicts over the definition of security, but neglects almost entirely the matter of how and why NTS issues are actually governed. Whether one views the rise of NTS as reflecting real-world changes that generate new threats (Dupont 2001; Brown 2003a; Mittelman 2010), or as a socially constructed phenomenon reflecting the agency of security officials or rising societal concern (Buzan et al. 1998; Bigo 2002; CASE Collective 2006), security analysts explicitly or implicitly expect a response from states commensurate with the urgent and dangerous nature of security threats. Yet very little of this literature explores how security problems, once identified, are managed in practice or how the systems established to manage them actually operate. That is, they neglect security *governance* (cf. Krahmann 2003).

This book emerges from our dissatisfaction with this treatment of NTS and with the general neglect of security governance. As a small group of scholars pioneering the study of 'security governance' have emphasised (see Bevir and Hall 2014), there is a qualitative difference between NTS and 'traditional' interstate security, which appears to require novel forms of governance and associated forms of politics. The traditional concept of 'international security', which concerns military relationships between states and state survival, reinforced the division of the world along the lines of territorial state boundaries. However, because NTS issues are typically viewed as transboundary in nature, they inherently problematise this division. Analysts and political leaders alike argue that sovereign state-based governance is no longer adequate and consequently demand new approaches capable of managing challenges that span state boundaries (e.g. Swain 2013). Accordingly, the questions of who will manage security, how and at what level are much more open-ended and contested than before. Thus, 'non-traditional' threats raise the possibility of 'non-traditional' forms of security governance (Bevir and Hall 2014: 17–26). Most security scholars overlook this because they treat NTS issues as just part of a growing 'laundry list' of states' security concerns and are disinterested in questions of governance.

Conversely, 'security governance' scholars observe that, particularly in the EU, as the identified range of threats and risks has widened, so have the actors and instruments tasked with managing them. Security policy formation and implementation are no longer the sole preserve of defence and foreign affairs ministries, nor are they constrained to the formal borders of sovereign states or multilateral organisations. Rather, to tackle complex problems that traverse such boundaries, power has been dispersed to other actors in the public and private sectors, and to levels above and below the nation-state (Krahmann 2003; Webber et al. 2004). Security is therefore pursued through 'multi-actor and multi-level forms of governance' (Schröder 2011: 34), involving 'administrative practices developed elsewhere in domestic and global governance, including markets, networks, joined-up or whole-of-government strategies and public-private partnerships, as well as old-fashioned, top-down rule by states and international organizations' (Bevir and Hall 2014: 26). These incisive observations – sadly ignored by most security scholars – characterise much of what is now done in the name of 'non-traditional security', as our wide-ranging case studies later demonstrate. However, the largely descriptive, 'pre-theoretical' literature on security governance provides no basis for explaining the wide diversity in security governance systems and outcomes (Christou et al. 2010: 342). It tends to focus on the EU, seeing it as a *sui generis* case, and thus concentrates on explaining why EU-like governance approaches do not emerge elsewhere. By contrast, we argue they *are* emerging elsewhere, even in the most unlikely places, demanding an explanation of their emergence and variety.

We therefore turn for guidance to theories of global governance, which have always sought to explain how transboundary challenges are managed. However, mirroring security studies' neglect of governance, these theories have generally neglected security issues. When NTS issues are considered, they are treated in a 'siloed' fashion. Scholars have, for example, considered global health governance and observed the securitisation of health, but they have not extended their insights into an account of security governance more generally. Instead, they often assume that what is happening in their 'silo' uniquely originates there, and is potentially colonising other silos. They claim, for example, that international security is becoming 'medicalized' (Elbe 2010a) or 'climatized' (Oels 2012), rather than seeing either health or the environment as just one of many areas susceptible to new, transboundary forms of security governance with many common features (Held and Young 2013).[1] More useful are general theoretical approaches – notably neo-Gramscian and poststructuralist theories – that identify, and seek to account for, these wider patterns and the emergence of multi-actor, multilevel governance systems.

We combine insights from these global governance theories with others from critical political geography and state theory to generate a novel theoretical framework for explaining how and why NTS issues are managed the way they are: the State Transformation Approach. In a nutshell, our argument is that, as security is becoming 'non-traditional', so too are states. Our approach focuses attention on how efforts to manage transboundary security threats do not simply involve empowering supranational organisations, but primarily seek to transform state apparatuses dealing with specific issue-areas and integrate them into multilevel, regional or global regulatory governance networks. For example, efforts to tackle the laundering of money associated with organised crime and terrorism do not involve the emergence of an authoritative international body that directly governs this issue-area, bypassing state institutions. Rather, states' domestic legal and regulatory arrangements are reorganised using international standards, and the responsible domestic institutions are networked into regional and global surveillance systems. These state apparatuses are thereby

---

[1] The *reductio ad absurdum* is a recent article proposing the 'rhinofication' of South African security as rhino poaching becomes securitised (Humphreys and Smith 2014).

rescaled – they no longer operate within a purely national setting, but are partly internationalised, imposing international disciplines on other parts of their states and societies, and networking with their counterparts across national boundaries. Rescaling may be driven, as in this example, by an international standard-setting organisation, but it could also be led by part of a formerly domestic state apparatus that has itself become transnationalised. For example, since the September 11, 2001 terrorist attacks, the Australian Federal Police (AFP), hitherto a domestic law enforcement agency, has become directly involved in the policing of states in Southeast Asia and the Southwest Pacific. This has, in turn, rescaled these states' police forces, as their priorities, procedures and laws have been amended to reflect the AFP's policy goals (Hameiri 2010: 117–45).

Because such changes in states' configurations and purposes reallocate power and resources, they are inherently contested, both during and after the transformation has occurred. The exact forms of NTS governance that emerge are an outcome of this contestation. The nub of this contestation is a struggle over the appropriate *scale* at which a problem should be governed. The claim that individual states cannot deal with problems like pandemic disease or transnational crime generates demands for new regional or global arrangements to tackle them. Although such demands may now appear commonsensical, just as what counts as 'security' is an inherently political and contested question (McDonald 2008), so too there is nothing natural or obvious about the level, or scale, at which an issue is governed. Different scales – local, provincial, national, regional, global and so on – privilege different interests and agendas; consequently, any attempt to shift governance from one scale to another typically elicits considerable political resistance. Reflecting their different material interests and ideologies, coalitions of socio-political forces form around different scalar arrangements and struggle to define governance approaches that best suit their preferences (Jones 2012; Hameiri 2013).

Conflicts are particularly likely to emerge around NTS governance because it typically affects economic interests directly. Problems like transboundary pollution, transnational crime, human trafficking and so on are frequently seen as being generated by rapid economic growth and intensifying interdependence, and thus as the 'dark side of globalization' (G8 1999; Smith 2001; see also Mittelman 2010). Furthermore, tackling these problems often directly affects the interests of particular industries. Thus, for example, whilst national and international public health officials may seek to contain diseases like avian influenza by promoting regionalised surveillance and biosecurity measures, this may potentially involve radical changes to the way in which poultry is produced. This will likely elicit resistance from agricultural interests and potentially industry regulators who fear a loss of power and influence. These groups may thus organise to preserve a local scale of governance or deflect governance rescaling onto less powerful actors. The regimes that emerge to govern NTS issues, and the degree of rescaling involved, thus reflect the contingent outcome of political struggles. These conflicts will also shape how these new governance systems function in practice, since affected interests will likely seek to mould their operation to their own benefit. Thus, socio-political conflict – and the wider power relations and political economy context in which it is rooted – ultimately determines how NTS issues are governed.

With significant exceptions, global governance scholars largely neglect the crucial dimension of state transformation. Their debates too often focus on whether or not national authority is being superseded by international authority – a 'zero-sum game' view of states 'versus' international organisations. In contrast, through studying NTS, we observe that the transformation of the state is the main process through which global governance is emerging. Efforts to manage NTS issues are not, we suggest, the sole or even the main driver of state transformation. They are both an outcome and further facilitator of ongoing, contested processes of state transformation, driven by evolving social conflicts and epochal changes in the global political economy, often glossed as 'globalisation'. The most important of these changes is the emergence of disaggregated, 'regulatory' forms of statehood and related models of international governance, including regulatory regionalism and multilevel governance. The State Transformation Approach therefore deliberately eschews treating security as a special domain isolated from wider struggles over power and wealth. It instead situates NTS, and its governance, firmly within these historically evolving dynamics.

We apply the State Transformation Approach to three NTS issue-areas – transboundary pollution, pandemic disease and transnational crime – in Southeast Asia and the Southwest Pacific. Specifically, we consider efforts to tackle 'haze' pollution and climate change associated with emissions from land and forest fires in Indonesia, measures to prevent and contain the spread of avian influenza (bird flu) in Thailand and Indonesia and the control of money laundering and terrorist financing in Myanmar and Vanuatu. We have selected predominantly Southeast Asian cases because they provide a 'hard' and rigorous test for our argument. The overwhelming majority of studies of Southeast Asian security cooperation emphasise regional states' persistent inability to collaborate effectively on NTS, particularly compared to more institutionalised groupings like the EU. This is frequently attributed to their attachment to 'non-interference' and 'Westphalian' sovereignty, which ostensibly impedes efforts to construct modes of governance appropriate for transboundary problems. Typically, Moon and Chun (2003: 107) assert that the 'naked pursuit of Westphalian sovereignty epitomize[s] the essence of Asian security' (cf. Jones 2012). Asia thus provides an extremely unlikely venue for the processes of state transformation and rescaling that we suggest are occurring. The existing literature on regional security generally neglects such processes, merely assuming they are not happening; it focuses virtually exclusively on formal, intergovernmental organisations and, observing their failure to acquire EU-like supranational powers, concludes that very little international security governance is actually occurring (e.g. Caballero-Anthony et al. 2006; Caballero-Anthony 2008; Caballero-Anthony and Cook 2013). The wider 'security governance' literature concurs that this region of 'Westphalian states' produces only '"weak" governance', if any at all (Kirchner 2007: 11–12; see also Weber 2011: 221; Breslin and Croft 2012: 11). Conversely, our case studies reveal that considerable rescaling efforts are underway – with varying degrees of success that are attributable not to an outdated attachment to sovereignty but rather to conflicts over the appropriate scale of governance. In fact, the invocation of national sovereignty forms part of these conflicts. Thus, we not only debunk the myth that Asia is somehow 'unique' but also use a general theoretical model, applied to Asian case studies, to shed light on a widespread phenomenon and generate insights of wider interest to students of International Relations (IR).

A narrow geographical focus is also necessary for practical reasons. First, it is needed to demonstrate how local socio-political conflicts shape the outcome of efforts to manage regional or global security challenges. Much of the comparative security cooperation literature focuses on intergovernmental dynamics and multilateral organisations, neglecting to explore how, or even whether, international initiatives translate into local actions. Doing this requires extensive, in-depth fieldwork and comprehensive area expertise. Second, we found that security governance outcomes display such enormous variety that one cannot meaningfully generalise about any given region and then compare it to others. Our case study of avian influenza, for example, identifies variation not only across Southeast Asia but also within individual countries – which is explained by local socio-political conflicts. Identifying and accounting for this micro level variation cannot be achieved through wide-ranging, but superficial, interregional comparisons. Moreover, such an approach would assume that variation is explicable by regional-level differences – for example, that Asian states are 'Westphalian' whereas European ones are 'post-Westphalian' (Kirchner 2007). Our case studies clearly demonstrate that such crude generalisations are not helpful for understanding variations in security governance.

Instead, we compare outcomes within and across single countries and, to provide a modest degree of external comparison, we include a case study from the Southwest Pacific, Vanuatu, in chapter five on money laundering. This is useful not only to consider anti-money laundering governance in an offshore tax haven, but also to contrast outcomes in 'Westphalian' Southeast Asia to those in a region of supposedly 'weak' states. Southwest Pacific states are typically presented as the polar opposite of East Asian ones: they are 'quasi-states' (Jackson 1990), lacking real substance and being dominated, or even extensively controlled, by Australia in a form of 'patron–client regionalism' (Firth 2008). Vanuatu should thus be very amenable to externally driven state transformation. Nonetheless, as we shall see, local power struggles still condition security governance outcomes, demonstrating the importance of the social conflict foregrounded in the State Transformation Approach.

Outline of the book

Part one contains our theoretical investigation of NTS governance. In chapter one, we engage with the literature on security and global governance. Although security studies has become increasingly sophisticated and provides a useful perspective on how the security agenda has widened, we argue it nonetheless remains limited for our purposes due to its relative neglect of governance. The security governance literature contains important empirical insights into the changing way in which non-traditional threats are managed. However, it lacks any articulated theoretical framework capable of explaining how new modes of governance are emerging and operating in practice. Studies of global governance, despite their own relative neglect of security issues, furnish some useful analytical insights for us, particularly neo-Gramscian and poststructuralist approaches. However, most theories remain limited by their inattention to the politics of state transformation that we recognise as an inherent part of efforts to govern transnational problems.

Chapter two combines relevant insights from existing IR literature with those from political geography, state theory and political economy to generate our framework for explaining NTS governance – the State Transformation Approach. Given the centrality of questions of scale to our perspective, we draw on critical political geography to begin analysing contestation over the level at which security problems should be understood and managed. To flesh out this contestation and pay due attention to the instruments and actors involved in rescaling efforts, we also use a particular branch of Marxist state theory – associated with the work of Nicos Poulantzas (1978) and Bob Jessop (2008) – and critical political economy literature. We argue that actual modes of security governance express the contingent outcomes of conflict between socio-political coalitions struggling to define the appropriate scale and instruments of governance in a given issue-area. These struggles are often rooted within, and always conditioned by, the broader context of the political economy and state–society relations.

Part two of the book applies this framework to our three case studies. Chapter three deals with the 'haze' problem in Southeast Asia, a recurring transboundary pollution event. Every year, thick smog from land and forest fires in Indonesia drifts into Singapore and Malaysia, causing serious public health problems and economic disruption, plus vast carbon dioxide emissions which contribute to climate change. We explore how a coalition of concerned actors – environment ministries, environmentalist non-governmental organisations (NGOs), international organisations and some international business groups – has promoted the rescaling of the governance of these fires, and land management more broadly, to the regional level. This has involved networking national and subnational institutions into regional and subregional fire-fighting arrangements and attempts to empower a group of experts to influence the deployment of international fire-fighting teams. However, this rescaling has been resisted by local and national officials and powerful business interests involved in illegal land clearance using fire, who prefer a local scale of governance which enables them to continue business as usual. The outcome of struggles between these rival coalitions is a highly constrained system of subregional governance which, despite some rescaling of state apparatuses, largely fails to tackle this NTS threat.

Chapter four explores the governance of Highly Pathogenic Avian Influenza H5N1 in Southeast Asia. H5N1, a zoonotic pathogen originating in poultry, was a major global security scare during the last decade, arousing fears of a worldwide pandemic that could kill up to 350 million people and profoundly disrupt the international economy (Davis 2005). This provoked frenzied efforts to construct internationalised systems of surveillance and control in outbreak countries, particularly Indonesia, which had the highest number of human deaths worldwide. As we demonstrate in studies of both Indonesia and Thailand, a considerable amount of rescaling of state apparatuses occurred. In Indonesia, international health agencies were networked into a new, multilevel governance system spanning local, provincial and national scales, into which international agencies were directly incorporated. In Thailand, international standards were rigorously enforced, resulting in a massive restructuring of the poultry industry, the source of the disease. However, in both cases, powerful forces linked with this industry determined the form and operation of rescaled governance institutions. In Thailand, the dominance of large, integrated, export-oriented conglomerates produced a system which further concentrated market power in their hands, practically eliminating the smallholder sector, while protecting the industry from detrimental international intervention. In Indonesia, the complex relations between large-scale, domestically oriented conglomerates and smaller-scale farmers produced a very different outcome. The commercial sector as a whole was protected, deflecting the rescaled governance institutions towards 'backyard' farmers. Accordingly, while H5N1 appears largely contained in Thailand, it remains a serious problem in Indonesia.

Chapter five considers efforts to tackle money laundering and the financing of terrorism. Money laundering is seen as inherently linked to the challenge of transnational crime and terrorism, and has therefore been extensively securitised, particularly after September 11. The push by developed states to rescale its governance has occurred largely through the Financial Action Task Force (FATF), which has prescribed regulatory instruments, standards and processes that all states must adopt and also monitors compliance through regional surveillance mechanisms. The FATF is considered one of the biggest success stories of global governance as its recommendations have been adopted by almost every country on earth. We explain this apparent success as a unique case, reflecting the particular political economy of global finance, which makes defying the FATF very costly. However, even here, when we explore the dynamics of the rescaling of security governance in two specific settings, a far more complex picture emerges. In Myanmar, although international standards have ostensibly been adopted, state apparatuses were rescaled only insofar as they empowered the central state against peripheral groups considered potentially disloyal to the ruling regime, whilst regime-affiliated groups were spared. In Vanuatu, despite formal adoption of FATF standards, actual compliance remains very limited because of strong links between the offshore financial sector and political elites. Although the offshore financial sector has severely declined, governance rescaling and foreign intervention has largely displaced money laundering activities into other spaces and sectors.

We conclude the book by comparing findings from across our cases, drawing out lessons for security studies and global governance and discussing the normative implications of the new modes of governance we identify. One important finding is that, although the transformation and partial internationalisation of state apparatuses is a key mode through which global governance is emerging, national and subnational governments remain extremely important as 'scale managers'. They do not simply 'lose' power to supranational bodies (or vice-versa) but continue to influence how far, and in what ways, the governance of specific issues is shifted to new levels and instruments. This is not, however, a simple matter of governments picking and choosing which issues are to be rescaled, as these processes are ultimately shaped by social conflict and wider political economy relations. Accordingly, global governance cannot be improved simply through better designed institutions or technocratic solutions. Attempts to change how any issue-area is governed are inherently political: because any governance system will advance certain sets of interests and ideologies over others, efforts to change them will always elicit contestation, which shapes the process of change and how new institutions operate. Accordingly, constructing new approaches to governing transnational issues must be regarded as a political project, not a technical one.

Finally, given this political character, different governance arrangements must be evaluated normatively in terms of whose interests and ideologies they advance. Although technocratic rule depicts itself as neutral, merely existing to solve problems efficiently, in practice it invariably advances sectional agendas and empowers unelected, unaccountable experts while insulating policymaking from democratic control. Similarly, resistance to this form of rule may also be driven by unsavoury and even predatory interests that benefit from the problems being addressed, though it may also reflect legitimate grievances by those bearing the costs of enhanced regulation. Who wins or loses depends on the specific power relations in a given issue-area and local context. It is not simply the case that 'good' international technocrats and norms ought to trump 'bad' domestic interests and 'outdated' notions of state sovereignty. As our case studies show, rescaling governance can seriously threaten the livelihoods of the poorest people in developing countries. Moreover, it can even be functional for conservative, authoritarian and/or predatory interests by constraining democratic contestation or enabling the construction of governance regimes that suit their preferences. Our normative judgements, therefore, depend on the particular societal groups advantaged or disadvantaged by specific modes of governance in given issue-areas. Moreover, we show that resistance to emergent forms of global governance need not, as is often thought, occur solely through 'global civil society' or idealised institutions of global democracy, but often occurs locally, through supposedly obsolete state institutions, despite considerable international pressure. Local institutions remain vital arenas for political contestation, offering hope for progressive agents who may want to 'think globally but act locally'.

PART I

Theory

1 | *Security and governance: existing approaches*

This book explains how particular non-traditional security (NTS) issues are governed and how the governance regimes that emerge operate in practice. The voluminous post-Cold War literature in international security studies has undoubtedly advanced our understanding of security, particularly of how issues become considered matters of security. Yet it still provides relatively little insight into how these issues are subsequently governed. Furthermore, beyond a small group of scholars who have pursued the question of 'security governance', security studies has not fully grasped how the qualitative distinction between traditional security and non-traditional security shapes how security is understood and managed. Typically, NTS issues are seen as merely adding to a laundry list of states' security concerns, and not as qualitatively distinct from traditional, interstate, military threats. This overlooks the way in which the transboundary nature of NTS issues inherently problematises territorial, state-based governance and generates demands for new scales of governance (Bevir and Hall 2014: 17–26). This in turn creates pressure for state apparatuses to be transformed through their insertion into new regional or global governance regimes.

A small but burgeoning body of 'security governance' literature is directly devoted to describing and assessing the rise of new modes of governance designed to tackle threats that appear to exceed the capacity of individual states to manage. However, this work is constrained by its emergence from the functionalist branch of European integration studies. While it rightly observes an important shift in European and trans-Atlantic security management, the failure of other regions to evolve EU-like institutions is perceived to signify a lack of security governance, which we see as empirically inaccurate. Moreover, the explanations offered for this supposed gap are, like the literature itself, 'pre-theoretical' (Christou et al. 2010: 344), offering an insufficient basis for explaining the widespread variation in NTS governance with which we are concerned.

Accordingly, we turn to the literature on global governance, where scholars have generated theoretical explanations of how and why certain transnational issues are, or are not, governed, with some also trying to explain how governance regimes operate in practice (see Weiss and Wilkinson 2014; Harman and Williams 2013). However, mainstream realist, liberal and constructivist approaches are limited by their tendency to dichotomise states and international organisations, which limits their ability to account for new, hybrid modes of governance that network together state and non-state agencies. Generally, they also neglect to explore how governance regimes function in practice. Furthermore, while some liberal scholarship is more attuned to state transformation through, for example, the rise of transgovernmental regulatory networks (Slaughter 2004), this process is typically seen as a functionalist response to rising interdependence, as in the 'security governance' literature. Examination of specific regimes problematises these mainstream theoretical explanations of how and why they arose.

More useful for our purposes are neo-Gramscian and poststructuralist approaches. These theories are more sensitive to how social contestation shapes the formation and operation of governance institutions and the different interests and ideologies privileged by particular regimes and scales. These theories also attend to the transformation of states involved in these developments, and the uneven, unstable and contradictory nature of governance outcomes. However, neo-Gramscians arguably overstate the unity, coherence and efficacy of global governance as an expression of dominant class interests. Conversely, poststructuralists overstate its fragmentation, fluidity and haphazardness because they neglect the role of structural constraints and material power relations in shaping regimes' formation and operation.

International security studies and non-traditional security

The widening and deepening of the international security agenda has prompted much debate and theory-building in security studies since the 1980s. This section explores how major approaches understand the rise of NTS and its politics. We particularly focus on broadly social constructivist accounts, notably the Copenhagen School (CS) of security studies, which identify security threats not as objective aspects of reality but as socially and politically constructed. These theoretical approaches have made a valuable contribution in analysing the rhetorical broadening of the security agenda. However, most scholars neglect to explore how new threats are actually managed once they are 'securitised'. Correspondingly, they fail to recognise that rhetorical securitisation does not necessarily entail the emergency responses they anticipate. Instead, we may observe varied, complex modes of governance emerging via securitisation, or sometimes no practical changes at all. A related problem is that most security scholars do not adequately recognise the implications of the qualitative distinction between NTS and traditional security: NTS threats are typically viewed as, at least potentially, transboundary in nature. As security governance specialists observe, this generates demands for new modes of governance that transcend the state-based approaches that securitisation scholars anticipate.

Reactions to the widening of the security agenda beyond interstate defence partly depend on whether scholars see '(in)security' as an objective condition or as socially constructed. Early debates largely revolved around whether 'security' should be broadened at all (Jahn et al. 1987; Walt 1991; Booth 1991). In the 'objectivist' camp, traditional realists argued that widening the security agenda risked making both scholarship and state policy incoherent. Others, however, saw the broadening of security as potentially emancipatory, allowing its focus to shift from the state to 'human security' (Booth 1991). Ultimately the 'wideners–deepeners' prevailed and the study of NTS is now firmly ensconced within security studies (Buzan and Hansen 2009: 44).

For realist 'objectivists', the rise of NTS simply reflects changes in the threat environment, particularly globalisation's impact in creating new risks, threats and vulnerabilities for states and people, to which governments must now respond (Dupont 2001; Brown 2003b; Mittelman 2010). In reality, however, many 'new' security concerns are not new at all; rather, they have recently come to be viewed – and managed – differently. For example, Spanish Influenza, which killed around fifty million people worldwide, was viewed at the time as part of the general misery of the Great War and its aftermath. Today, however, Spanish Influenza is constantly invoked by public health practitioners and policymakers to justify intrusive 'pandemic preparedness' measures and interventions to prevent a similar catastrophe (Wraith and Stephenson 2009). Similarly, money laundering is an age-old practice, and was not even criminalised anywhere until 1986 in the US. It was only thereafter that money laundering began to be treated as a matter of international security (Hülsse 2007: 166).

More promising, then, is scholarship that recognises the historically evolving, socially constructed nature of security. From this perspective, security threats are not objectively given but reflect intersubjectively shared understandings, in which something is discursively framed as posing an existential threat to some valued referent object (Buzan et al. 1998). This 'securitisation' process has been the focus of a large body of constructivist and poststructuralist scholarship. By focusing on the creative agency of policy elites, they offer a more compelling explanation of how new issues are added to the security agenda. However, despite their sophisticated and significant contribution to security studies, including to our argument, these approaches are far less helpful in explaining how security threats are *governed*; indeed, most scholars working in this tradition have largely neglected this question altogether. Our discussion focuses most heavily on the highly influential CS. The CS pioneered the study of 'securitisation', and much recent literature has developed in relation to it. Our evaluation of the CS draws on relevant insights from other critical approaches, but also explains why these, too, inadequately address the issue of security governance. In particular, by focusing on the expansion of the 'field' of security professionals, the 'Paris School' offers a more promising explanation of the widening of the security agenda and security governance (CASE Collective 2006). However, its neglect of broader socio-political and economic dynamics leads it to over-privilege the agency of a narrow set of agencies.

The Copenhagen School and the study of securitisation

The CS has played a crucial role in rejuvenating security studies. Nevertheless, the agenda it sets and the analytical tools it employs tell us only a limited amount about the securitisation of NTS. Copenhagen scholars have focused on identifying *how* problems become security issues, through changes in discourse. However, given this limited research agenda, they do not attempt to explain *why* this happens or how security issues are subsequently *governed*. In particular, they do not adequately appreciate how the transboundary nature of NTS creates qualitative distinctions in the way insecurity is managed.

The CS's major conceptual contribution is the notion of 'securitisation'. It is through inventing this concept that the narrowers/broadeners debate was resolved by fixing *form*: 'whenever something took the form of the particular speech act of securitisation, with a securitising actor claiming an existential threat to a valued referent object in order to make the audience tolerate extraordinary measures that otherwise would not have been acceptable, this was a case of securitisation' (Wæver 2011: 469). Reflecting the broader constructivist turn in International Relations (IR), Copenhagen scholars rightly argued that the broadening security agenda did not simply reflect objective shifts in the threat environment but was instead being socially constructed.

Copenhagen scholars' theorisation of this development profoundly shaped their subsequent *problematique* and research agenda. For them, the securitisation process is fundamentally discursive: drawing on language theorist J.L. Austin, Wæver (1995) defines securitisation as a 'speech act'. A speaker's success in securitising a given issue depends on certain facilitating conditions, including their requirement to follow 'the grammar of security', their relationship to their audience and the features of the alleged threat (Buzan et al. 1998: 33). When successful, the speaker transforms the issue into a matter of 'security', placing it atop the political agenda and legitimising the use of extraordinary resources and measures to tackle the 'threat', including the suspension of normal political rules and procedures. This implicitly invokes Schmitt's understanding of the sovereign's right to declare a 'state of exception' (Ciuță 2009: 306–7). This emphasis on 'speech acts' focused subsequent analytical attention on this 'productive moment . . . of securitisation' (Wæver 2011: 468). Although this generated many interesting studies, it also significantly limited the CS's scope of inquiry.

First, as many critics argue, the 'speech act' theory of securitisation wrongly emphasises utterances at the expense of other important dimensions of securitisation, such as images, unstated sentiments, physical action and security practices (Williams 2003; Balzacq 2005; McDonald 2008). A point often missed by these critics, however, is that emphasising discourse without reference to material context also presents 'securitisation' as a timeless, generic process, as applicable to the Soviet Union during the Cold War as it is to HIV/AIDS today.[1] NTS issues are merely added to a growing 'laundry list' of security concerns, but the basic model of security remains unchanged: 'the structure of the game is still derived from the most classical of cases: war' (Wæver 1995: 54).

Thus, Copenhagen scholars do not adequately recognise the implications of the qualitative distinction between traditional and NTS issues: the latter are explicitly *transboundary* in nature. Security has had a transnational dimension in the past, of course. The Cold War, for instance, involved struggles between contending social forces and their associated ideological, political and economic projects that were, in important part, fought out transnationally (Jones 2013). However, this was nonetheless predominantly expressed in a firmly 'national' and international form of security politics: state-based arms racing, military alliances, nuclear deterrence and so on. The prevailing international order strongly affirmed the inviolability of postcolonial borders and sovereign states (Barkin and Cronin 1994). Accordingly, even where interventions occurred, they were temporally bounded, aiming to (re)produce a political order desired by the intervening power before it withdrew (Colás 2008). Conversely, today the *transboundary* nature of NTS issues generates demands for very different modes of security governance. For example, Dupont (2001: 8) argues that: 'deforestation results not only in the loss of a valuable resource for a local community or particular state. It can also trigger catastrophic flooding across national borders and contribute to widespread pollution and climate change that, in turn, may cause food shortages, population displacement, economic damage and death.' Such framing of NTS issues intrinsically raises questions of *scale*: they posit that threats have expanded in scope, beyond the national level, and urge commensurate shifts in governance to manage the problem. Typical is Mittelman's (2010: 164–5, 172) claim that:

Nontraditional threats, including climate change, pandemics, transnational crime, and cross-border terror emanate from above and below the nation-state. Thus, there cannot be a neat separation between national and global security. Nor is there a sharp division between internal and external security. Sundry threats at home have extraterritorial dimensions . . . national security

---

[1] Some poststructuralist definitions of discourse claim to encompass the material or institutional contexts in which frameworks of meaning are embedded (see **Poststructuralist (governmentality) approaches to global governance**, below). Here we refer to the constructivist use of 'discourse' to denote speech acts.

and global security, often regarded as counterpoints, are becoming a single stream. This evolving configuration may best be described as *postnational security* . . . [requiring] multilevel global governance.

Similar views are frequently echoed in policy documents. The UN High-Level Panel on Threats, Challenges and Change (2004: 1) states: 'Today's threats recognise no national boundaries, are connected, and must be addressed at the global and regional as well as the national levels. No State, no matter how powerful, can by its own efforts alone make itself invulnerable to today's threats.' Such formulations directly challenge the division between domestic and international politics. As the UK's National Security Strategy asserts, today 'when it comes to national security, foreign and domestic policy are not separate issues, but two halves of one picture' (Cabinet Office 2010: 5). As security governance scholars have observed, then, 'global interdependences and expanding security agendas [have] create[d] a demand for new forms of governing' (Ehrhart et al. 2014a: 121; see also Bevir and Hall 2014: 17–26).

These 'new forms of governing' do not simply involve discursive shifts within a fundamentally unchanging form of security politics, with national elites seeking to persuade national audiences of the need for emergency measures at the national level to tackle new threats, as CS scholars imply. Rather, it often entails efforts to build new, multilayered governance arrangements more fitting to the transnational scale of the problem. For example, because of the highly integrated nature of financial markets, it is argued that money laundering associated with transnational crime and terrorist financing cannot be tackled by states acting individually. Consequently, a global regulatory regime has been promoted to harmonise anti-money laundering governance worldwide (see chapter five). As we elaborate below, this push to *rescale* governance beyond the national level is the main means by which NTS issues are sought to be governed today.

Although the CS does provide some treatment of 'scale', it is merely a synonym for 'size' or extent – the number of actors, referent objects and threats loaded into a single securitisation process. The concepts of 'regional security complexes' and 'macro-securitisations' were developed to label mid- to large-scale agglomerations of security concerns, understood as hierarchical, top-down groupings that 'incorporate, align and rank the more parochial securitisations beneath' them (Buzan and Wæver 2009: 253; see also Buzan and Wæver 2003).

For the CS, then, scale denotes a 'level of analysis/aggregation' (Buzan and Wæver 2009: 259). This notion of scale does not approximate the more sophisticated concept used by political geographers, who have demonstrated that governance is not simply hierarchically 'stacked', but occurs at multiple scales simultaneously and is also rescaled, that is, it shifts to new spatial configurations. Consider the FATF's anti-money laundering regime, which is simultaneously global, regional and local. Globally, it is centred on the FATF as a universal rule-setting body. Regionally, monitoring and enforcement occur through FATF-style regional bodies whose membership cuts across traditional regional organisations and are thus irreducible to existing 'regional security complexes'. Locally, national state apparatuses are transformed to enact FATF disciplines. Such arrangements are seen as necessary precisely because NTS issues appear to operate simultaneously at the local/domestic, regional and global levels, requiring novel, multilevel, multi-scalar forms of governance (Eriksson and Rhinard 2009). Moreover, these arrangements are typically issue-specific and not subsumed into existing multilateral security organisations.

Secondly, as poststructuralist and Paris School critics argue, the CS's definition of securitisation excludes a great deal of contemporary security practice. The CS contends that, to retain conceptual coherence, the notion of 'security' can only apply to issues identified as constituting an existential danger to something else. But the majority of 'new' NTS issues are not actually described or governed as if they are urgent, existential threats but rather as *potentially* existential dangers, or *risks*. As Beck (1999) argues, recently, policymakers and ordinary people, particularly in the West, have become preoccupied with new kinds of risks like climate change, global pandemics or terrorism. Such risks have a low probability of occurring, but are seen to have potentially catastrophic consequences, defying conventional forms of management, insurance and compensation. Despite these potentially existential dangers, the management of these issues rarely resembles the emergency politics of mass mobilisation and 'extraordinary measures' associated with traditional securitisation. Instead, it involves the creation of enhanced systems of detection and management, underpinned by technical, managerial and scientific expertise.

Consequently, securitising NTS issues does *not* necessarily involve legitimising or taking exceptional measures. Instead, as the emerging literature on European security governance has observed, it often involves extending into security management 'practices developed elsewhere in domestic and global governance, including markets, networks, joined-up or whole-of-government strategies and public-private partnerships' (Bevir and Hall 2014: 26). This typically bureaucratic and technocratic approach requires neither the assent of an identifiable audience, as 'speech act' theory supposes (Balzacq 2008), nor a break with politics as usual (Stritzel 2007: 367). For instance, the risk of terrorists using aircraft in their attacks was addressed after September 11 by extending pre-existing forms of surveillance and policing to civil aviation (Aradau and van Munster 2007). The securitisation of migration after September 11, with its discourse of exceptional threats, has also been managed through a routinised, bureaucratised form of border management, with emergency measures applied only infrequently (Neal 2009). Similarly, a study of the 'apocalyptic' discourse around global warming in the UN Security Council found that, rather than 'exceptional measures ... the securitisation of climate change seems to reinforce the mundane routine practices of risk management ... "banal" political measures' associated with 'precautionary and preparatory' logics, to be negotiated among UN member-states (Methmann and Rothe 2013: 105, 107, 117).

Importantly, this extension of pre-existing modes of governance into the security field also involves their application to new *spaces* of governance. For example, the risk of terrorism has been addressed partly through extending US bureaucratic security checks along a '"virtual border ... designed to operate far beyond US boundaries" enabling the [Department of Homeland Security] to "assess the security risks of all US-bound travellers and prevent potential travellers from reaching [physical] US borders"' (Amoore 2006: 337). Similarly, the 2010 US Nuclear Posture Review (NPR) is concerned less with the threat of interstate nuclear confrontation than the risk of terrorists and rogue states acquiring nuclear weapons (US DoD 2010a). Correspondingly, the NPR abandons the Cold War policy of deterrence in favour of a risk-management approach, involving a wide range of checks and controls across the public and private sectors to regulate the movement of dangerous components, materials and technologies, not only in the US but also in other countries. These examples illustrate the shift towards risk management, the transnationalisation of security governance and also, crucially, its incorporation of, or even leadership by, private actors, including businesses (see also Aydinli 2010a; Abrahamsen and Williams 2011; Hönke 2013).[2]

Wæver (2011: 474) concedes that the rise of such practices 'represent[s] a serious challenge to securitisation theory'. Nonetheless, he prefers to retain a narrow definition of securitisation, even if the 'utility and power' of 'the theoretical model contracts', leaving it to others to theorise risk management as a distinct phenomenon. Yet, the line between securitisation and risk management that Wæver seeks to defend theoretically is hard to draw in reality, even from within the CS's model. The 2001 invasion of Afghanistan demonstrates that even when exceptional powers of war-making are sought, they are often justified with reference to managing or eliminating risks, such as potential future terrorist attacks emanating from within Afghanistan's borders. Furthermore, military intervention was only the first step in a longer-term process of international 'state-building', involving a wide range of governance actors. Moreover, as Aradau and van Munster (2011) observe, even the Cold War – the CS's prime example of 'macrosecuritisation' (Buzan and Wæver 2009) – was ultimately made governable through managing the risk of nuclear war (see also McDonagh and Heng, in press). Today, the US Department of Defense (US DoD 2010b: 89) explicitly adopts a 'Defense Risk Management Framework' proclaiming that 'risk management is central to effective decision-making and is vital to our success'; the UK's National Security Strategy relies upon a 'National Security Risk Assessment' (Cabinet Office 2010: 25) and the EU's Internal Security Strategy deploys a 'risk management policy linking threat and risk assessments to decision-making' (European Commission 2010a: 4). Refusing to acknowledge this real-world merging of risk and security seems tantamount to burying one's head in the sand.

This further relates to our third and main criticism, the CS's disinterest in explaining security governance. By 'governance' we refer to a wide range of activities, performed by a diverse range of public and

---

[2] This does not imply that all security issues are now governed in this manner; it is the peculiarly transboundary nature of NTS threats that makes such arrangements appear particularly necessary. Thus, the transnational governance of nuclear weapons still coexists with the interstate Non-Proliferation Treaty process, because the threats associated with these weapons are not exclusively transboundary. Although governance arrangements have evolved in traditional areas of defence (Krahmann 2003), statist approaches still persist in many areas.

private actors, which include defining the nature and sources of security problems, devising plans and policies to ameliorate them, engaging in the actual management of these issues and auditing security practitioners' performance. These issues are unfortunately marginal to the CS's research agenda. Copenhagen scholars are implicitly interested in the question of '*what difference does securitisation make*[?]' because 'it is the effects that securitisation has that make it attractive (or not) for various actors to pursue' (Wæver 2011: 476, original emphasis). However, Copenhagen scholars apparently believe that securitisation co-constructs threats, referent objects and the means to tackle threats simultaneously; that is, security governance is discursively generated as part of the 'speech act' (Buzan et al. 1998: 26). It is intrinsic to the securitisation process that successful securitisations enable extraordinary measures. Beyond this, Copenhagen scholars pay little attention to what governance arrangements – if any – actually emerge.

In practice, however, as our case studies illustrate, discursive changes do not automatically generate changes in governance, and certainly not emergency measures. Indeed, sometimes surprisingly little action is taken. For example, in Southeast Asia, the World Health Organization (WHO) and regional governments have discursively securitised infectious diseases yet, in practice, little concerted action has ensued (Caballero-Anthony 2008; see also Caballero-Anthony and Cook 2013). Similarly, given the 'apocalyptic discourses' apparently securitising environmentally induced migration, from the CS's perspective, 'it is not immediately understandable why . . . a looming catastrophe [is actually addressed] with the calm, moderate, incremental mechanisms of governance' (Bettini 2013: 131). Since they define the very purpose of securitisation as being 'to make the audience tolerate extraordinary measures' (Wæver 2011: 469), Copenhagen scholars may simply dismiss such outcomes as cases of 'failed' securitisation. Yet, as we have argued, this wrongly neglects a vast array of policies and activities that *do* nonetheless flow from the discursive identification of threats, but do not approximate 'extraordinary measures'.

Moreover, the CS's fixation on the 'productive moment' of securitisation leaves it struggling to explain – rather than merely to lament – gaps between apparently successful securitising discourse and actual governance, and has meant that it has not developed any theoretical apparatus capable of explaining the particular forms that security governance takes in practice (Jones 2011).[3] One might argue that the issue of governance is deliberately excluded from the parsimonious 'securitisation' model. But this is a significant limitation since governance outcomes exhibit wide variety – even within a single country – which demands explanation. As chapter four demonstrates, for example, the arrangements established to tackle avian influenza in Indonesia operated intensively in some areas, but barely touched others.

The 'Paris School' has addressed security governance more directly than the CS. Paris scholars operate with Bourdieu's concept of the 'field' and Foucault's work on 'governmentality', risk and discipline. They emphasise the role of professional networks of security practitioners, which attempt to define and manage threats and risks through their positions as experts, and their capacity to create and govern borders (CASE Collective 2006: 457). This focus on security professionals' concrete practices means that the Paris School does explore the relationship between how security is broadening and how it is governed. Security's expansion is explained by the increasing integration of the disparate agencies into a single 'field' of 'security', diminishing differences between threats and placing all security issues onto a continuum of traditional and NTS issues (CASE Collective 2006: 459). Paris scholars argue that security governance is shaped by power struggles between the agencies incorporated into the security field, coupled with the context and nature of the security issue (Balzacq 2005). Security is thus theorised in terms of the real practices of state apparatuses, not simply political elites' 'speech acts'. These useful insights partly inform our own approach, elaborated in chapter two.

However, by focusing almost exclusively on power struggles among security bureaucracies, the Paris School potentially over-privileges the agency of an even smaller number of people than the CS. Missing is any sustained examination of the relationship between the security 'field' and its socio-political and economic context, producing an exaggerated emphasis on the agency of a few government 'securocrats'. Ironically, given their emphasis on 'fields', they generally fail to appreciate how the rise of NTS has dramatically widened the range of actors involved in security politics and governance, well beyond traditional security

---

[3] The single attempt to stretch the CS approach to include governance outcomes merely adds an atheoretical description and evaluation of them to the core concern with securitising discourse and audience acceptance (Christou et al. 2010).

agencies like police, militaries and border agencies. The US Department of Defense (US DoD 2010b: 74), for example, asserts that the 'security sector' now 'includes the defense and criminal justice sectors, government management and oversight bodies, and civil society', describing it 'as a system of systems that demands interagency partnerships'. Similarly, the UK National Security Strategy adopts a 'whole-of-government approach' involving 'all government departments and agencies' (Cabinet Office 2010: 34). This is part of a secular shift from 'government' to 'governance', with authority being dispersed to a wide range of actors across the public–private divide (Bevir and Hall 2014). Accordingly, studying a narrow range of actors without investigating how their agency is constrained by wider societal dynamics is a flawed approach. Some Bourdieusian scholars are rightly recognising this secular shift: for example, Abrahamsen and Williams (2011) brilliantly demonstrate how the incorporation of private security companies into the 'field' of security professionals is creating a new 'global security assemblage'; yet, as Hönke (2013: 7) notes, they still pay inadequate attention to other local actors and conditions that shape actual governance outcomes on the ground.

Consider, for example, the contrasting responses to the outbreak of Severe Acute Respiratory Syndrome (SARS) in Canada and China. In the 'global city' of Toronto, reflecting the legacy of neoliberal state reforms, health officials enjoyed considerable autonomy from central government and economic interests and moved swiftly to enhance biosecurity measures in line with WHO demands (Ali and Keil 2009). Conversely, in China, where SARS originated, provincial and national governments were concerned about its effects on economic growth targets and completely blocked public health officials from sharing information with the WHO, even denying the disease's existence for two months (Fidler 2003a; Stevenson and Cooper 2009). Clearly, the autonomy of security professionals to pursue their preferred policies varies widely, depending on state forms and local political-economy relations. As Joseph (2010: 225) observes of the misapplication of Foucault's governmentality concept in IR more broadly, the Paris School's social ontology is thus too narrow, its usefulness limited to describing security governance in a small number of advanced capitalist states and societies. Even then, it does not identify what attributes of these particular societies apparently grant security professionals such relative autonomy.

Furthermore, much like the CS, by depicting securitisation essentially as the incorporation of new issues into a widening spectrum of security, Paris scholars also miss the implications of the transnational character of NTS threats. Coupled with its neglect of the broader context of security politics, this leaves the Paris School struggling to explain why border-spanning securitisations occur in some places or around certain issues, but not elsewhere.

What we take from the CS and its constructivist and poststructuralist critics, then, is the notion that security is socially constructed; that it refers to, at least potentially, existential dangers; that securitisation inherently empowers some actors at the expense of others; that discourse plays some role in defining security; and that networks of experts and officials are an important aspect of security governance. However, these approaches neglect important aspects of contemporary security politics. Although the term 'securitisation' is useful to denote the discursive identification of issues as security threats, this 'productive moment' neither determines nor explains what happens next. It often does not generate 'exceptional measures' but is instead followed by a wide variety of governance responses that these constructivist and poststructuralist approaches cannot – indeed, do not attempt to – explain. Consequently, we use 'securitisation' in this study only in the loosest sense, not that intended by Copenhagen scholars, to denote a process by which NTS issues are understood and governed as security problems. In our usage, this process is only ever partially discursive; more importantly, it involves efforts to construct new modes of governance claimed to be appropriate to the scale of the problem. To understand how NTS issues are managed in practice, we need a framework capable of explaining these efforts and their outcomes. To assist in this, we now turn to literature that has sought to explain why and how transnational issues are governed.

Global governance theories and their limitations

The neglect of governance by security scholars reflects IR's long-standing division between the 'high' politics of international security and the 'low' politics of international political economy (Keohane and Nye 1977: 23). Security, traditionally associated with interstate threats, is not typically thought to involve transnational problems of the sort requiring global governance. And, given security's association with state survival, most security scholars assume that states would not surrender control over security to international institutions or other groups. Thus, they simply do not imagine there is much transnational security governance to investigate. This view has begun to be challenged by 'security governance' scholars, who observe the emergence of new modes of governance to manage transnational threats in the trans-Atlantic area. However, this subfield's origins in European integration studies have constrained its development into a fully theorised approach capable of explaining variation in NTS governance across time and space.

The wider literature on 'global governance', while generally (though not entirely) neglecting security, has nonetheless focused considerable attention upon explaining the management of transnational issues in 'low' politics, such as the economy, the environment or human rights. Notwithstanding some claims that global governance is transcending IR to become its own theoretical field (e.g. Rosenau 2007; Weiss 2013), in reality, most work is either atheoretical or falls into IR's broad schools of thought.[4] Thus, our discussion of this material is organised around realist, liberal, constructivist, neo-Gramscian and poststructuralist approaches. Notwithstanding some differences, for the sake of brevity, we also subsume power-based, interest-based and norm-based regime theories – the precursors of 'global governance' theory – into the realist, liberal and constructivist approaches, respectively. Although each approach has its strengths, none is fully compelling or capable of explaining the sheer variety of governance outcomes visible around NTS. Realist approaches explain governance regimes as reflecting the interests of powerful states, but this leaves them incapable of explaining instances where regimes do not work as apparently intended. Liberal approaches suffer from a similar predicament because they explain governance outcomes as attempts to solve collective problems by powerful states, or as functional responses to challenges arising from growing global interdependence. Constructivists argue that governance regimes express the adoption of particular norms and ideas by states and international organisations, but do not adequately explain why particular norms are adopted over others. Neo-Gramscian and poststructuralist approaches are more

---

[4] Even Rosenau's (2007) anti-theoretical discussion, for instance, uses the notion of 'spheres of authority' developed by constructivists Hall and Biersteker (2002).

useful. However, neo-Gramscians arguably overstate the unity, coherence and efficacy of global governance as an expression of dominant class interests. Conversely, poststructuralists overstate the fragmentation, fluidity and haphazardness of governance outcomes.

Security governance

In the last decade, a small but burgeoning literature has emerged to recognise and assess 'the expansion of security threats and risks, and the proliferation of actors and mechanisms to address them' (Sperling and Webber 2014: 129). It makes a signal contribution merely by insisting that security is now managed through a wide variety of novel mechanisms, not merely 'exceptional measures'. However, the utility of this literature as a general framework for explaining the emergence and variability of these new mechanisms is constrained by its intellectual origins in functionalist accounts of European integration. Security governance is not seen as a general phenomenon requiring generalised theoretical explanations, but as an extension of EU-style governance into the security field. Consequently, when looking for security governance elsewhere, the absence of EU-style multilateralism is taken to indicate an absence of security governance. This causes security governance scholars to overlook modes of governance beyond formal multilateral institutions. It also leads them to focus on explaining the relative lack of EU-like institutionalisation outside of Europe. Given the subfield's lack of theoretical development – as recognised by its own proponents (Christou et al. 2010; Ehrhart et al. 2014a) – this generates merely an *ad hoc*, under-theorised listing of factors favouring or constraining the emergence of security governance, such as the presence of 'Westphalian' or 'post-Westphalian' states. This approach cannot account for observable variation within regions, or even within a single state.

Security governance scholars were the first to recognise that the shift from 'government' to 'governance' is occurring in the apparently unlikely domain of security (Krahmann 2003: 9–21). Their basic claim is that, confronted with 'new threats' and 'wicked problems', 'the state had to change' and 'could not go it alone' anymore; power has consequently been dispersed to a much broader range of public and private actors who now collaborate in networked, multilevel arrangements to form, and implement, security policy (Bevir and Hall 2014:

17–26; see also Kirchner 2007: 7–8; Kirchner and Domínguez 2011a: 1; Aydinli 2010b: 1). These empirical observations are almost exclusively based on the European and trans-Atlantic experience (Krahmann 2003; Webber et al. 2004). Reflecting an underlying functionalist orientation, security governance is seen to emerge from the extension of European integration and the 'Europeanisation' of governance into the security domain. Accordingly, much of this literature is devoted to describing and evaluating the efficacy of these arrangements. However, these scholars have noted the difficulty in extending EU-style security governance to former Soviet spaces (Wagnsson et al. 2009; Schröder 2011), and have contrasted this approach to those applied where governments seem less willing to disperse authority to diverse actors operating at multiple levels (Kirchner and Domínguez 2011b; Breslin and Croft 2012).

This intellectual trajectory – from the EU outwards – has kept the study of security governance 'pre-theoretical' (Christou et al. 2010: 342), as its own proponents readily admit (Ehrhart et al. 2014a). 'Security governance' has been grasped overwhelmingly as an empirical phenomenon: the term is a 'heuristic device' used to elucidate departures from traditional defence and security policies (Kirchner 2007: 18; Sperling and Webber 2014: 127). Accordingly, most studies are overwhelmingly descriptive, focusing on 'mapping security provision at the regional level' and evaluating its 'functional efficiency' (Sperling and Webber 2014: 129). Thus, most debates within the subfield focus on what 'counts' as security governance (Adler and Greve 2009; Kirchner and Domínguez 2011a; Breslin and Croft 2012; cf. Sperling and Webber 2014), or on the relative merits of the governance arrangements established (Daase and Friesendorf 2010; Ehrhart et al. 2014b). As Sperling and Webber (2014: 128–9) state, the subfield 'is not ... theoretically innovative ... [it] makes no significant stand-alone theoretical claims' and remains caught in a 'trap of "pre-theory"'. Accordingly, it is neglected by both major fields of IR (Christou et al. 2010). More importantly, it has not developed the theoretical tools necessary for explaining the emergence and variation in NTS governance with which we are concerned.

This is particularly apparent in recent work exploring security governance beyond Europe. Because scholars' understanding of security governance as an empirical phenomenon is so bound up with the EU's functional integration, the non-existence of European-style, deeply multilateralised regional institutions in other regions is assumed to indicate the absence or weakness of security governance (Kirchner and Domínguez 2011b; Breslin and Croft 2012). The study of security governance thus dissolves into comparative regionalism, asking why, given the presence of new threats and risks, other regions are not developing 'better' modes of governance. This has generated an *ad hoc*, atheoretical listing of factors seen to enable or constrain the emergence of security governance. Sperling and Webber (2014) aggregate these factors into the 'degree of "post-Westphalianism"', determined by the level of shared threat perceptions, the nature of external interests and the nature of local states – whether they are 'penetrated' by non-state actors and how far they maintain Westphalian 'sovereign control' (Kirchner and Sperling 2010). This boils down to the rather circular claim that non-European regions do not evolve European-style security governance because their states are not like European ones: the 'Westphalian states of Eurasia are trapped by the logic of anarchy', leading to '"weaker" forms of regional security collaboration' (Kirchner and Domínguez 2011a: 14).

There are at least two serious problems with this Eurocentric approach. First, it wrongly equates security governance with security multilateralism. In reality, security governance need not map onto or be part of formal regional organisations. Precisely because NTS issues are seen as transnational and not confined to predefined territories of states or regions, new modes of governance are often established around particular threats or risks, establishing new spaces of governance. For example, the EU's own Cocaine Route Programme is an interlinked chain of projects aimed at transforming governance in the territories through which cocaine is smuggled into Europe – Latin America and West Africa – in order to disrupt this illicit flow (Sandor 2014). Because the governance arrangements are constructed around the transnational flow itself, they do not map onto, and would never be captured by, surveys of either European, African or Latin American regional security organisations.

Second, the crude dichotomy between 'post-Westphalian' Europe and 'Westphalian' or 'pre-Westphalian' states and regions elsewhere overlooks, and thus cannot explain, considerable variation within these spaces. Even within the EU, not every security issue is managed in the way that security governance scholars would anticipate. The EU's supposedly 'post-Westphalian' member-states frequently play 'sovereignty games', strategically relaxing or flexing their sovereignty to promote or resist transnational European governance initiatives in line with their interests and agendas (Adler-Nissen and Gammeltoft-Hansen 2008). Moreover, the world's supposedly 'Westphalian' states do not uniformly reject security governance. As all of our case studies demonstrate, even in the Asia Pacific – supposedly home to the most hidebound Westphalian states of all – there is ample evidence that non-traditional modes of security governance are emerging. They are not simply absent; rather, as in the EU, they are variegated, sometimes within even a single country. As chapter four shows, Indonesia accepted extensive international involvement in recasting its domestic institutions, with overseas agencies becoming directly embedded into disease control systems; but these were active only in certain economic sectors. Moreover, simultaneously, the government declared 'sovereignty' over viral samples, refusing to share them with a long-established international surveillance system (Hameiri 2014). Clearly, this complex variegation cannot be explained by crudely labelling states 'Westphalian' or 'post-Westphalian', but only by drilling down to the divergent interests, agendas and contestations that shape outcomes. However, the *politics* of governance construction is typically excised from the predominantly functionalist–technocratic security governance literature (Ehrhart et al. 2014b). This leaves the subfield without the theoretical resources needed to explain such variation, even if it could recognise it.

The security governance subfield therefore offers only limited assistance to the present study. Its major contribution is the crucial empirical observation that security governance has broadened beyond statist 'exceptional measures', involving new actors and mechanisms imported from other issue-areas. However, its theoretical underdevelopment leaves it incapable of explaining variation in the form and operation of security governance mechanisms. Accordingly, we now turn to consider explicitly theorised explanations of transnational governance.

Realist approaches to global governance

Realists focus on the role of powerful states in promoting or thwarting the formation of international regimes (Paterson and Grubb 1992; Barkin and Shambaugh 1999; Hyde-Price 2006). If dominant states favour a regime's formation, it will occur and be effective, and vice-versa. Institutions are seen as little more than tools manipulated by powerful states, which support or discard them in accordance with their interests (e.g. Mearsheimer 1994/95; Sterling-Folker 2005; Drezner 2007). The realist approach can thus explain why governance systems emerge around certain issues and places but not others, without resorting to the problematic characterisations of statehood used by security governance scholars.

Perhaps the most significant recent realist study of global governance is Drezner's (2007) *All Politics Is Global*. Dismissing the relevance of non-state actors, Drezner views the support of the great powers, specifically the US and the EU, as necessary for forming effective international regulatory regimes:

> Great powers – defined here as governments that oversee large internal markets – remain the primary actors writing the rules that regulate the global economy. The key variable affecting global regulatory outcomes is the distribution of interests among the great powers. A great power concert is a necessary and sufficient condition for effective global governance over any transnational issue. Without such a concert, government attempts at regulatory coordination will be incomplete, and non-state attempts will prove to be a poor substitute (Drezner 2007: 5).

Drezner argues that domestic factors shape state preferences, specifically industries' costs of adapting to proposed regulations and their capacity to exercise 'voice' or 'exit'. But once state preferences are locked in, he maintains, international bargaining explains international regulation, not domestic preferences. Indeed his case studies spend little, if any, time explaining domestic preferences, focusing instead on proving the necessity of great-power concerts.

Putting Drezner's narrowly economistic framework for reading state preferences aside, his explanation for the emergence and efficacy of international regulatory regimes is not persuasive. Simply put, regulatory regimes and governance institutions established by the great powers often *do not* work as intended (Reich and Lebow 2014). Like many other realists, Drezner completely ignores the implementation phase, merely assuming that, once regulatory standards are in place, governance simply 'happens', because the great powers want it to. This reflects global governance theorists' surprising neglect of how, or indeed whether, international regimes actually influence local processes and outcomes.[5]

---

[5] Rare exceptions include Victor et al. (1998), Brown Weiss and Jacobson (2000) and Underdal and Hanf (2000). However, such accounts are typically highly technical, avoiding essential questions of power and politics: cf. Ferraro (2014).

Drezner's own example of financial regulation clearly demonstrates this problem. Andrew Walter (2008) shows that East Asia's adoption of international financial regulatory standards, as advocated by the great powers through the International Monetary Fund (IMF) and the Financial Stability Forum, amounts to little more than 'mock compliance'. As Walter observes of Indonesia, the state worst hit by the 1997–98 Asian financial crisis and thus the one with the least apparent capacity to resist great-power pressure:

[A] combination of pro-compliance domestic and external forces promoted a considerable degree of formal compliance with international banking supervision standards... however... the actual behaviour of public and private actors in Indonesia subsequently diverged from this formal commitment... That these banks remained highly prone to fraud and corruption since the crisis suggests that the root cause of substantive compliance failure has been a set of deeply ingrained collusive relationships between government, bureaucracy, and the private sector... [S]trikingly, given the claims of much recent literature about the power of external forces to promote policy convergence, domestic politics trumped compliance pressures from the IFIs [international financial institutions], bilateral creditor governments, and private creditors (Walter 2008: 76–7).

Thus, even if great-power preferences could explain the emergence of particular regimes, they clearly do not explain how they operate in practice.

Realists' impoverished, state-centric view of politics, which ignores the multiple actors contesting (and possibly disregarding) the formation and operation of governance regimes, also constrains their ability to explain compliance gaps. Realist scholar Sterling-Folker (2005: 23) rightly says that 'Global governance will always be produced by the choices and actions of... relatively powerful groups.' Yet, the focus of realist scholarship, including Sterling-Folker's own, is actually on 'sovereign political units', that is, states, not social groups (Sterling-Folker 2005: 18). Realists thereby ignore the fact that different parts of states may have, and pursue, different interests, including by promoting or resisting international regulation. To continue the banking governance example, otherwise relatively weak Indonesian technocrats exploited international pressure to adopt international standards in order to strengthen their position against better-entrenched predatory interests associated with the Suharto regime. The IMF also saw its intervention in these terms (Walter 2008: 51–2). However, they were ultimately foiled by a countervailing alliance between powerful governmental and bureaucratic actors and private-sector interests. Such internecine struggles are occluded by realism's state-centric ontology.

Liberal approaches to global governance

Liberal global governance scholars generally accept the realist assumption that states are self-interested actors, but argue that rising interdependence, stemming from intensifying global economic flows, creates stronger incentives to collectively govern transnational problems than realists acknowledge. As in the security governance literature, global governance regimes are thus essentially viewed as a functionalist response to common challenges. To explain variations in governance outcomes, liberals often focus on identifying the institutional design, rules and norms that produce effective regulation and/or incentives for states, and sometimes relevant non-state actors, to cooperate (Gehring 1994; Rittberger and Mayer 1995; Abbott and Snidal 2009). This is essentially the 'new institutionalism' transposed to the international level, with rational choice approaches dominating (e.g. Kahler and Lake 2009; Büthe and Mattli 2011). The resultant emphasis on institutional design and tweaking cost–benefit matrices tend to marginalise politics and contestation (e.g. Keohane and Martin 1995; Boehmer et al. 2004; Tavares 2010). Indeed, liberals often view politics as problematic: shifting from national to international or global regulation is often promoted as a means to bypass national-level 'vested interests', 'spoilers' and 'rent-seekers' who resist progressive change (Kahler and Lake 2009).

Some liberal scholars have recognised the importance of domestic politics for achieving compliance with global governance regimes (Dai 2005; Linos 2007; Mattli and Woods 2009). Mattli and Woods (2009: 12), for example, attempt to incorporate domestic contestation into an explanation of how regulatory governance outcomes may vary from 'pure capture regulation to common interest regulation'. Regulatory outcomes are explained as reflecting the balance between 'demand' – the degree of societal enthusiasm for regulatory change – and the 'supply' of institutions 'within which the demand for regulatory change is formed, implemented, monitored, and enforced' (Mattli and Woods 2009: 43). Global regulation, they argue, often faces higher risk of capture than national regulation because global institutions usually lack transparency, due process and mechanisms of accountability, and because of the uneven distribution of the requisite expertise and capacities that enable participation in them.

Despite usefully underscoring how political contestation shapes regulatory outcomes, their treatment of this remains limited. First, as the authors themselves concede, the distinction between 'capture' and 'public interest' is objectionable. The only social cleavage countenanced by Mattli and Woods (2009) is essentially between 'rent-seekers', who selfishly subvert regulation, and 'the public', which is viewed as an essentially amorphous mass, implicitly desirous of 'good' regulations, with no inherent social or ideological divisions. In reality, societies always contain diverse interests that are differentially affected by regulations; one does not have to be a 'rent-seeker' to fear detrimental consequences of new regulations and thereby resist them (Cheng and Ngo 2014). Moreover, real social divisions undermine Mattli and Woods' neat distinction between institutional context (the 'supply' side) and interest groups (the 'demand' side; see also Dai 2005). As our banking reform example illustrates, state institutions are not neutral arenas where interest groups contest regulatory proposals. Instead, actors located in state apparatuses often form alliances with agents outside the state, affecting how these institutions operate. A final and related drawback is Mattli and Woods' exclusive focus on formal multilateral organisations; they thereby fail to consider how state apparatuses are being transformed as part of new, transnational governance initiatives.

Some liberal scholars are much more sensitive to this latter development. International legal scholars, such as Slaughter (1997, 2004) and Chayes and Chayes (1995), have examined the recent emergence of new 'transgovernmental' networks of regulators and experts. These scholars describe very important changes in states' internal configuration and the formation of transnational networks between state apparatuses, international organisations (IOs) and non-governmental organisations (NGOs). However, they typically see these developments as a functional response to increasing international interdependence, and as normatively desirable, without considering the political implications of the rising power of experts who are not democratically accountable (cf. Kennedy 2005; Davis et al. 2012). Indeed, this functionalist approach tends to neglect politics altogether and thereby lacks the theoretical apparatus capable of explaining variation in state transformation and governance outcomes across time and space, beyond broad assertions of the significance of 'political will' and 'state capacity'.

Constructivist approaches to global governance

Constructivist scholars focus on the processes constituting the interests, identities and values pursued by states and their extension into international governance regimes. Constructivists particularly emphasise the role of 'epistemic communities' and 'norm entrepreneurs' in defining problems and how they should be governed (Haas 1989; Adler 1992). These actors are seen to employ persuasion or socialisation to change states' and people's understandings and therefore behaviour (Keck and Sikkink 1998; Barnett and Finnemore 2004; Avant et al. 2010). Once they successfully institutionalise a norm internationally, a 'norm cascade' ensues, followed by the norm's internalisation by states. Thereby, international norms 'become more important than domestic politics', acquiring a 'taken for granted' quality as a new standard of appropriate behaviour and thereby causing states to comply with new global rules (Finnemore and Sikkink 1998: 896, 900, 902). For constructivists, then, global governance is produced when small groups of transnational activists and experts successfully promote new norms or shared understandings of a transnational problem and possible solutions to it.

For our purposes, constructivist approaches have some useful insights. First, they recognise how governance regimes may reflect experts' framing of certain issues as *requiring* new forms of governance, which in turn further empowers those experts (Haas 1989). We concur that such empowerment of experts should not be treated as natural or commonsensical. Constructivists also recognise that new 'levels' of governance – notably the global level (Adler 1997; Hoffmann 2005) – are not natural, but must be constructed discursively. We agree that the fact that an issue traverses borders does not mean it will automatically be understood or governed as a transnational matter, and that scales of governance are also not natural, but socially and politically constructed.

However, the explanatory mechanisms used by constructivists cannot systematically explain divergent outcomes in the governance of transnational issues. Why is it, for example, that Asian governments have mostly implemented, or are in the process of implementing, FATF's 40 Recommendations on combating money laundering and terrorist financing (see chapter five), but campaigns designed to prevent environmental degradation have had relatively little purchase (see chapter three)? Why does one set of knowledge, ideas, norms, rules or authority prevail over another in particular circumstances? Why does a 'taboo' emerge to prevent the use of some deadly weapons, but not others (Price 1997; Tannenwald 2005)? Similarly, why is the idea of a global or regional scale compelling at some times and for some issue-areas, but not others? Likewise, how do some small expert groups become 'global governors' (Avant et al. 2010) whilst others do not? Constructivists explain the capacity of small groups of activists and technical experts to make innovations in governance as something inherent to their expertise, the moral force of the norms they promote or their persuasive power. In reality, however, experts are not always listened to, and 'persuasion' and 'socialisation' do not always work. As Walter's (2008) discussion of banking reform showed, international norms do not always trump domestic politics. Moreover, despite Darwinian claims that the 'better norm' in an issue-area is 'naturally selected' to become 'dominant' (Florini 1996: 364), in reality the 'good'-norm entrepreneurs favoured by constructivists frequently encounter rivals promoting 'bad' norms, who often thwart efforts to govern serious problems such as arms trafficking (Bob 2012).

Although constructivists may insist that 'ideas do not float freely' (Risse-Kappen 1994), and claim to include both discursive and material forces in their analysis (Wendt 1999), in practice, their focus on small groups of moral or expert agents denudes their explanatory framework of the broader social, political and economic forces that enable the realisation of one set of ideas whilst disabling others. The triumph of one norm over another in establishing institutions like the International Criminal Court is instead attributed to its supposed moral status as the better argument (Deitelhoff 2009; cf. Hanrieder 2011). Similarly, resistance is explained purely ideationally, as a clash between local and foreign norms (Checkel 1998: 6; see also Acharya 2004, 2009b; Merry 2006). But it would surely strain credibility to argue, for example, that climate scientists and concerned NGOs' failure to promote a global climate change mitigation regime merely stems from moral or argumentative weakness or a clash with local norms, without considering the material context of their campaign, particularly a global capitalist economy driven by the consumption of fossil fuels.

Attempts at constituting new framings and scales, empowering experts and so on can only be properly understood when considered as part of broader contestations over power and resources, which shape the relative strength and authority of different groups and the ideas they are promoting (cf. Bieler 2001; Bieler and Morton 2008).

However, constructivist analyses typically avoid discussion of material power relations and specific social forces in a misguided quest to prove that norms 'matter' more than interests. Barnett and Finnemore's (2004: 45) treatment of the IMF is a particularly egregious example. They argue that developments within 'the IMF's expert authority prompted shifts in its mission', from helping states achieve full employment in the immediate post-war decades to pursuing neoliberal structural adjustment in the 1980s, for example. This shift is attributed to intellectual developments internal to the IMF, legitimated externally by 'economic analysis that is accepted by a large number of economists in many countries' and enacted through the 'persuasion and education' of target governments (Barnett and Finnemore 2004: 45, 48, 68). There is no mention whatsoever of the material context and drivers of this shift: the 1980s' third-world debt crisis, which prompted structural adjustment interventions to rescue overexposed Western banks at the expense of developing-country governments and peoples. There is also no recognition of how structural adjustment was actually pursued: not simply through 'persuasion and education' but rather coercion – strict conditionality imposed on IMF loans to crisis-hit states. Barnett and Finnemore (2004: 68) imply that none of this matters because, if the IMF lacked normative 'authority' stemming from its expert status and merely demanded reforms because powerful states insisted, 'borrowers would rebel, [and] publics in G7 states would mobilise in protest'. But in fact borrowers did rebel, not least because their own publics 'mobilised in protests' (widely described as 'IMF riots'), later followed by anti-IFI demonstrations in Western states. The smooth constructivist world of 'authority', 'socialisation' and 'persuasion' does not countenance such violent strife.

Another weakness of constructivism is the tendency to treat the state as a 'black box' (Bulkeley and Newell 2010), and as a coherent or unitary actor, albeit one whose interests and identities can change. By adopting realist statism – an explicit commitment of Wendt (1999), who even theorises the state as a person (Wendt 2004) – constructivists assume that the basic nature of states is static. There is no investigation of the historical evolution of state forms, or of specific state apparatuses and their relations with particular societal forces. Commensurately, there is also frequently a sharp separation in this literature between states, IOs and NGOs, with IOs and NGOs' roles being limited to attempting to socialise or persuade states to accept new norms (Wapner 1996 is an exception). Constructivists thereby neglect the transformation and rescaling of state apparatuses, including their networking with IOs and NGOs, which, as some liberals observe, are crucial processes through which the governance of transnational issues actually occurs.

Finally, as with the other approaches surveyed above, constructivists provide little sense of how and why – or indeed whether – governance actually works (Bulkeley and Newell 2010). Until extremely recently, constructivists paid virtually no attention to what happens after norms are supposedly 'internalised'. They have typically supposed that governance simply 'happens', because contestation over norms is assumed to end during the 'institutionalisation' phase and, having internalised the norms, actors should logically behave in accordance with them (Finnemore and Sikkink 1998; Risse-Kappen et al. 1999). Constructivists thereby neglect the material conditions and power relations that actually make normative regimes efficacious, or inefficacious, in different contexts. Wiener (2008), for example, attributes variance in EU governance to the degree of cross-border interaction between bureaucrats, which determines whether shared understandings of 'contested norms' are generated. The 'evolving and changing power position' of officials is, however, explicitly 'left to one side' (Wiener 2009: 191). In another example, Sharman (2011a) claims that the normative power of the FATF to damage states' 'reputation' compels them to adopt its Recommendations for combating money laundering. But he does not adequately recognise that the FATF's capacity to inflict reputational damage stems from a very specific political economy context – the sensitivity of investors, operating in highly fluid global capital markets, to risk indicators like the FATF's 'blacklist' – and is not generalisable beyond this case (see chapter five). Such concerns are absent from, for example, the international market for palm oil, and so 'shaming' those engaged in environmentally destructive production has no such effect (see chapter three). And despite its unique context, actual compliance with FATF rules – as Sharman himself observes and our cases studies further demonstrate – is feeble.

Again, if FATF's 'norms' really had the independent capacity to 'socialise' regulators and 'persuade' states, we should not observe this outcome.

A few constructivists have been forced to recognise and explore the 'compliance gap' between norms and actual state practice, which their earlier models could not explain (Risse-Kappen et al. 2013). This has compelled them to recognise the importance of not merely ideational but also *material* power relations in the socialisation process, including changing incentives, international economic coercion and domestic political struggles (Deere 2009; Risse-Kappen et al. 2013; Betts and Orchard 2014). Although this is welcome, constructivist theorising of these factors remains thin and underdeveloped. Consequently, constructivism remains of questionable value.

Neo-Gramscian approaches to global governance

Neo-Gramscian scholars view global governance as expressing the agency of specific social forces and dominant class strategies, particularly the rise of a transnational capitalist class promoting the intensification of neoliberal globalisation (Gill 1995; van der Pijl 1998, 2012; Overbeek 2005). From this perspective, global governance is a hegemonic project driven by dominant class fractions – notably high finance – and their 'technopol' allies in governments and bureaucracies, designed to intensify commodification, reduce barriers to capital and increase profits at the expense of other social groups. Accordingly, neo-Gramscians tend to focus on global *economic* governance and peak institutions, like the World Bank, IMF, World Trade Organization and EU, in spreading and locking in neoliberal 'discipline'.

We see considerable utility in neo-Gramscian contributions for our purposes. First, these scholars were among the earliest to highlight transformations in statehood and the transnational networking of agencies to create new governance systems (Cox 1981; Cox and Sinclair 1996). They demonstrate that global governance occurs not simply through erecting supranational authorities but also by reconfiguring domestic state apparatuses to advance particular global agendas (Sassen 2014). This is a profoundly important insight that is central to the approach developed in this book. Furthermore, neo-Gramscians rightly link this process to transformations in the global political economy, which appropriately historicises developments in global governance, rather than presuming a timeless, unchanging international system. Global governance regimes are also usefully seen as complexes of ideologies, material conditions and institutions, thereby eschewing the mainstream IR perspectives' misguided focus on just one or two of these elements in isolation (Cox and Sinclair 1996).

Second, neo-Gramscians foreground contestation over global governance, theorising this as social conflict rooted in concrete, material contexts (Gill 2002, 2008). The neoliberal governance project is seen as being attached to, and driven by, the interests and ideologies of specific social forces, not merely small bands of 'norm entrepreneurs' (Bieler 2001; Bieler and Morton 2008). Moreover, this class project is not smoothly realised through 'persuasion' and 'socialisation'; other social forces resist and contest it, shaping the outcome. Thus, governance systems like the EU are shaped by conflict between transnational capital and nationally based labour movements (Bieler and Morton 2001; van Apeldoorn 2002; Bieler 2005). Accordingly, there is no expectation that governance will be automatic, smooth or stable, as mainstream IR approaches imply; instead it will be contested and contingent, and could possibly break down, leading to further restructuring (Brenner et al. 2010).

Third, neo-Gramscians avoid reified categories and simplistic distinctions between states and societies, or the domestic and the international. They recognise that the processes driving global governance are simultaneously inside and outside the state, are local and global and occur at different scales (Sassen 2014). In terms of scale, neo-Gramscians acknowledge the disjuncture between territorially based governance and the global capitalist economy that global governance seeks to manage (Gill 1992). Neo-Gramscians also recognise the stakes involved in shifting decision-making and authority to post-national scales; these are not functional, teleological processes or technocratic tweaks, but involve shifting the locus of authority, undermining democratic accountability and depoliticising important issues, by removing economic governance from the purview of representative institutions and establishing a neoliberal 'economic constitutionalism' (Gill 1992, 2002).

Neo-Gramscian perspectives become less persuasive, however, when we attempt to apply their ideas to NTS issues, or to other non-economic global governance concerns. Virtually all neo-Gramscian literature focuses on the economy (e.g. Overbeek 2005; van Apeldoorn et al. 2007; Gill and Cutler 2014a), which makes it easier to argue that global governance is merely 'the political-judicial counterpart to disciplinary neoliberalism' (Gill and Cutler 2014b: 6), directly servicing the economic interests of dominant classes. This is less compelling in other issue-areas. Cox, for example, has been criticised for treating the state's military-security role as 'merely a function of political economy' (Schechter in Cox and Schechter 2002: 4). Where neo-Gramscians have focused on security issues, they tend to critique the insecurities generated by neoliberal capitalism, or the growing privatisation of security provision (e.g. Gill and Bakker 2003; van der Pijl et al. 2004). They have not yet sought to explain the governance of particular security issues, and it is not clear that class interests would translate as directly here as neo-Gramscian accounts sometimes imply.

Take, for example, the issue of infectious disease control, which we explore in chapter four. Certainly, claims are made that the WHO's declaration of a state of emergency to tackle the H1N1 'swine flu' pandemic in 2009 was partly motivated by its overly cosy relationship with big pharmaceutical companies, which undoubtedly profited from the worldwide rush to purchase countermeasures and vaccines (see Durodié 2011). Davies (2010) also argues that funders have pressured the WHO since the 1980s to promote the neoliberal restructuring of developing countries' health systems. Chorev (2012) argues, however, that the WHO has quite successfully repelled these pressures, despite resultant funding cuts and the WHO's partial eclipse by the World Bank as a significant health donor. The link to a hegemonic class project becomes even less convincing when we consider the WHO's increasingly important role in emergency pandemic preparedness and response. For example, the WHO's declaration of travel embargoes in response to the 2003 SARS outbreak caused a serious economic shock to the affected Asian countries and the Canadian city of Toronto, and therefore to the global circulation of capital (Abraham 2007). It would, therefore, be dubious to argue that the WHO is little more than a mechanism for promoting a worldwide neoliberal project on behalf of a dominant transnational capitalist class. Although the WHO arguably moved to contain SARS to protect core capitalist economies from exposure, it did so by harming economic interests operating elsewhere. This suggests that, at the very least, different governance arrangements may benefit different class fractions, operating at different scales and with different sectoral interests, rather than expressing the interests of a hegemonic, transnational bourgeoisie.

While, theoretically, nothing in the Gramscian approach would fore-close analysis along such lines, in practice, there is an unfortunate tendency to depict global governance as part of a relatively unified and coherent system of class domination or 'hegemony', a global 'disciplinary' system compelling compliance from all states (Gill 1995). Despite ostensibly accepting that the 'new constitutionalism' is 'not a uniform force field' but is variable and 'contingent', neo-Gramscians nonetheless present it as 'part of a broader supremacist... project of rule associated with extending the power of capital and the geopolit-ical reach of the US, and... creating a global plutocracy' (Gill and Cutler 2014b: 6, 14). Arguably, this overstates the coherence and evenness of processes of global economic transformation and does not adequately consider transnational or local resistance, variega-tion, adaptation and experimentation (see Ong 2006; Brenner et al. 2010). In neo-Gramscian accounts, 'resistance' generally means resis-tance to neoliberalism, whether progressive or reactionary, with anti-globalisation protestors or organised labour as oft-used examples (Gill 2002, 2008; Bieler and Morton 2001; Gill and Cutler 2014a). They have not yet explored the way in which powerful capitalist interests, transnational or local, may selectively embrace neoliberalism or global governance in some cases, but resist it and attempt to reshape it when their own interests are threatened (cf. Harvey 2005).

In summary, despite its considerable strengths, the neo-Gramscian framework has not yet developed to adequately explain security gover-nance. A looser, middle-range theory is required that does not subsume all modes of governance into a single hegemonic project, but is focused more on specific struggles around particular issue-areas.

Poststructuralist (governmentality) approaches to global governance

Poststructuralists study how global governance is produced, particu-larly as it transforms subjects and practices. They typically see global governance as a form of 'governmentality' – the modern urge to order and rule, not necessarily through coercion, but through the use of discourses, understood as power–knowledge constructs, to cultivate subjects who will govern themselves in particular ways (Dean 1999).

While Foucault devised this concept to explain early-modern European statecraft, some argue that it has recently been extended internationally, including to the regulation of developing countries (Lipschutz with Rowe 2005).[6] In global governance, governmentality is typically understood as explicitly neoliberal, promoting the production of self-regulating, entrepreneurial, risk-managing subjects and the creation of market dynamics (Larner and Walters 2004a; Ong 2006; Methmann et al. 2013a). Poststructuralists also analyse global governance as the internationalisation of 'biopolitics' – the modern drive to improve the population's well-being (see Duffield 2007; Lakoff and Collier 2008). Combined with the neoliberal ethos, this produces an emphasis on best-practice codes, measurement, benchmarking and market mechanisms in regimes like the Millennium Development Goals or carbon-trading markets, which depoliticise the deeper roots of the problems being governed (Löwenheim 2008; Methmann et al. 2013a). Nonetheless, poststructuralists do not present global governance as being shaped by an underlying structure, either in the global political economy or class relations, or the international states system. Rather, poststructuralists perceive a patchwork of partial and even contradictory initiatives, reflecting various power plays by diverse actors.

For the purposes of this book, poststructuralist approaches have some merits. They emphasise the highly problematic, messy and unstable nature of the 'assemblages' formed in international governance. This 'bricolage' (Cerny 2010) seems to capture much of what we see empirically. As even mainstream commentators note, we do not observe coherent world or even regional government, but nor is governance left entirely to states; instead, a revived 'neo-medievalism' exists, with cross-cutting networks claiming authority and exercising varying levels of efficacy across different spaces (e.g. Zielonka 2007). Poststructuralist approaches also transcend rigid local/global and public/private distinctions, being sensitive to complex arrangements operating at multiple scales simultaneously (e.g. Heng and McDonagh 2008; Hansen and Salskov-Iversen 2008). They emphasise that governance scales are not pre-existing, with governance merely shifting from one already established level to another, but have to be *constituted* through the production of new networks and knowledge (Larner and Walters 2004b: 14). They also reject the constructivist dichotomies between states, IOs

[6] For a critique of applications of Foucault in IR, see Joseph (2010).

and civil society, observing that civil society actors can actually form part of governing regimes and play a key role in depoliticising them, rather than simply being 'good guys' spreading 'good' norms (Sending and Neumann 2006; Jaeger 2007). Poststructuralists also avoid presenting a zero-sum power struggle between states and supranational bodies, instead observing how some forms of international governance can actually re-empower particular state interests (Valverde and Mopas 2004: 236; Sending and Neumann 2006; Rajkovic 2012). Their emphasis of the unevenness and selectivity of neoliberal good governance is also more sensitive than neo-Gramscian scholarship to how *some* spaces or issues may be subjected to global rules and forces while others are not. Neoliberalism is not presented here as a hegemonic, all-consuming project, but as a logic that is selectively embraced and therefore highly variegated (e.g. Ong 2006). A few poststructuralists also explore how local practices cause governance outcomes to vary (Valverde and Mopas 2004: 245). Finally, poststructuralists are particularly alert to how grasping problems as 'risks' leads to new 'risk-management' regimes, which in turn empower actors like technical experts (Heng and McDonagh 2008; Jaeger 2010; Hansen 2011).

Nonetheless, poststructuralist approaches have drawbacks, limiting their analytical utility. If neo-Gramscian approaches suffer from a tendency to view global governance as a coherent, top-down class project, the poststructuralists' problem is the exact opposite. Their overemphasis on the fluid, haphazard nature of global governance misses the broader structural forces that powerfully shape, and even determine, outcomes (Brenner et al. 2010). By depicting 'governmentality' as a massive series of messy experiments, poststructuralists miss the broader structural transformations that have fostered the rise of global governance and set its general contours, ensuring that outcomes are not as indeterminate, open-ended and 'radically unstable' as they suggest (Methmann et al. 2013b: 7). Although some poststructuralists engage with political economy and therefore do not operate entirely at the discursive level (e.g. Lipschutz with Rowe 2005; Ong 2006), their general aversion to discussing social structure tends to overlook or unduly marginalise the structural constraints and embedded power relations that arguably shape governance outcomes in different contexts.

Even some poststructuralist scholars have been strongly critical of governmentality approaches' neglect of questions of agency and social and material context. As Larner and Walters (2004b: 4) argue, governmentality 'describes a political process without agency, contexts, conditions or interactions'. Dale (2004: 184) similarly criticises a 'tendency . . . for abstract nouns, rather than individual or collective agents, to be the subject of sentences'. But the poststructuralists making these criticisms often have a very limited social ontology themselves, focusing, for example, solely on bureaucrats or security professionals (Dale 2004: 181; Bigo 2002; CASE Collective 2006). Indeed, when poststructuralists criticise a lack of concern for 'contexts, conditions or interactions', they usually refer to a lack of *discursive* contextualisation, such as a failure to consider the 'interplay' of different discourses, or how specific governmental 'technologies' may clash with other political rationalities (Mert 2013; Dale 2004: 185). Although poststructuralists often claim that their notion of 'discourse' encompasses material dynamics, in reality, their work tends to neglect it entirely: 'the dominant perspective is that [focusing] on speech and language' (Methmann et al. 2013c: 254–5).

This leaves poststructuralists exposed to many of the criticisms we earlier levelled at constructivists. Poststructuralists often *describe* the rise of particular discourses, but rarely if ever *explain* why one becomes dominant. Although poststructuralists, like constructivists, eschew linking discourses to material determinants, refusing to analyse them as 'ideology' (Methmann et al. 2013b: 6), they develop no other explanations. Governmentality theorists themselves concede that their approach 'entails a move of "bracketing" the world of underlying forces and causes, and instead examining the different ways in which the real has been inscribed in thought' (Larner and Walters 2004b: 16). But for those interested in causes, this generates very dissatisfying, descriptive treatments. Thus, for example, Wolf (2013) rightly identifies that the governance of climate change is extensively marketised, but several hints that this serves the interests of powerful states and economic actors are not built into any explanation for this outcome or any assessment of its structural determinants. Instead, in line with the poststructuralist emphasis on radical contingency, he incongruously suggests that climate governance's 'future direction is wide open' (Wolf 2013: 54). Conversely, as Lohmann (2013) shows, one cannot understand why environmental problems are governed through market mechanisms, or how these mechanisms actually operate in practice, without considering the dominant role of finance capital, financialisation, accumulation crises and other material drivers.

The exclusive concern with discourse, moreover, neglects or produces misguided accounts of real-world contestations over governance innovations. The linguistic turn has largely generated 'armchair research' focusing solely on texts and failing to examine real-world practices, merely assuming that governance outcomes are shaped by the discourses being studied (Neumann 2002). Ironically, considering the discussion in some governmentality scholarship of 'hybridity' and 'bricolage', many accounts depict these discursive 'technologies of power as all pervasive and universal in their effects' (Dale 2004: 185). When poststructuralists do study contestation, they again focus on contending discourses, for example, indigenous versus Western systems of meaning or political rationalities (Li 2007). Accordingly, poststructuralists overlook the capacity of local elites to *instrumentally* adopt, adapt and subvert regulatory interventions for their own ends (Hameiri 2010), often by forming tactical, cross-cutting coalitions of local and international actors that are otherwise ideologically incompatible (see Hughes and Hutchison 2012).

Conclusion

This chapter surveyed existing approaches to security and governance to identify their utility and limitations for explaining the emergence and operation of NTS governance regimes. We began with an assessment of the securitisation literature. We took from existing constructivist and poststructuralist work the notion that security is socially constructed; that it refers to real or potential existential dangers; that securitisation inherently empowers some actors at the expense of others; that discourse plays some role in defining security and that networks of experts and officials are an important aspect of security governance. But, we argued, these approaches cannot explain the form that NTS governance takes in different issue-areas and places; indeed, this is rarely their aim.

We then considered the security governance literature. This makes an important contribution by recognising how the expansion of security threats and risks that are supposedly beyond the capacity of individual states to manage has been responded to by dispersing authority to new actors and mechanisms operating below, alongside and above the state. However, the subfield's functionalist origins leave it without a robust theoretical basis, restricting it to a particularly atheoretical form of comparative regionalism that cannot adequately explain observable

variation in real-world security governance. To progress, the study
of security governance needs a better theorisation of how governance
regimes are constructed and why they operate the way they do.

To this end, we surveyed the literature on global governance.
Although largely unconcerned with security, this field has endeav-
oured to explain how transnational issues are governed, with some
approaches also examining how governance regimes work in practice.
We explored realist, liberal, constructivist, neo-Gramscian and poststructuralist (governmentality) approaches. While each offers useful
insights, we found neo-Gramscian and poststructuralist approaches
most applicable to our concerns. Scholars in these traditions are sensitive to the social contestation that drives the formation and operation
of governance institutions, and the possibility of governance being
contested across multiple scales. They also attend to the transformation of states involved in new modes of governance, and the uneven,
unstable and contradictory nature of governance outcomes. Both have
their weaknesses, however, with neo-Gramscians often overstating the
unity, coherence and efficacy of global governance as an expression of
dominant transnational class interests, and poststructuralists tending
to overstate the fragmentation, fluidity and haphazardness of governance outcomes because of their neglect of structural constraints and
material power relations.

Having examined the strengths and weaknesses of existing approaches, the next chapter builds on insights selected above to elaborate our own State Transformation Approach to explaining NTS
governance.

2 | *The state transformation approach*

This chapter develops our framework for understanding how non-traditional security (NTS) issues are governed in practice: the State Transformation Approach (STA). The STA overcomes the limitations of existing approaches by bringing together the hitherto largely discrete literatures on governance and security, and adds important new insights from political geography, state theory and the study of new modes of governance and regulation.

The STA starts from our observation that 'traditional' and 'non-traditional' security issues are qualitatively distinct, requiring novel modes of governance rather than simply extending the logic of war to new issues, as the Copenhagen School suggests. Traditional securitisation, which focuses on interstate conflict, tends to reinforce the organisation of world politics along the lines separating states. However, NTS issues are typically viewed as at least potentially transnational and thus beyond the capacity of individual states to manage, requiring new, post-national governance responses. Although this claim is practically axiomatic in both public discourse on NTS issues and in the relevant specialist literatures, its significance for theory-building has largely escaped scholars of international security.

From this observation, we proceed in three theoretical steps in the following sections. First, drawing on critical political geography, we theorise the political process that drives the emergence of NTS governance as a kind of *politics of scale*, involving contestations over the appropriate scale at which a particular NTS problem should be managed, as well as over the governance instruments and actors seen as best suited to manage the issue. The securitisation of NTS issues comprises not merely the discursive identification of threats, but also claims that existing, nationally based forms of governance are inadequate, and related efforts to construct new modes of regulatory governance at other scales. Crucially, this does not necessarily mean shifting the locus of authority to pre-existing supranational institutions at the regional or global levels, but rather the *rescaling* of parts of the national, or in some cases subnational, state, so that these are removed from a purely domestic context and are integrated into regulatory regimes operating on a regional or global scale. This process often involves the production of *new* spaces and scales of security governance that are depicted as more suitable for the issue at hand. For example, the main locus of anti-money laundering efforts in Southeast Asia is not the formal regional organisation, the Association of Southeast Asian Nations (ASEAN), but the Financial Action Task Force-affiliated Asia Pacific Group on Money Laundering (APG), which is a far wider geographic entity with a narrow regulatory focus. Moreover, as critical political geographers note, the scale at which any issue is governed is not natural or pre-given but, because it privileges different societal interests and agendas, is always contested.

Our second move, therefore, is to theorise this contestation over scale as part of a wider politics of state transformation. Rescaled NTS governance does not seek the usurpation of state power by international organisations, but rather the reconfiguration of state powers, institutions and processes to enact international plans for containing and managing NTS threats. Accordingly, state transformation is at the heart of NTS governance. Our conception of state transformation deploys a Marxist understanding of the state, as theorised by Nicos Poulantzas (1978) and Bob Jessop (1990, 2002, 2008). In contrast to mainstream, statist, International Relations (IR) approaches, we view the state as a social power relation, expressing the agency, interests and ideologies of specific socio-political forces, particularly classes and class fractions, in given historical contexts. Political outcomes, including governance outcomes, are thus understood as the contingent products of struggles between contending forces. State *transformation* thus refers not merely to changes in states' institutional architecture, but also to a broader institutionalised and/or routinised transition in the distribution and (re)production of political power within particular states, which is always partial among different socio-political groups. Attempts to rescale NTS governance are just one manifestation and driver of this broader phenomenon; accordingly, we situate it within its context theoretically and historically. We thereby present attempts to transform state apparatuses to create transnational NTS governance arrangements as a conflict-ridden form of state transformation.

Third, we understand the outcomes of efforts to construct NTS governance as being determined by socio-political conflict, which is shaped by broader structural constraints. Specifically, whether and how security governance is rescaled, and how governance regimes operate in practice, reflect the contingent outcomes of dynamic contestations between socio-political coalitions, whose relative strength is shaped by the broader political economy context and wider social power relations. This is an ontological commitment, shaped by our adoption of Marxist state theory, but also reflects the specific nature of NTS issues. NTS threats are widely depicted as undesirable side effects of economic development, 'the dark side of globalization' (G8 1999; Smith 2001; Mittelman 2010). The extension of global trading and financial networks, for example, is often thought to facilitate the expansion of international criminal activities and terrorism. Consequently, efforts to combat NTS threats are depicted as 'wars of globalization' (Andreas 2013: 22). Because addressing NTS issues frequently involves efforts to regulate the economic activities seen to produce, exacerbate or facilitate them, they often affect important economic interests, which vary by issue-area. Sectors and companies whose interests are served or threatened by governance innovations will thus naturally join, or even form, coalitions to contest the rescaling of governance. That NTS issues are intrinsically related to the economy does not, however, mean that governance outcomes are dictated by the most significant economic actors, as their relative strength and capacity to attract necessary support from other powerful actors in business, government or civil society varies considerably depending on the historical development of state–society and class relations.

Non-traditional security and the politics of scale

Our key starting point is that the securitisation of NTS issues does not merely add to a 'laundry list' of security problems for states; it is a qualitatively distinct process, requiring a new framework for analysis. This is because the securitisation of NTS issues inherently problematises the conventional notion that world politics is organised along the territorial borders separating states. Migration induced by climate change, for instance, is assumed to 'have destabilising impacts well beyond the areas impacted by displacement', creating a spillover or 'domino effect'; as the 2007 Stern Review put it, environmental crises 'in the developing world may have knock-on consequences for developed economies, through disruption to global trade and security ... population movement and financial contagion' (Bettini 2013: 127). This transnational aspect of NTS challenges leads most observers to conclude that 'the changing nature of threats ... has largely surpassed the capacity of individual states to efficiently perform their traditional task of providing security to their citizens' (Kirchner and Domínguez 2011b: 1), generating demands for 'intricate and extensive forms of cooperation' across borders (Sperling and Webber 2014: 135). This framing of NTS issues as not merely existentially dangerous, but also as transnational and therefore beyond the capacity of individual governments to avoid and manage, is a central feature of the politics of NTS securitisation. This framing has theoretical, not just rhetorical, significance. It intrinsically raises questions of *scale*: the argument made is that, as threats have expanded in scope, beyond the national level, commensurate shifts in governance must follow to adequately manage them. In other words, governance must be *rescaled* to fit the scope of the threat.

This *rescaling* of NTS issues – the scope of the threat, its referent object and its governance – is the most crucial aspect of their securitisation. Indeed, their relocation beyond the national scale, though not necessarily altogether out of the hands of state actors, partly constitutes their securitisation, while the discourse of threat helps rationalise the rescaling of governance to other levels and undermines resistance to this process. Importantly, this does not simply mean shifting the issue into regional intergovernmental forums, for example, but can involve the rescaling of particular state apparatuses themselves by inserting them into, or making them answerable to, international or transnational governance systems.

This process of rescaling is always contested, involving subjective political strategies, rather than simply being a rational response to an objective threat environment, because different scales always privilege different interests and ideologies – a point we elaborate below. The politics of NTS thus involves different coalitions of actors, typically spanning state and society, struggling to define the nature of the problem and the appropriate scale at which it should be governed. The securitisation process may involve discursive strategies but, contra the Copenhagen School, is not limited simply to (indeed, may not even involve) demanding exceptional measures and, to yield real-world effects, also involves going beyond discourse to materially produce new governance arrangements or rescale existing ones.

IR scholars are notoriously blind to the role of space in politics, typically taking the territorial configuration of 'nation-states' for granted and ignoring the contested processes through which these configurations have historically been created and transformed (Agnew 1994). Conversely, critical political geographers have long argued that space and society are mutually constituted. Power relationships run through the construction of space, and, in turn, the spatial organisation of political and economic governance helps (re)produce particular power relations in society (Massey 1992; Harvey 2006). At the most basic level, the extent of the territory over which a state exercises sovereignty has enormous repercussions for the number of people sharing particular identities, the type and amount of natural resources available, the size of internal markets, the number of political actors with citizenship rights, the extent of their networks and so on. Consequently, 'the extensiveness of a territory can play a crucial role in determining the balance of power among competing territorial groups and institutions' (Miller 2009: 54).

Accordingly, attempts to manipulate space and its political consequences – 'territorial politics' – are a crucial, but oft-neglected, aspect of social and political struggle. Societal and state actors frequently pursue 'territorial strategies . . . mobilising state institutions to shape and reshape inherited territorial structurations of political-economic life, including those of state institutions themselves' (Brenner and Elden 2009: 368; also Keating 2009). These strategies are constrained by existing institutional arrangements, including established international borders, national sovereignty and international law, which in themselves are manifestations of earlier contested processes of territorialisation (see Tilly 1992). Yet, if successful, transformations of the spatial configuration of political and economic rule can have profound consequences. For example, the designation of parts of the national territory as 'offshore' industrial zones dramatically affects class struggle by disadvantaging organised labour groups which depend upon national legal protections and bargaining institutions, while advancing the interests of corporations seeking to reduce the cost of production (Lillie 2010).

The different interests and ideologies advanced by particular territorial configurations become particularly clear when considering the

issue of 'scale', a term political geographers use to denote a socio-
politically constructed configuration of social, political and/or territorial space. Whether a political issue is defined as urban/local, provincial, national, regional, global and so on is not neutral but, because
each scale involves different configurations of actors, resources and
political opportunity structures, always privileges certain societal interests and values over others. Together with the nature of the socio-
political coalitions that organise around different scales, it is one of
the most important factors that determine the outcome of social and
political conflicts over a given issue. Precisely because the scale of
governance matters so much, actors will typically attempt to rescale
issues as a way of (re)producing particular power relations favourable
to themselves and their allies, while other actors and coalitions will
resist such efforts if they are deleterious to them. For example, authoritarian local officials will often try to maintain a local scale of governance to preserve their dominance, whilst their weaker opponents
will seek to redefine contentious issues as a matter for national politics in order to widen the scope of conflict and draw in allies to tilt
the balance of forces in their favour (Gibson 2012; see also Gough
2004). This strategy of 'scale-jumping' – shifting political contestation
to a different scale to bring in new actors and resources – has been
used by movements as disparate as the Zapatistas, labour unions,
indigenous peoples' organisations, feminists, environmentalists and
living wage campaigners (Leitner and Sheppard 2009: 233). Importantly, this is not limited to merely shifting an issue between predefined territorial levels, but can involve efforts to produce entirely
new scales designed to create political traction, like city-regions, ethnically based transboundary communities or cosmopolitan 'one world'
framings.

Crucially, there is no scale at which it is 'natural', 'better' or 'more
progressive' to govern a particular issue; there are only scalar arrangements that advance some groups' agendas and interests better than others. Consequently we should not assume that those promoting global
governance are 'good guys' while those resisting by trying to maintain a national scale of governance are 'bad guys'. As we shall see,
for example, in chapter five, highly authoritarian elites in Myanmar
have harnessed rescaling to marginalise social and political opposition. Moreover, the politics of scale need not take a dichotomous,
for-or-against, all-or-nothing, form: contestation could instead revolve

around the degree and form of rescaling and the practical operation of rescaled institutions. A constrained form of rescaling can serve conservative and authoritarian interests well: by internationalising governance in certain domains, it may deprive opposition groups of future opportunities to contest these policy areas (Hameiri 2010: Ch. 7). Similarly, in our case study of money laundering (chapter five), there is such overwhelming pressure to rescale governance that contestation concerns not whether to rescale, but rather how far. Powerful groups also seek to mould how transformed governance apparatuses operate in practice, to suit their interests.

Although the study of territorial politics typically focuses on domestic political struggles (e.g. Keating 2008; Gibson 2012), there is no reason why the governance of particular issues cannot be rescaled to levels beyond state borders: there is no 'initial moment that creates a [timeless] framework or container within which future struggles are played out' (Brenner and Elden 2009: 367). Indeed, the presentation of NTS issues as 'transnational' is itself to insist on governing them outside of national frameworks, although not necessarily by non-state actors. This is often missed by security governance scholars, who present such demands simply as a necessary, functional response to globalisation, and claim that 'the altered threat environment has called forth a particular type of response' (Sperling and Webber 2014: 128). Yet, as chapter one notes, many of today's threats are not new; they are understood and managed differently. Claims to the contrary are actually part of this redefinition of security challenges. One example of how such redefinitions alter practice is the revised 2005 International Health Regulations (IHRs) of the World Health Organisation (WHO). These reflect the perception that the incidence and severity of emerging infectious diseases has intensified and therefore that the older IHRs, dating from 1851, which sought to coordinate intergovernmental cooperation on disease control at border crossings, were no longer effective or adequate (Fidler 2007; Davies 2012). Instead, the new IHRs go much deeper to specify the domestic health systems, capacities and processes that each country must develop to comply with the international pandemic preparedness framework. The WHO, in this regime, is not so much a supranational body amalgamating or overriding national governments' authority, but a regulator, evaluator and coordinator for a range of ostensibly national authorities being networked across borders towards common goals.

ımple reveals that the rescaling processes associated with lve not merely rescaling the scope of particular issues but ıpparatuses tasked to deal with them. From this perspective, ics of NTS differs radically from that of traditional security. sing NTS issues does not simply add to a list of security concerns for states whose fundamental nature remains unchanged. Rather, by virtue of their transnational nature, the securitisation of NTS issues is part of a process of state transformation.

State transformation and the governance of non-traditional security

State transformation is the crucial mechanism through which the rescaling of NTS governance occurs. This perspective is a fundamental departure from mainstream security studies, which – unlike some scholarship in political science, globalisation studies and political geography – typically depicts states as fixed and unchanging. This section outlines our understanding of state transformation as a political project driven by particular socio-political interests as part of wider struggles over power and wealth. The demand for and construction of new, transnational modes of governance to address NTS is not occurring in a vacuum. Rather, it is part of a much broader transformation of political life, in which the national scale of governance is being 'relativised', permitting new experiments with multilevel, networked forms of governance. This transformation is itself associated with epochal shifts in the global political economy and local socio-political power dynamics. Thus, rather than analysing the state transformation of NTS governance in isolation, this section situates it historically as an outcome and further accelerant of wider structural changes in global politics.

At the most basic level, 'state transformation' refers to the political, legal and institutional reconfiguration of state power and apparatuses. It involves changes to the authority of and relationships between different agencies and actors, potentially across the public–private and domestic–international divides. Existing agencies and functions may be destroyed or amended and new ones created, while patterns of authority and control are reallocated. 'State transformation' thus denotes a wide range of innovations, including the redistribution of powers across state agencies, the outsourcing of authority to quasi-autonomous or private actors, decentralisation to subnational units and upward delegation to supranational agencies. In mainstream political science, particularly EU studies, 'state transformation' is often used to denote several of these processes occurring simultaneously, and the networking of public and private actors in complex, multilevel governance arrangements. The concept thus refers to the replacement of traditional, Weberian state forms, based on hierarchical, territorially bounded 'command-and-control' systems, by more fluid, overlapping patterns of rule involving the continuous negotiation of authority between diverse actors at multiple scales (Hooghe and Marks 2003; Slaughter 2004; Pierre and Peters 2005).

On this basis, Sørensen (2004), for example, divides the world into 'post-modern', 'modern' and 'pre-modern' forms of statehood, with EU members seen as the most advanced manifestation of transformed, 'post-modern' statehood, because they have pooled their sovereignty in many issue-areas. Emerging powers, like China and India, are viewed as 'modern', given their concern to protect national sovereignty and emphasis on growing national military prowess. Failing peripheral states are viewed as 'pre-modern', unable even to bring their national territory under centralised control (see also Cooper 2000). This typology is alternatively presented in terms of post-Westphalian, Westphalian and pre-Westphalian states (Hettne 2010), which, as we have seen, is also used in the literature on security governance.

Institutionalist approaches like Sørensen's helpfully transcend the stale debate on whether globalisation 'strengthens' or 'weakens' states in 'zero-sum' terms, and are descriptively potentially useful. However, they do not adequately explain why transformations occur in some contexts, but not others. The descriptive labelling of entire states as transformed – 'post-modern' or 'post-Westphalian' – and of others as 'non-transformed' – pre-modern, 'pre-Westphalian' or 'Westphalian' – neglects the fact that considerable internal transformations along 'post-modern' lines are occurring within states typically characterised as 'modern' or 'Westphalian', such as China and India (e.g. Rudolph and Rudolph 2001; Zheng 2004; Dubash and Morgan 2013), while in 'post-modern' Europe, resistance to transnational governance occurs in many issue-areas, with sovereignty being surrendered or flexed depending on the interests at stake (Adler-Nissen and Gammeltoft-Hansen 2008). That transformations in statehood are clearly contested and uneven is precisely what our approach focuses on and seeks to explain.

In our more flexible formulation, state transformation is fundamentally a political project driven by particular interests and manifested in institutionalised, or routinised, shifts in the manner in which political power is distributed and (re)produced within particular states. This process can also involve, as it does in the politics of NTS, territorial politics. There are three aspects to this transformation: shifts in the *location* of state power, meaning the institutions and modes of governance through which it is exercised; in the *ideological rationalisation* for the use of state power; and in the *actors and agencies* exercising state power (Hameiri 2010). Consider, for example, the widely observed rise of quasi-autonomous non-governmental organisations ('quangos') in advanced capitalist states. This has involved shifting the location of state power out of central government ministries into the hands of semi-autonomous, issue-specific regulatory bodies. It has been rationalised through discourses of market-facing efficiency – claims that 'bureaucratic' government control is less effective, costlier and more susceptible to undesirable political 'interference' than light-touch regulation by non-political actors with issue-specific expertise. The shift has disempowered central ministries (and, by extension, the electorate), which have lost many of their direct mechanisms of control over socio-economic processes, while empowering a new caste of technical experts. In some issue-areas, quango-style regulation has also become both privatised and internationalised, shifting the scale of governance. For instance, the Forest Stewardship Council, a non-profit private body, strongly influences the governance of forestry and wood products by convening business and environmentalist NGOs to govern global supply chains, cutting across established national boundaries.

As the foregoing hints at, although state transformation has institutional manifestations, more importantly, it reflects and further entrenches fundamental shifts in social power relations that condition how state power is arranged and used in practice. These shifts – which are heavily contested – are the STA's primary focus. This emphasis reflects a Marxist theorisation of state power developed by Poulantzas (1978) and Jessop (1990, 2002, 2008). Here, the state is viewed not merely as a set of institutions, agencies and actors, but primarily as a social relation and expression of power. State power is understood as a set of complex and dynamic social and political relationships that shape the form and operation of state institutions (see Hewison et al. 1993: 4–5). Conflict among historically specific coalitions of social and political forces, rooted primarily in the political economy – classes, class fractions, distributional coalitions and other societal groups – is consequently crucial for understanding why particular state forms and institutions emerge, and for explaining how they function in practice.

The chief insight of this state theory is that states and their institutions are never neutral but always express a 'strategic selectivity', being more open to certain societal forces pursuing particular strategies than to others and thereby systematically privileging some interests and agendas over others (Jessop 2008). Most generally, the underlying dependence of capitalist states upon the expansion of capitalist economies to generate employment and government revenue means that the interests of the capitalist class, or of particular fractions thereof, are systematically privileged over the interests of other groups (see Jessop 1990; Panitch and Gindin 2012). More specifically, the particular societal interests privileged in any given period express the outcome of historical struggles to restructure state apparatuses.

This theoretical approach sheds important light upon the origins, nature and potential trajectory of contemporary transformations in statehood, helping us to set the rise of transboundary NTS governance in its proper historical context. As many scholars note, policymaking is increasingly being reallocated from democratically elected governments to non-elected experts, networked with their peers across borders, with the central state's role being redefined as a coordinator and regulator of a range of private and semi-private governance actors (Slaughter 2004; Pierre and Peters 2005; Vibert 2007). This process of state transformation emerged from the uneven and contested dismantling of many of the institutions of the post-war welfare state in the West, and the subsequent spread of new governance models to other parts of the world. The institutions of the welfare state reflected a Keynesian–Fordist 'compact' between capital and labour within nationally based industrial societies, designed to avoid repeating the instability and resort to radical politics experienced in the 1930s, particularly in the context of the early Cold War (Jayasuriya 2006). Accordingly, national representatives of business and workers were inserted directly into 'corporatist' governing institutions, and an unprecedented share of economic output was allocated to wages (Stilwell and Jordan 2007: 22; European Commission 2010b: 92;

Federal Reserve Bank of St. Louis 2013). In the 1970s, however, Western capitalism entered a period of sustained crisis marked by declining profit rates and rising unemployment. Rising wage rates and union power became a liability for capitalist expansion. The transformations in statehood that followed were aspects of political projects designed to restore, or in some cases (e.g. China and Russia) create, capitalist class power (Harvey 2005; Jessop 2002).

Whether pioneered by overt attacks on organised labour by the 'new right', as in Thatcher's Britain and Reagan's US, or by parties ostensibly of the centre-left, state 'reforms' since the 1970s have consistently sought to undermine the post-war Keynesian settlement and re-establish state–society relations around new ideas of market participation and competition, captured in Cerny's (1997) concept of the 'competition state', or Jessop's (1993) notion of the 'Schumpeterian workfare state' (see also Hay 1996). Whether we employ these labels, or the commonly used 'regulatory state' (Majone 1994), all highlight the institutionalised marginalisation of hitherto-central political claims based on material inequality. Government's function has been redefined from securing a political accommodation between competing domestic interests to facilitating market-led development, providing regulation and managing risk. The state has retreated from directly securing many social, economic and political objectives to merely setting broad goals and elaborating regulatory frameworks for myriad public and private bodies to operate within (Jayasuriya 2001). Accordingly, corporatist state apparatuses have been dismantled or sidelined, marginalising the actors they once empowered, such as nationally based industrialists and organised labour (Jessop 2002). Authority has been dispersed to diverse governance actors, often operating outside the official boundaries of government. These transformations have been crucial in limiting the range of issues contested through the institutions of representative democracy, and have given considerable power to unelected experts – public and private – to define and govern particular issues (Swyngedouw 2005; Vibert 2007). They have also played an important part in shifting the axes of contestation over social policy from left–right to supranational–subnational, making the politics of scale intrinsic to this process (Linos 2007).

This disaggregation of statehood carries enormous consequences for international politics, including in relation to NTS. The diminished role of central administrations and the expanded responsibility and autonomy of other public and private agencies has permitted and encouraged the latter to engage with their counterparts across international borders to devise common solutions to shared problems (Jayasuriya 2001). Thereby, complex governance structures have emerged, networking together governmental, intergovernmental and non-state actors operating simultaneously across several scales. For example, central banks and financial regulators are now increasingly independent of governmental control, and no longer simply operate nationally. They are instead networked with their counterparts and private-sector bodies across borders, establishing regulatory codes that seek to govern spaces and flows well beyond their own formal jurisdictions. These networked, multilevel arrangements have established new 'transnational regulatory regimes' or 'regulatory regionalism', operating not as supranational organisations transcending state power, but instead working through transformed – rescaled – state apparatuses that are no longer purely domestic in nature (Eberlein and Grande 2005; Hameiri and Jayasuriya 2011). Although such arrangements are often presented neutrally, as simply being more 'efficient', their net effect is to further weaken the power of organisations like trade unions, whose power depends upon national political and legal institutions, and which have typically sought to expose questions of economic governance to wider, democratic contestation (Gill 1992; Lillie 2010). This is why, according to Murphy (2000: 794), the biggest winners in global governance have been 'global private authorities', like bond-rating agencies, self-regulating bodies and business cartels. Meanwhile, organisations that are more representative or corporatist, like the International Labour Organization, or more devoted to economic development, like UNCTAD, have been sidelined.

These transformations, and the demise of traditional left–right sociopolitical contestation (Giddens 1994), promote and have been supported by material shifts in the political economy, commonly described as economic globalisation. One important transition has been from Fordist to post-Fordist forms of production (Jessop 1993). Post-Fordism often involves complex, transnational production chains that improve corporations' leverage vis-à-vis both national governments, which increasingly struggle to regulate and tax multinational enterprises, and the working class, which has been rendered fragmented and politically disorganised. A second important structural transformation has been the massive growth of financial capitalism and its deep embedding within contemporary class relations. In the US, for example, the share of manufacturing in corporate profits declined from around sixty per cent in the 1960s to about five per cent by 2007, while the share of finance increased from less than ten per cent to approximately forty-five per cent (Harvey 2010: 22). Declining wages and job security were initially offset through expanded consumer credit, though this eventually contributed to the current global financial crisis (Crouch 2011), while the financialisation of workers' lives has made political counter-mobilisation even harder (Martin et al. 2008). Meanwhile, resources and power have become massively concentrated: just 0.7 per cent of the global population now control 44 per cent of global wealth (Credit Suisse Research Institute 2014: 24).

The opportunity to experiment with new modes of transnational governance has been further facilitated by associated shifts in elite and popular attitudes towards the national and other scales. Key among these is the 'relativisation' of the national scale. The dominance of the national scale as the appropriate level at which political, economic and security issues should be governed, which IR scholars usually see as a timeless fact of life (Agnew 1994), now appears more as a feature of a particular historical moment, consolidated through the 'long nineteenth century' (Hobsbawm 1962, 1975, 1987) and reaching its zenith in the early post-war decades. The Keynesian–Fordist domestic settlement, supported by the Bretton Woods institutions, affirmed the primacy of national money over international currency and established the individual and social wage as the basis of domestic demand. These priorities 'were reflected in the primacy of national economies, national welfare states, and national societies managed by national states concerned to unify national territories' (Jessop 2009: 99). Internationally, this was reflected in a strong determination to uphold state sovereignty and existing territorial borders, including those bequeathed to post-colonial states (Barkin and Cronin 1994), and by an understanding of international security as being fundamentally interstate in nature. Today, however, the national scale is no longer automatically assumed to be the best level at which issues should be governed. Yet, no other scale – whether local, regional or global – 'has acquired a similar dominance. Instead, different economic and political spaces and forces located at different scales are competing to become the primary or nodal point of accumulation and/or state power' (Jessop 2009: 99). As Krahmann (2003: 12) observes of security governance, the '"upward" shift [of policy-making arrangements] does not represent a substitution of the state as central authority by international institutions, which would suggest centralization at a new level, but typically marks the dispersion of political authority between governments and their international organisations'. This relativisation of scale also offers important new opportunities for scale-jumping and struggles over inter-scalar articulation.

The securitisation of ostensibly transnational issues is further prompted and legitimised by the related emergence of new 'spatial imaginaries', through which political thought and identities are recast (Larner and Le Heron 2002). Partly as a result of the creation of global market forces, capitalist interests and state managers encourage citizens to perceive and adjust their social and economic life in the context of global economic competition, creating a strong sense of the planetary scale on which economic flows now operate. This is reinforced by popular and scholarly discussion of 'globalisation'. State managers experimenting with transnationalised forms of governance promote new regional imaginaries to cultivate popular legitimacy for their projects, such as a 'European' identity or an 'ASEAN community'. Environmentalist NGOs and scientists construct 'bioregions' that cut across domestic jurisdictions, encouraging us to imagine ourselves as part of regional or global ecosystems. And urban political elites and finance capital promote imaginaries of 'global cities' – better connected to far-flung urban centres than their own hinterlands.

The profusion of such post-national spatial imaginaries creates a far broader subjective sense of interconnectedness across space and of greater vulnerability to far-away developments, while implicitly or explicitly depicting nationally based governance as fundamentally inadequate for the challenges we face. This promotes the identification of NTS issues as being intrinsically transnational in nature and thus requiring rescaled forms of governance. For instance, although terrorism is often presented as a 'new' transnational threat, in reality, it is an old threat whose imagined scale has mirrored the rise and fall of the national scale. In the nineteenth century, where transnational empires were common and national states had yet to consolidate, elites understood terrorism as a transnational problem, generating 'embryonic' transnational governance, including cross-border policing. In the twentieth century, however, the problem was downscaled to a national problem to be addressed through national measures. However, with the relativisation of the national scale from the 1970s onwards, terrorism was once more depicted as a trans-boundary threat requiring transnationalised governance approaches (Aydinli 2010b: 8–18). Tackling such issues has also become politically important in the context of the spatial imaginary of a 'world risk society' (Beck 1999). With the demise of class struggle as the animating force of politics, political elites increasingly seek to mobilise support through appealing to and seeking to manage the widespread fear and insecurity accompanying the more precarious and individuated nature of contemporary social and economic life (Furedi 2005).

These epochal changes in statehood, governance and scale, initially emerging in the West, where they were driven largely internally by political responses to the 1970s capitalist crisis, have subsequently spread to non-Western regions through a variety of different mechanisms. This trend is visible even in Asia, traditionally understood as a region of 'strong', 'Westphalian' states. Here, state transformation has generally not been driven by efforts to undermine organised labour, which was largely crushed by Cold War authoritarian regimes. It is rather associated with the transnationalisation and regionalisation of production networks and investment driven by extra-regional firms and by East Asian state and state-linked capitalist interests. State transformation was also promoted by the 1997–8 Asian financial crisis and the associated crisis of the developmental state project, and the need to accommodate political demands from new groups emerging through decades of sustained economic growth (Jayasuriya 2005; Jayasuriya and Rodan 2007). Accordingly, we can observe in Asia a similar process of the state's role being redefined as coordinating and regulating a much wider host of governance actors (Minogue and Cariño 2005; Bach et al. 2006). Even in countries like China, the national government's authority has been radically reduced, with extensive decentralisation to provincial governments, special administrative regions and formally state-owned enterprises, generating an unruly *de facto* federation that is likened to the EU (Breslin 2007: 69; see Zheng 2004, 2007). Moreover, increasingly these disaggregated public and private actors are networked regionally at multiple levels (Jayasuriya 2009; Hameiri and Jayasuriya 2011; Tun Myint 2012). For example, the Chinese provincial government of Yunnan takes a leading role in the Greater Mekong Subregion, where it coordinates vast infrastructural developments with local and national governmental agencies of other states, alongside state-owned and private businesses (Su 2012). As we argue at length in this book, similar processes are visible in relation to NTS. For example, 'hybrid forms of maritime security governance', involving corporations, NGOs, governmental actors and multilateral organisations, have emerged to tackle NTS threats like smuggling, human trafficking, piracy and illegal fishing (Liss 2013).

In Africa and the Southwest Pacific, where most so-called 'fragile' states are located, state transformation processes are often more externally driven. They have partly been facilitated by structural adjustment programmes imposed by international financial institutions (IFIs), and subsequent 'good governance' aid programmes, which have shifted from discrete, time-bounded interventions to ongoing projects of state transformation (Williams 2013). These initiatives promoted a dismantling of developmental state apparatuses and the extensive privatisation of assets, businesses and public services from the 1980s onwards, with the state retrenching to a more 'regulatory' model (Harrison 2004, 2007; Dubash and Morgan 2013). State transformation has also been pursued via Western state-building interventions designed to contain threats and risks emanating from social and political instability in these countries, often by substantially internationalising key government agencies (Hameiri 2010). For example, national treasuries are increasingly subject to transnational regulation, including private regulatory projects like the Extractive Industries Transparency Initiative, and the direct insertion of overseas personnel to supervise budgetary processes – producing 'shared sovereignty' over vast swathes of governmental activity (Krasner 2004). Security governance, too, has become increasingly privatised and globalised (Abrahamsen and Williams 2007). The recently announced US Security Governance Initiative, for example, seeks to bolster ministries of justice and international peacekeeping forces across eleven key African jurisdictions to combat terrorism and transnational crime, creating a 'network of US-backed security partnerships stretching from Morocco to Pakistan' (Ignatius 2014). Interventions in the Pacific, meanwhile, have already seen overseas police and judges being inserted into law enforcement agencies, whose priorities and procedures are reorganised to tackle problems of concern to external powers, rather than pressing domestic issues (Hameiri 2010).

Dubash and Morgan (2012) rightly observe that, in developing countries, relatively intense distributional conflicts often compromise or overwhelm regulatory state apparatuses. This is certainly a pattern we observe in our case studies. However, Western regulatory states are themselves hardly immune from corruption, regulatory capture and the subversion of public governance for private ends. This is simply a reminder that all state forms represent contingent outcomes of social and political conflicts and that, despite their claims to neutrality, efficiency and serving the 'public good', regulatory states privilege certain societal interests over others. Moreover, even amidst intense distributional struggles in the global South, networked, multilevel and transnational modes of governance are increasingly visible (Dingwerth 2008; Hameiri 2009a; Leonard 2009).

To summarise, the politics of scale around NTS governance is not a unique phenomenon, but part of broader transformations in the global political economy and statehood that have occurred in recent decades. The politics of NTS is not a singular driver of state transformation, but one specific manifestation of these processes, both reflecting the existing disaggregation of governance and spurring it further. The framing of NTS issues as transnational in nature and as requiring governance systems which map onto these problems reflects the relativisation of scale, with the national level no longer being seen as the most appropriate one at which to manage collective problems. Yet, because different scalar framings and governance arrangements are not neutral, but always privilege certain interests and agendas over others, they are always contested in practice. We now turn to theorise this contestation, which determines how far NTS governance is rescaled, and how it operates in practice.

The political economy of non-traditional security

This section describes the STA's third and final element, elaborating the guidelines for case study analysis. So far, we have argued that the politics of securitising NTS issues manifests as attempts to shift the scale at which these issues are governed to new scales and modes of governance seen as better suited to managing transnational problems, and that these rescaling efforts take the form of state transformation, underpinned by changes in the political economy and social power relations. We develop this further by arguing that the outcome of such rescaling efforts, as well as how rescaled modes of security governance work in practice, is determined by the contingent outcomes of struggles between socio-political coalitions supporting or resisting rescaling. In turn, the nature and relative strength of these coalitions is shaped by the political economy of the particular sector and economic activity that rescaling would affect, within the broader context of capitalist development and the social and political power relations running through a particular state and society.

This analytical perspective flows naturally from our choice of state theory, but is also important given the specific nature of NTS. If states are expressions of social power and exhibit strategic selectivity, then political analysis must involve carefully identifying concrete social and political forces and their interrelations in particular contexts, and tracing how these shape political outcomes. However, a political economy analysis is particularly warranted for NTS. For many policymakers, and for analysts adopting a broadly realist ontology, the rise of NTS issues on the security agenda stems in important parts from accelerating economic globalisation processes, particularly since the late 1980s. The end of the Cold War is seen to have undermined the sense of 'ontological security' – the knowledge of what to expect – associated with the stable geopolitical structures of bipolar rivalry, making policymakers and citizens more attuned to other security threats and risks (Giddens 1991: 35–69). Moreover, it is commonly argued that intensifying global economic flows impose real and very serious pressures on the natural world, generating unintended consequences like environmental degradation or deadly new pathogens (Brower and Chalk 2003; Davis 2005; Elbe 2008). Furthermore, the transportation and communication technologies that are produced by, and further facilitate, globalisation are also seen to enable the spread of problems like pandemic disease, and to afford new opportunities for transnational terrorist and criminal groups to organise and strike (Libicki 2001; White House 1998).

Since many issues presented as NTS threats are perceived as direct or indirect products of economic activities, efforts to manage them will inevitably carry potentially significant implications for the activities concerned. They may challenge existing accumulation regimes and attendant social and political power structures, and therefore touch on the specific interests of particular industries and sectors. Seeking to interdict transnational terrorist financing affects banking and financial institutions; containing the spread of animal-to-human disease engages agricultural interests; tackling environmental degradation threatens the operations of polluting industries. Business and related actors are therefore likely to be strongly involved in struggles over the rescaling and transformation of NTS governance. In any given case, how particular sectors and segments of industry relate to the issue and how rescaling security governance will affect their interests will shape to what extent they will promote or oppose such moves, and how. As noted in chapter one, as the security agenda becomes non-traditional, broadening into other areas and touching on new interests, so too does the composition of actors involved in security politics and governance.

The success of industry interests in attaining desired governance outcomes depends on the broader political economy and state–society relations. Where an industry (or part of it) is dominant, is able to form broad alliances with other powerful societal groups and/or has privileged access to state institutions, it may be able to successfully promote, curtail, or resist rescaling, or limit rescaling to less powerful parts of the sector and society, in line with its interests. Its capacity to do so is likely to revolve around several political economy factors.

The regional or global political economy of the issue-area is of particular importance because it shapes the costs and benefits for different actors associated with particular governance scales. For example, global governance networks like the Forest Stewardship Council (FSC) and the Roundtable on Sustainable Palm Oil (RSPO) promote environmentally friendly production of wood and palm oil, respectively, by certifying firms that satisfy their sustainability criteria. The FSC is substantially more successful than the RSPO because, since a sizeable global market for sustainable wood products exists, export-oriented wood producers have embraced the global scale of governance. Conversely, the market for sustainable palm oil is tiny and the fastest-growing export markets are economies like China's, where sustainability concerns are minimal. Consequently, the world's largest palm oil industry, Indonesia's, has withdrawn from the RSPO to promote a much weaker, national-scale certification scheme instead. In rare cases – as in our study of money laundering (chapter five) – global market pressures are so overwhelming that total resistance to rescaling becomes too costly, constricting contestation to the degree of rescaling and the operation of rescaled institutions.

Local political economy factors and state–society relations are also critical in shaping business actors' attitude towards and ability to influence rescaling. These include the industry's contribution to the domestic economy and government revenues, its perceived importance in relation to ideological goals like 'national development' and its specific, historically constituted relationship with the state and key agencies and groups within it.

The latter point is particularly important because, notwithstanding all the changes discussed above, governments – far from being completely sidelined as hyper-globalists suggest – retain a key role as 'scale managers' (Peck 2002: 340). As the emphasis on state *transformation* suggests, states are not simply 'losing' power in a zero-sum sense to supranational bodies; rather, institutions previously confined to a national scale are being rescaled. Despite the relativisation of the national scale, by virtue of their formal sovereignty, resources and institutional capacities, national governments retain considerable influence over the level at which issues are governed (Mahon and Keil 2009). They may, for example, curtail the transnational activities of subnational units, or bargain with international donors to limit or redirect governance interventions. Because central government indifference, if not active buy-in, is typically necessary to achieve desired outcomes, this grants considerable power to actors with influence over this tier.

However, in line with the 'strategic selectivity' of state institutions, access to their 'scale management' function varies considerably and is itself shaped by the broader political economy and socio-political power relations. As we have seen, states' strategic selectivity reflects social and political conflict and consequently varies considerably over time and space. It also varies across state institutions. Far from being unified, coherent entities, as mainstream theorists suggest,

The sheer unwieldy character of states' far-flung parts, the many fronts on which they fight battles with groupings with conflicting standards of behaviour, and the lure for their officials of alternative sets of rules that might, for example, empower or enrich them personally or privilege the group to which they are most loyal, all have led to diverse practices by states' parts or fragments. Various parts or fragments of the state have allied with one another, as well as with groups outside, to further their goals. Those practices and alliances have acted to promote a variety of sets of rules, often quite distinct from those set out in the state's own official laws and regulations (Migdal 2001: 20).

Thus, it is not unusual to see some state agencies and their societal allies promote rescaling, while other powerful social groups, whose interests are threatened by such moves, simultaneously find influential allies elsewhere in the state apparatus to assist them, generating complex, internecine struggles spanning state and society. For example, in responding to H5N1 avian influenza, the Indonesian Ministry of Health (MoH) resisted international intervention in late 2006 when it refused to share virus samples with the WHO and expelled the US Naval Area Medical Research Unit from the country. Simultaneously, however, the MoH, supported by veterinarians, encouraged other international interventions that helped it establish some control over local-level animal health surveillance. Meanwhile, powerful poultry industry interests supported the more industry-friendly Ministry of Agriculture in seizing control of and terminating the unpopular policy of poultry culling (Hameiri 2014). Contending interests and alliances among different state apparatuses and societal groups thus produced an incoherent, uneven governance outcome.

Finally, and importantly, the contestation of rescaling does not stop with the establishment of rescaled governance institutions, but continues thereafter to influence how these apparatuses actually operate in practice. As policy studies have long noted, even if ideal policies are enacted, during the implementation phase, the allocation of costs and benefits is often dictated by patronage networks, ethnic, personal or other particularistic coalitions spanning state and society (Grindle 1980). Thus, even if they failed to dictate the degree and form of rescaling that occurred, powerful economic players enjoying close links to state actors may be able to constrain or subvert the operation of rescaled governance institutions through coercion, corruption or other forms of regulatory capture. Indeed, rather than overt political opposition, such subversion could be the primary means by which rescaling is resisted (Ferraro 2014: 57–8, 61–2).

Thus, exploring how corporate interests and influence, market dynamics and class power shape outcomes is essential to explaining why governance regimes so often fail to meet their ostensible objectives, rather than simply lamenting this fact and issuing naive recommendations for additional effort or institutional fixes. As Lohmann (2013: 82) comments, such shortcomings are too often depicted as 'irksome pathologies or side issues. When such phenomena persist despite their supposed "abnormality", well-intentioned mainstream observers find themselves at sea, impotent to suggest any solutions other than more "political will" or better technique' (see, for example, Weiss 2013: 149).

Given the importance of the political economy context in shaping the relationship of particular socio-political forces to a given NTS issue-area, and also their capacity to influence the formation and operation of governance regimes, we closely analyse this aspect of NTS politics in our case studies. How a given NTS issue is produced by economic activity and how efforts to tackle the problem impinge on different sectors is identified, along with the specific state–society relations that provide the context for struggles over the rescaling of governance.

Conclusion

This chapter outlined the STA, a new, mid-range framework for explaining how NTS issues are governed in practice. The STA charts a middle path between the neo-Gramscian and poststructuralist approaches discussed in chapter one, because it is sensitive to the complexity and diversity of the interests involved in shaping NTS governance and to the structural, material context within which new modes of security governance emerge, develop and function. It consists of three theoretical moves. First, we argue that questions of scale are central to the politics and governance of NTS, but that the scale at which particular issues are governed is not neutral, as different scalar arrangements involve different configurations of actors, resources and political opportunity structures, and always privilege certain societal interests and values over others. Second, we located the politics of scale associated with NTS as part of a wider context of state transformation. Drawing on the state theory of Poulantzas and Jessop, we defined state transformation as institutionalised and/or routinised shifts in the distribution, production and reproduction of state power in particular states. The widely observed rise of new forms of disaggregated, regulatory statehood and the associated 'relativisation' of the national scale of governance are, from this perspective, linked to the contested and uneven demise of the post-war Keynesian state, in the context of a deep crisis of Western capitalism and commensurate shifts in the global political economy. The politics and governance of NTS are a particular manifestation, as well as a driver, of such processes of state transformation. Finally, we argued that the form and operation of NTS governance in particular contexts is shaped by struggles between coalitions, encompassing parts of states, business, NGOs and IOs. The constitution and relative power of these coalitions and their orientation to rescaling are shaped by the political economy of the sector concerned and the broader context of the social and political power relations running through state and society. What we *do not* argue is that powerful business interests always resist attempts to rescale governance or introduce more stringent regulation. We also do not argue that the outcomes of struggles over NTS governance are determined by the size of affected industries, or that capitalist interests simply dictate outcomes. As our case studies clearly demonstrate, the particular, historically constituted relationship between the state and the industry concerned, as well as the varying capacity of business interests to form coalitions within and outside the state, mean that outcomes are driven by the political actions of real actors in dynamic contexts and the contingent outcomes of socio-political conflicts are not determined *a priori*. Nevertheless, the range of possible outcomes in NTS governance is strongly conditioned by the political economy, and is therefore structurally constrained, rather than being entirely voluntary or open-ended.

PART II

Case studies

3 | Governing transboundary pollution: Southeast Asia's haze

The earliest calls to include nontraditional issues on the security agenda referred to the environment, and by the late 1990s the Copenhagen School had firmly identified it as a 'sector' of international security (Ullman 1983; Mathews 1989; Buzan et al. 1998). While initial securitising moves reflected concern with rainforest and ozone depletion and the 1986 Chernobyl disaster, climate change has undoubtedly been decisive, spurring many important states and international organisations to identify environmental degradation as a security threat. The 1994 German Defence White Paper was the earliest to do so, insisting that 'risk analysis...must be based on a broad concept of security' including 'ecological trends'. The EU Commission's *Strategic Objectives 2005–2009* warned that 'environmental crises' generated 'cross-border threats' (Brauch 2005: 26–7, 58). In 2007, the British government initiated the first UN Security Council discussion of climate change, amidst claims that it was partly driving the war in Darfur. In the same year, Al Gore and the Intergovernmental Panel on Climate Change (IPCC) were jointly awarded the Nobel Peace Prize, implying that environmental degradation was now a threat to international peace. The IPCC's 2014 report explicitly made this claim, adding a chapter on the security implications of climate change for the first time. Indeed, by then, leading states had already securitised climate change. The UK's 2008 National Security Strategy identified it as 'potentially the greatest challenge to global stability and security, and therefore to national security' (Cabinet Office 2008: 18). In the same year, Australia's prime minister declared climate change the 'most fundamental national security challenge for the long term future' (Rudd 2008). Even the US, typically seen as an environmental laggard, has gradually followed suit. The Pentagon initiated climate change scenario planning in 2003; the 2006 National Security Strategy included 'environmental destruction' as a non-traditional issue that if 'left unaddressed...can

threaten national security' (White House 2006: 47); and the 2010 Quadrennial Defense Review explicitly discusses 'environmental security',
stating that 'climate change will shape the operating environment, roles
and missions that we undertake' (US DoD 2010b: 84).

Environmental securitisation has largely been driven by neo-
Malthusian narratives, which depict human societies, particularly in
developing countries, as exhausting their natural environments and
being overwhelmed by the consequences, resulting in civil unrest,
armed conflicts, mass migration or even – in the most alarmist formulations – civilisational 'collapse' (Diamond 2005). Because these bleak
scenarios risked prompting a militarised response from powerful states
to contain the 'spillover', some ecologists resisted environmental securitisation altogether (Deudney 1990). However, others have promoted
an alternative 'human security' framework, which seeks to mitigate
environmental risks faced by the most vulnerable. Reflecting a key
premise of the State Transformation Approach (STA), in this formulation, the *transboundary* nature of environmental degradation renders
militarised, state-based responses ineffectual. Thus, Dalby (2009: 6–7,
75, 132) argues that, given the 'global scale' of environmental change,

the simple geography of protecting domestic spaces from external threats ...
is no longer adequate ... The global economy spreads [environmental] conflicts across national boundaries, so impacts of consumption in one place
are frequently displaced into other states and regions ... [Consequently,]
national frontiers cannot be taken as the given categories for political
action.

These contrasting approaches to environmental security have merged
over the last decade. The claim that environmental security cannot be
managed at a national scale is now widely echoed by policymakers.
For example, in 2009, US President Barack Obama declared: 'every
nation on this planet is at risk. And just as no one nation is responsible for climate change, no one nation can address it alone' (Webersik
2010: 111). Accordingly, the governments of many powerful states
now suggest that their security depends on preventive, ecological risk
management in 'fragile' states, rather than the *post hoc* military containment of 'spillover' from environmental conflicts. Environmental
security is consequently pursued by transforming governance arrangements within vulnerable states to improve resource management, prevent climate change and develop resilience to climate-induced disasters.

This state transformation is generally overlooked by the literature on global environmental governance, which tends to focus on formal intergovernmental bargaining and regimes. Yet, since many such regimes involve establishing targets, standards and guidelines for domestic governance and networking institutions across state borders, they too are implemented through state transformation.

To illustrate this shift and explore its constraints, this chapter uses the STA to analyse efforts to govern Southeast Asia's most serious environmental security problem: the 'haze'. This euphemism denotes a thick, acrid smog arising annually from land and forest fires in Indonesia, which drifts into the territory of neighbouring states, particularly Malaysia and Singapore. The haze causes widespread socio-economic harm, serious health problems and massive disruption to trade, investment, travel and tourism, and it also contributes significantly to climate change. In 1997, one of the worst years, fires killed around 500 people, haze harmed the health of 70 million people and the total socio-economic and environmental cost was estimated at US$9.3 billion (Qadri 2001: 52, 54). The carbon dioxide released comprised an estimated thirteen to forty per cent of the total global emissions from fossil fuels in that year (Page et al. 2002). By 2010, Indonesia was the world's third largest carbon dioxide emitter after the US and China, with land and forest fires comprising eighty-five per cent of its emissions (McCarthy and Zen 2010: 156; Luttrell et al. 2011: 14). Accordingly, the haze has been directly linked to the threat of climate change. Unsurprisingly, regional states have identified the haze as a significant transboundary security threat (ASEAN 2006a). Considerable attempts have been made to construct a regional multilevel governance system for fire suppression and land management to mitigate the risk of fire, involving the transformation and rescaling of Indonesian domestic institutions.

However, these rescaling efforts, and the operation of rescaled institutions, have been shaped by intense contestation, rendering ASEAN's haze regime highly uneven and often ineffective. This contestation is rooted in the political economy of Indonesia's plantation sector, where operators often use fire to clear land cheaply. They typically enjoy impunity due to the sector's entrenched corruption and patronage relations, which were exacerbated by Indonesia's post-1998 decentralisation. Politico-business networks have resisted governance rescaling that would threaten their interests, and deflected rescaled governance apparatuses away from commercial plantations while co-opting fire-fighting teams to work on their plantations. Blame for the haze, and governance interventions, has been deflected onto politically and economically weaker actors: smallholders and subsistence farmers. Although these groups do burn land, they are not primarily responsible for major fires and, due to their poverty, they lack alternative methods to clear land. Consequently, the haze regime's operations are largely counterproductive and ineffective.

The chapter comprises two subsequent sections. The first examines the rise of 'environmental security', showing how the neo-Malthusian and human security approaches merged into a thrust to transform governance in environmentally at-risk jurisdictions. The second section presents the haze case study, describing the rescaling efforts undertaken in Indonesia, and then illustrating how the political economy and state–society context have moulded governance outcomes.

The securitisation of the environment

Scholars generally agree that environmental degradation is objectively occurring – rather than being socially constructed – and demands a response. There is considerable debate, however, over how the threat and response should be framed. Early securitising moves established a durable, neo-Malthusian narrative linking ecological crises to armed conflict and environmental migration from developing countries. Some environmentalists rejected this approach, fearing an inappropriately militarised, statist response. Others promoted a 'human security' approach, which involves assisting the vulnerable, rather than treating them as a threat, and promotes the rescaling of governance institutions to better fit the scale of the problem. These two approaches have gradually merged. Tackling environmentally induced transboundary threats is now widely seen to require addressing vulnerabilities in other states by transforming their internal governance.

The rise of environmental security

The rise of environmental security is often attributed to growing concern, since the 1970s, about acid rain, nuclear power, rainforest destruction, ozone depletion and global warming, suggesting that human-induced environmental degradation has directly precipitated the environment's securitisation. However, like most NTS issues, threats emanating from environmental change are neither entirely new nor solely associated with contemporary globalisation. European imperialism considerably altered the environment by transmitting diseases, importing new species and creating new agrarian ecologies, thereby killing and displacing tens of millions of people (Crosby 1986). Similarly, the British Empire's creation of global cereal markets caused famines that killed millions in the late nineteenth century (Davis 2001). The environment–security nexus was even discussed at the height of the Cold War, with the health consequences of nuclear fallout helping to generate the 1963 Partial Nuclear Test Ban Treaty (Brauch 2005: 59; Dalby 2009: 37).

However, the notion of environmental security only gained serious currency as the Cold War's ideological conflict dissipated. Following the 1986 Chernobyl disaster, Soviet premier Mikhail Gorbachev proposed 'ecological security' as a top international priority. His foreign minister declared in May 1989 that 'the traditional view of universal security based primarily on military means of defence is now totally obsolete and must be urgently revised'. He proposed creating a UN Environmental Security Council and a UN Centre for Emergency Environmental Assistance, a 'group of international experts... [comprising] a rapid response force' – quickly dubbed 'green helmets' (Dabelko 2008: 36–7). The 1987 Brundtland Commission report also proposed expanding security 'to include the growing impacts of environmental stress – globally, nationally, regionally, locally', placing the threat of 'environmental ruin worldwide' alongside that of nuclear war (Brauch 2005: 27). Subsequently, many environmentalists promoted environmental securitisation to redirect political attention and resources to their cause (e.g. Westing 1986; Holst 1989; Mathews 1989). 'Environmental security' also appealed to conservative Western elites seeking new bases for domestic and foreign policy as the force of anti-communism dwindled. Having defeated the British trade union movement, for example, Prime Minister Margaret Thatcher embraced environmental degradation as a 'new threat' supplanting communism (Harrabin 2013). Later, other conservatives also framed 'the environment' as a 'hostile power', 'filling the hole' left by the collapsed Soviet Union (Kaplan 1994: 54–5).

This post-ideological convergence, backed by important scientific bodies like the IPCC, has fostered growing elite consensus around climate change as the ultimate threat to humanity, including even many corporate actors. Capitalist state managers initially resisted radical environmentalists' demands, insisting on balancing environmental protection with continued economic growth (Bulkeley 2001). However, over time, businesses in important sectors like insurance, finance and energy have found ways to extract profits from the scarcities, subsidies and markets introduced to mitigate environmental degradation (Heartfield 2008; Newell and Paterson 2010). Influential interventions like the Stern Review have also framed climate change as both an economic threat and a business opportunity (Stern 2007). Accordingly, powerful corporate actors have joined the chorus for 'environmental security' by demanding a global regulatory framework to create investor certainty and preclude competition from less strictly regulated firms and jurisdictions (IIGCC et al. 2009). This reconciling of environmentalism and capitalism enabled Western governments to look more favourably on 'environmental security', and also profoundly shaped environmental governance, as discussed below.

Promoters of 'environmental security' have always confronted the dilemma of its divisibility. Environmental security may appear indivisible: since the 'biosphere' is global, its degradation anywhere can be seen as threatening people everywhere, not just those within particular state boundaries. As Mische (1989: 394–6) asserted: 'the Earth does not recognise security as we know it . . . The sovereignty of the Earth is indivisible'. However, many aspects of environmental security are, in fact, divisible. For example, less developed countries, which contributed least to climate change, are most likely to suffer its effects. Rising sea levels threaten Pacific Island states far more than others since, unlike developed countries, they cannot afford technological adaptations to defend their low-lying territories. Accordingly, some realists argued that the environment is not a security concern for the major powers (Levy 1995).

Environmentalists have therefore emphasised the *transboundary* threats arising from ecological degradation to encourage governments and people in wealthier states to care about the issue. This involved reviving previously discredited Malthusian arguments that resource exhaustion would lead to societal collapse, 'spilling over' into threats to international security. In a typical account, Mathews (1989: 168, 170) warned that global warming could disrupt Western economies and endanger 'the vastly disproportionate share of the world's economic wealth that is packed along coastlines'. More seriously, ecological crises cause 'economic decline [which] leads to frustration, resentment, domestic unrest or even civil war', particularly in developing countries where 'weak central governments will be least able to adapt'. Western states should be concerned, she argues, because '[e]nvironmental refugees spread the disruption across national borders', where they inflict further ecological damage. Similarly, Homer-Dixon (1991: 113) argued that environmental crises could spark civil unrest, revolution and takeovers by 'extremist, authoritarian' forces, which would use external aggression, chemical weapons and 'nuclear blackmail'; thereby, 'the interests of the North may be directly threatened'.

Despite extensive criticism of the assumed linkages between ecological degradation and conflict (see Kahl 2006), this neo-Malthusian narrative became central to environmental securitisation. The spectre of 'environmental refugees' surging across state borders was particularly widely invoked, with the UN Environment Program (UNEP) anticipating 200 million by 2050 (see Hartmann 2013: 94–6). Resource conflict and scarcity were also supposedly central in the so-called 'new wars' induced by globalisation (Jung 2003; LeBillon 2005; Kaldor 2007). In a widely cited article, Kaplan (1994) argued that environment degradation was '*the* national security issue of the twenty-first century'. While the West could adapt, the 'Hobbesian' global South would not. It would become 'increasingly ungovernable', subject to 'anarchic implosion[s] of criminal violence', 'ethnic and regional splits', 'Muslim [*sic*] fundamentalism' and 'disease', with mafias, Islamist terrorists, drug cartels and 'tribes' roaming dangerously across borders, sparking 'subnational' wars and state collapse.

Governing environmental security: struggles over scale and instruments

This depiction of environmental threats as transboundary in nature generated demands to rescale governance beyond the national level. However, this was far from uncontested, underscoring that rescaling is a political move, not a straightforward functional response.

For conservatives and realists, environmentally induced conflicts and migration potentially provided a post-Cold War mission for states' redundant military apparatuses. Neo-Malthusian narratives meshed neatly with growing concern about the security risks emanating from 'failed states' and attendant demands for military intervention and enhanced border security (Brock 1997; Esty 1999; Smith 2007). However, environmentalists attacked this statist approach, arguing that national security apparatuses' focus on interstate violence was inappropriate and counterproductive. For example, Deudney (1990: 464, 475) insisted that environmental threats were not 'particularly "national" in character' but were 'often oblivious of the borders of the nation-state'. He rejected the notion of 'environmental security' altogether, warning environmentalists not to 'dress their programmes in the blood-soaked garments of the war system'.

However, most environmentalists instead sought the benefits of securitisation but promoted *transnational* forms of governance over traditional security responses. Using a logic later extended to all NTS issues, they argued that environmental threats' transboundary nature rendered state-based governance defunct, requiring rescaled, intrusive modes of governance that empowered technical experts and encompassed other societal actors:

> The majority of environmental problems demand regional solutions which encroach upon what we now think of as the prerogatives of national governments ... because the phenomena themselves are defined by the limits of watershed, ecosystem, or atmospheric transport, not by national borders ... No one nation or even group of nations can meet these challenges, and no nation can protect itself from the actions – or inaction – of others ... [Environmental security requires] the remodelling of agriculture, energy use and industrial production ... development assistance ... transferring technology ... new institutions and regulatory regimes ... a more active political role for biologists and chemists ... [and] a more involved and constructive role for the private sector (Mathews 1989: 173–6).

Similarly, even while rejecting 'securitisation', Deudney (1990: 465) promoted a highly interventionist governance agenda for which nationally based defence institutions were clearly inappropriate, arguing that 'aspects of virtually all mundane activities ... must be reformed. The routine everyday behaviour of practically everyone must be altered. This requires behaviour modification *in situ*'.

This agenda has been pursued through the framework of 'human security', rather than 'national security' (Matthew et al. 2010; Brauch et al. 2011). This concept was first popularised by the UN Development Program, which identified environmental change as one of six key challenges to human security (UNDP 1994). Human security advocates present environmental degradation as one of several 'threats without enemies' (Prins 1993), to be addressed not militarily, but by improving environmentally threatened states' capacity to prevent and withstand ecological disasters, thereby reducing individuals' 'vulnerability'. This emphasis resonated with the use of 'vulnerability' by environmental scientists and risk assessors, particularly those focusing on natural disasters. Rather like neo-Malthusian narratives, their technical studies linked ecological crises to threats by arguing that the interaction of environmental 'hazards' with individual 'vulnerabilities' created 'risks' – which needed to be mitigated. This 'hazard–vulnerability–risk' model was increasingly adopted by UN and EU policymakers (Brauch 2005: 31–59). This approach has been powerfully reinforced by scientists' presentation of climate change as the ultimate 'risk' to mankind. While not presently endangering everyone, climate change is nonetheless presented as demanding preventive action to avert future apocalyptic outcomes. This understanding has spurred a 'risk-management' approach to environmental security which emphasises 'building resilience . . . preventing and anticipating dangers rather than on reactions after the event' (Dalby 2009: 135).

Accordingly, rather than statist, 'national security' measures, this approach emphasises 'the need to change government policy, to change the rules and to enforce management standards within territorial jurisdictions', often involving 'technical debate, standards, measurements, evaluations, and assessments based on numerous quantifiable factors' (Dalby 2009: 162). It pursues environmental security by transforming governance in at-risk jurisdictions, creating multilevel regimes that advance international environmental agendas and prevent Malthusian outcomes. In a typical account, Scheffran (2010: 754–6) urges policymakers to:

create and reinforce multilateral regimes that involve cooperation between states and non-government actors from the local to the global level . . . that combine sustainable environmental policy, development policy and preventive security policy . . . [and] migration policy . . . A high priority should be given to stabilising fragile and weak states that are threatened by climate change . . . The[ir] capacity to manage environmental risks must be maintained and reinforced.

Thus, the initially antagonistic neo-Malthusian and human security approaches to environmental security have gradually merged in the policy networks of important states and international organisations. Although the environment continues to be securitised using neo-Malthusian narratives, policy prescriptions now emphasise the transformation of governance in other jurisdictions.

This is clearly apparent even in US policy. In an influential report, the US Center for Naval Analysis (2007: 6–7, 47) depicted environmental crises as generating 'widespread political instability and the likelihood of failed states' and 'large numbers of . . . refugee[s]'. However, it did not recommend enhancing national defences but rather suggested the US 'assist nations at risk [to] build the capacity and resiliency to better cope with the effects of climate change'. Similar analysis emanated from the influential Council on Foreign Relations (Busby 2007). This approach has gradually been mainstreamed into security planning. The 2006 US National Security Strategy suggested that 'environmental destruction' could 'overwhelm the capacity of local authorities . . . requiring a larger international response', including military intervention (White House 2006: 47). However, the 2010 Quadrennial Defense Review (US DoD 2010b: 85–7) shifted to a preventive approach. Using neo-Malthusian tropes, it presented climate change as 'contributing to poverty, environmental degradation and the further weakening of fragile governments . . . [which] will increase the spread of disease, and may spur or exacerbate mass migration'. However, to address such risks, it endorses not toughened border protection, but 'proactive engagement with these countries' to 'help build their capacity to respond'. Although the Pentagon had earlier promoted inter-military 'environmental security cooperation initiatives', its new, expansive agenda underscored the need to 'work collaboratively, through a whole-of-government approach', drawing many other actors into security governance.

European agencies also adopted this approach. The German Advisory Council on Global Change (2008: 2) warned that climate change could 'lead to the further proliferation of weak and fragile statehood and increase the probability of violent conflicts', the impact of which 'can transcend borders . . . swiftly expanding the geographical extent of crisis and conflict'. It suggests mitigating this risk through enhancing global environmental cooperation, adapting developing countries' governance and resource management structures, stabilising weak states through development assistance and creating transnational legal and surveillance regimes to manage environmental migration and other crises (ibid: 7–11). In securitising 'environmental crises', the EU Commission's *Strategic Objectives 2005–2009* followed this approach, promoting intervention 'at all stages: risk prevention, early warning, [and] crisis management' to counter 'cross-border threats' (Brauch 2005: 58). Similarly, Britain's 2010 National Security Strategy states that 'climate change and resource scarcity . . . increases the likelihood of conflict, instability, and state failure', as well as increased human displacement. Emphasising the 'spillover' consequences, the Strategy warns: 'this instability can spread from one country to another', adding that 'failing states . . . provide the environment for terrorists to operate as they look to exploit ungoverned or ill-governed space'. In response, Britain aims to 'tackle the causes of instability overseas in order to prevent risks manifesting themselves in the UK' (Cabinet Office 2010: 10, 16–18, 28). UK environmental security policies have consequently emphasised measures to 'build . . . developing country adaptive capacity and resilience . . . preventing [the need for] more expensive military interventions' later (Harris 2012: 8).

Emerging environmental security regimes

Accordingly, emergent environmental security governance differs considerably from traditional security governance. So-called 'green helmets' have been proposed three times since the 1980s, with some even demanding 'ecological interventions' (Eckersley 2007). However, one-off 'emergency' interventions in sovereign states are not the mainstream response. Instead, alongside pursuing intergovernmental environmental agreements, powerful states and international organisations now seek to rescale governance to fit the scope of ecological threats, and to transform developing countries' environmental governance on an ongoing basis. Environmental security practices thus 'involve highly complex political and diplomatic interventions in difficult and highly charged internal resource management issues . . . [spurring] reforms . . . to improve social resilience and prevent conflict' (Mabey 2008: 8). This typically involves diverse governance actors, often led by development agencies, reflecting the mainstreaming of climate change adaptation and risk management into many of their policies (Vandeweerd et al. 2011), and the widely observed merging of security and development (Duffield 2007). Britain's Department for International Development (DFID), for example, devoted £2.9 billion from 2011 to 2015 to enhancing environmental security in developing countries.

Reflecting the presentation of environmental insecurity as transboundary in nature, governance interventions frequently seek to rescale governance beyond the national level to fit the scope of environmental problems. This expresses the emergence of new spatial imaginaries with environmental rather than socio-political bases, like ecosystems, habitats and bioregions. For example, the ministerial-level Nile Basin Initiative aims to develop shared river-usage policies among eight riparian states to reduce resource conflict (Dabelko 2008: 41). River basin-scale conflict resolution mechanisms are also being promoted in the Kura-Aras and Mekong basins (Vandeweerd et al. 2011: 1309). In Latin America, transboundary governance is developing around bioregions like the Mesoamerican Biological Corridor, which has integrated conservation projects into 'one transborder unit', and the La Plata river basin, where five riparian states jointly govern natural resources (López 2010). In Southeast Asia, the US Agency for International Development (USAID) has promoted 'landscape scale' conservation efforts and 'ecoregional plans', and cooperation is emerging around three transboundary ecosystems: the Greater Mekong Subregion, the Heart of Borneo and the Coral Triangle (Rhee et al. 2004; Ardiansyah and Putri 2011). The British ministries of defence and foreign affairs and DFID (2004) jointly run the African Conflict Prevention Pool, which aims to build regional 'conflict management capacity' and promotes the 'regional management of resources and stability' to prevent resource scarcity and conflict escalating into warfare. As the STA emphasises, rescaling governance to new levels, while presented as commonsensical, is actually highly political, involving the reallocation of power and control over resources. As Finley-Brook (2007: 105–6) notes:

Large-scale conservation efforts may privilege transnational institutions at the expense of local groups . . . [They] frequently incorporate vast regions often without local support. State resource management may be extended to areas where it has a poor record of respecting local rights . . . A landscape-level approach may also be used as an excuse to maintain control of natural resources at higher government levels.

Any analysis of environmental security governance must therefore foreground likely inter-scalar contestation. It must also be sensitive to how 'transfrontier' environmental interventions that may appear to weaken state sovereignty could actually bolster the authority of particular state apparatuses and the interests they serve (Lunstrum 2013).

As the STA also emphasises, rather than establishing supranational bodies or enabling intervention, governance rescaling relies upon the transformation of state apparatuses to pursue internationally determined plans, standards and goals. The Mesoamerican Biological Corridor project, for instance, is largely pursued through the harmonisation of domestic laws, the reconfiguration of local livelihoods and governance and 'the replication of development planning according to global agendas' (Finley-Brook 2007: 117). Similarly, an 'environmental security strategy' spanning Southeastern Europe, the Caucasus and Central Asia, developed by the Organisation for Security Cooperation in Europe, the UNEP and the UNDP, operates through coordinated 'policy development and implementation . . . institutional development, capacity-building and advocacy' (Brauch 2005: 21). In the Caribbean, DFID is promoting a 'regional climate resilience implementation plan', from which twelve subsidiary national plans will be developed and implemented (DFID Caribbean 2012). DFID also seeks to cascade goals and processes downwards from the regional level in South Asia, where it seeks to integrate climate change mitigation into 'urban, regional and national development planning' (DFID Asia Regional Team 2012). Similarly, the EU's Forest Law Enforcement, Governance and Trade (FLEGT) programme reorganises institutions relevant to forestry in developing countries, building their capacity to engage with regional governance initiatives around illegal logging and timber smuggling (European Commission 2003).

Reflecting how transforming such state apparatuses touches directly on the political economy of natural resource use, governance rescaling efforts like these face intense contestation during their creation and implementation. Any attempt to improve environmental security inevitably touches on powerful corporate interests, since it is their resource-depleting and polluting activities that degrade the environment. However, given the collapse of existing alternatives to neoliberal capitalism, environmental governance is predominantly market-based: it seeks to work with, rather than against, the grain of corporate interests. Among the domestic governance transformations specified by FLEGT, for instance, is the creation of a certification scheme for sustainably harvested wood, which attracts a premium in EU markets. Similarly, the UN's Collaborative Program on Reducing Emissions from Deforestation and Degradation seeks to prevent climate change by creating market-based governance systems to measure and certify carbon reductions and to trade carbon permits (Lohmann 2013). Such approaches, and the associated emergence of 'green capitalism', undoubtedly smoothed the course of environmental securitisation, yet also reflect a significant capitulation to private power, channelling environmental governance along lines unthreatening to, or even beneficial for, dominant corporate interests (Levy and Newell 2005). The central role allocated to private-sector agents in designing and implementing these regimes, and the weak, regulatory role assigned to states, also enables business organisations to morph governance arrangements to suit themselves, often with perverse outcomes. Various carbon-trading schemes, for instance, have created bonanza profits for financiers and polluting industries, but no real reductions in carbon dioxide emissions (Gilbertson and Reyes 2009).

Over the last two decades, then, environmentalists' neo-Malthusian advocacy of 'environmental security' and the perspectives of security practitioners within important states and international organisations have substantially merged. Although the Malthusian framing of environmental degradation as causing conflict and mass migration risked reinforcing statist, 'national security' apparatuses, its reframing as a transboundary problem requiring transnational governance arrangements ultimately won out. This is largely because neo-Malthusian rhetoric meshed with Western states' growing concern with 'failing states', which are widely seen to require capacity-building interventions to manage the security risks emanating from poorly governed spaces (Hameiri 2010). This has deflected scrutiny from Western capitalism – historically the main source of environmental degradation – and even opened up new avenues for capital accumulation. Commensurately, the environmental security agenda is now pursued not through UN Security Council interventions, nor merely through negotiations for international environmental treaties, but through the transformation of state apparatuses in at-risk countries, networking them across state borders and directing them to enhance regional and global environmental security using internationally specified guidelines.

Having outlined the rise of the environment as an NTS issue and the form its governance takes, we can now apply the STA to a case study to show how NTS governance in practice is shaped by dynamic contestation rooted in the political economy of the issue-area.

Southeast Asia's haze problem

Southeast Asia's rapid and rapacious mode of capitalist economic development has generated widespread environmental degradation since the 1960s. The region's problems, which often have transnational drivers and repercussions, include extensive deforestation, the pollution of rivers and seas and chronic urban and industrial pollution, including annual transboundary 'haze' pollution caused primarily by fires in Indonesia.

As elsewhere in the world, environmentalists and scholars have promoted the securitisation of such issues in an attempt to prioritise conservation over environmentally destructive economic growth (Dokken 2001). Deploying the neo-Malthusian narratives described earlier, they have appealed to conservative elites' fears of social unrest by suggesting that environmental problems destabilise societies, economies and polities (e.g. Clapp and Dauvergne 2003; Dupont and Pearman 2006; Jasparro and Taylor 2008). In its extreme form, this narrative raises the spectre of ecologically 'failed' states. Busby (2007: 8), for example, argues that climate change 'might further destabilise Indonesia', suggesting that a 'weak' government response to environmental crisis 'could encourage separatists or radicals to challenge the state or launch attacks on Western interests'. While avoiding such alarmism, Southeast Asian governments have nonetheless identified ecological degradation as a regional security threat (ASEAN 2006a). Indonesia's environment minister has securitised the haze as a 'serious threat' to the economy, public health and the environment, while President Susilo Bambang Yudhoyono declared 'war against haze' (Sijabat 2006; *Straits Times* 24 April 2006). However, this discursive securitisation – despite its apparent acceptance by domestic audiences[1] – has not generated the national or regional 'emergency' measures anticipated by the Copenhagen School framework. Consequently, scholars using this approach frequently lament – but struggle adequately to explain – the gap between discourse and action, blaming 'under-securitisation', lack of political will and/or ASEAN's outdated attachment to state

[1] The proportion of Indonesians favouring environmental protection over economic growth and employment rose from forty-six per cent in 2007 to sixty-one per cent in 2012 (Pew Research Center 2007: 19, 2010: 69). By 2012, eighty-one per cent of Indonesians favoured immediate steps to prevent climate change, with either low (forty per cent) or significant (forty-one per cent) costs (Hanson 2012: 17).

sovereignty (e.g. Dokken 2001; Elliot 2007; Yanga 2013). Arguably, however, this very common argument – which recurs in our case study of infectious disease (chapter four) – overlooks the transnational, regulatory forms of governance emerging in this region, and neglects the deeper constraints they face.

The securitisation of the haze reflects the general pattern of environmental securitisation and transnational governance described above. As with other issues, environmentalists securitised the haze to promote conservation. As one NGO leader recalls, when they framed the destruction of Indonesia's forests as a biodiversity issue in the 1980s, 'no one wanted to listen'; but following the 1997–8 haze, they 'presented peat fires as a threat to health and the economy – this is what got attention . . . [This] was very strategic. Without it, we would never have got . . . agreement at the ASEAN level and national-level actions' (Parish 2012). ASEAN now identifies haze as one of six major transboundary security threats affecting Southeast Asia (ASEAN 2006a). Fires and haze are presented as 'threatening . . . natural resources and ecological functions . . . the socio-economic structure of settlements in the region . . . endangering the health of the population', and threatening wider international society by contributing to climate change (ASEAN 2007a: 4). Presenting Indonesia's fires as creating a transboundary threat also transformed a national issue into a regional one, requiring transnational governance. As one Malaysian official explains: 'with the environment, you cannot draw a border – you cannot say, "here is Malaysia; here is Indonesia" when it comes to air quality' (Malaysian Environmental Official 2012). ASEAN's Environment Ministers accordingly resolved in 1997 that 'haze mitigation efforts should be carried out at the ASEAN level due to its transboundary nature' (Varkkey 2014: 2). However, this has been pursued not by endowing ASEAN with the supranational authority to intervene in Indonesia but primarily by promoting the rescaling and internationalisation of forest and land governance within Indonesian territory.

The first subsection below describes these efforts. Since the late 1990s, over forty international projects have sought to improve, rescale and internationalise Indonesia's forest and land management practices, including via ASEAN. However, governance outcomes remain both meagre and unbalanced, with the haze persisting annually. The second subsection identifies two key explanatory factors: the political economy of Indonesia's forestry and plantation sectors and the post-Suharto decentralisation process. The third subsection shows how these factors and associated socio-political contestation have shaped and undermined the governance of this NTS issue. The final subsection explores two bilateral governance interventions in depth to further illustrate these constraints.

Governing the haze

Like many NTS 'threats', the haze is not new. Land and forest fires have occurred in Indonesia since the late nineteenth century (Varkkey 2013a: 2). There were seven serious haze episodes from the 1970s to the late 1990s, with the Asian Development Bank (ADB) estimating that the 1982–3 fires were actually the most costly (Qadri 2001: 36, 54). What *is* new is the attempt to govern this problem transnationally. These efforts have been spearheaded by the Singaporean, Malaysian and Indonesian environment ministries, supported by international institutions including the UNEP, the ADB and the ASEAN Secretariat, multilateral and bilateral donors and international and local environmentalist NGOs. The haze regime they have incrementally established has involved creating regional goals, policies and surveillance mechanisms and promoting the transformation and rescaling of domestic governance to conform to regional standards of land and forest governance.

Initially, these plans sought to suppress the fires causing the haze. The first significant step was the 1995 ASEAN Cooperation Plan on Transboundary Haze Pollution. This established a regional surveillance and reporting mechanism, with 'national focal points' reporting to a newly established ASEAN Specialised Meteorological Centre (ASMC) using regional metrics for air quality and fire danger. The ASMC also began directly monitoring fires region-wide using satellite imagery. ASEAN requested international donor support for national and regional capacity-building, and proposed strengthening the ASEAN Institute of Forest Management's role in developing governance processes (ASEAN 1995). The 1997 Regional Haze Action Plan went further, directing ASEAN governments to develop national-level plans to suppress fires, the contents of which were specified in considerable detail, including legislative changes and measures to strengthen fire-fighting capacities (ASEAN 1997). These tentative steps began establishing regional expectations and directing the transformation of domestic institutions to meet them – an incipient form of regulatory regionalism (see Hameiri and Jayasuriya 2011).

The ADB, engaged to 'operationalise' the 1997 Plan, intensified this development. At the regional level, it promoted 'risk pooling', establishing two Sub-Regional Fire-fighting Arrangements (SRFAs) to pool national fire-suppression capabilities for transboundary deployment during emergencies. More importantly, the ADB promoted the further transformation of domestic governance apparatuses to serve regional goals. It specified a regional framework to 'serve as a model' for governments' domestic programmes; the harmonisation and integration of national action plans; structures linking village-level fire-management institutions 'all the way up to the regional level'; and directed subnational monitoring institutions to report to the ASMC (Qadri 2001: xviii, xx, xxviii, xxxviii, 91, 119, 146–51). In 1999, ASEAN also issued its 'zero burning guidelines', a regional ban on the use of fire for land clearing, which national-level authorities were instructed to enact legislatively and enforce (ASEAN 2003). To implement this multilevel governance system, US, European and Australian donors were engaged to help craft and implement Fire Suppression Mobilisation Plans in Indonesian provinces and districts, create fire surveillance and mapping systems designed by technical experts and provide local training and capacity-building. Thirty-five donor projects had been launched by 1998 (Dennis 1999).

The early 2000s saw a shift towards risk management, emphasising the prevention rather than mere suppression of fires, and further attempts to empower technical experts. The 2002 ASEAN Agreement on Transboundary Haze Pollution (ATBHP) deepened regulatory regionalism, legally obliging national authorities to prevent and monitor transboundary haze pollution, respond to demands for information and enact regional regulations through domestic legislation, reporting their progress to an ASEAN Coordinating Centre. The Centre would be responsible for assessing the 'risks to human health or the environment', while national authorities were to 'identify, manage and control risks' and create mechanisms to admit regional assistance (ASEAN 2002: 5–9). In 2005, the ASEAN Panel of Experts on Fire and Haze Assessment and Coordination was established to provide 'rapid independent assessment and recommendation for the mobilisation of resources during impending critical periods' (ASEAN n.d.). The Panel would deploy automatically whenever the ASMC detected a particular number of hotspots (Oon 2010: 7), assess fires and issue recommendations for national and international responses. This empowerment of technical experts aimed to neutralise Indonesian resistance to the deployment of international fire-fighters, and enhance pressure on domestic institutions to respond.

The 2003 ASEAN Peatland Management Initiative and the 2005 ASEAN Peatland Management Strategy (APMS) consolidated the turn to risk management and technical expertise by focusing on the governance of peat forests. When drained for agriculture, peat is highly fire prone. Peat fires cause up to ninety per cent of transboundary haze (Varkkey 2013b: 680). They can burn underground for months, can only be extinguished by torrential rain and release vast quantities of carbon dioxide. Indonesia has the world's largest peat forests, holding an estimated fifty-seven billion tonnes of carbon – comparable to the Amazonian rainforest's eighty-six billion – making its degradation, at the annual rate of one billion tonnes of carbon, a major threat to climate stability (Olbrei 2013). Despite these factors, and its relatively poor fertility, peatland is attractive for agribusinesses to develop plantations on because it is typically more sparsely populated than mineral soil, and thus involves fewer land conflicts. Indeed, the World Bank promoted peatland conversion throughout the 1980s, generating widespread degradation and frequent fires.

The APMS consequently sought to embed international standards into Indonesia's peatland governance systems to reduce the incidence of fires. Networks of technical experts were created to craft these guidelines, including the ASEAN Social Forestry Network, ASEAN Expert Group on International Forest Policy Processes and ASEAN Knowledge Networks on Forest Law Enforcement and Governance and Climate Change. Along with best-practice guidance for sustainable peatland management and fire control (e.g. Adinugroho et al. 2005), these groups developed ASEAN Criteria and Indicators for Sustainable Management of Tropical Forests, and a regional Monitoring, Assessment and Reporting Format for Sustainable Forest Management based on International Tropical Timber Organisation standards. Fire Danger Rating Systems were also created to predict fire risk and guide mitigation efforts. The APMS directed national agencies to pursue 'the objectives of the regional plan', specifying ninety-eight detailed policy measures to be enacted (ASEAN 2005b: 11–21). The APMS also amended the regional zero-burning policy, permitting 'controlled burning' by low-risk, small-scale farmers but maintaining zero-burning for plantations, where fire posed a greater risk (ASEAN 2004a). The APMS is now being implemented through several donor initiatives under the ASEAN Peatland Forestry Project. These include projects by the Singaporean and Malaysian environment ministries to improve governance in two fire-prone Indonesian provinces (DoE 2009; NEA 2009).

The APMS also specified the multilevel and rescaled institutions through which regional governance should operate. The APMS promotes the spatial imaginary of an 'ecosystem approach' and the involvement of diverse governance actors at multiple scales, facilitating 'multi-stakeholder participation, inter-agency and inter-sectoral coordination' at 'the community, site-level, country, sub-regional and regional levels' (ASEAN 2006b). It specifies an ambitious, multilevel governance structure involving regional coordination, technical support and implementation by the Global Environment Centre (GEC), a regional NGO, input from an advisory group of world experts and the involvement of international donors in building governance capacity (Figure 3.1).

As a result of these efforts, Indonesian governance has been substantially transformed, rescaled and internationalised. Indonesia is now subjected to extensive international surveillance, with satellite imaging of 'hotspots' collected and disseminated via the Internet. During haze episodes, the Indonesian government submits weekly or daily situation reports to ASEAN, depending on the hotspot levels detected by the ASMC, with ninety-five per cent of these sent on time (ASEAN Secretariat Official 2011). During major haze episodes, regional apparatuses have also been activated. Malaysian fire-fighters were deployed to Indonesia in 1997, 2001, 2002 and 2005 (Zukarnian 2012). In 2006, the ASEAN Panel of Experts (PoE) deployed three times to Indonesia, and Jakarta requested Singaporean and Thai helicopters to help water-bomb hotspots (ASEAN Secretariat Official 2011). Regional regulations have also been embedded into domestic laws and regulations. Burning land has been outlawed, with the burden of proof placed on defendants and stiff penalties for violators. Agricultural development on deep peat has been banned, and all controllers of land are required to maintain fire-prevention and fire-suppression capacities (Varkkey 2013a: 6). APMS regulations have been incorporated into a National Wetlands Action Plan and a Peatland Action Plan, which

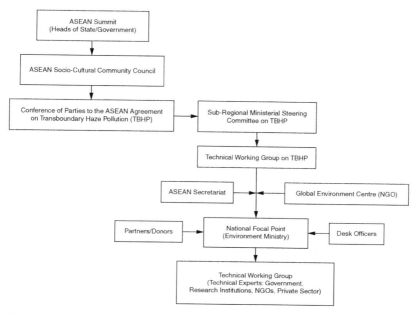

Figure 3.1 ASEAN Peatland Management System (adapted from ASEAN 2007a: 22–4).

are being disseminated to subnational officials. In 2006, Indonesia also adopted a National Plan of Action on Haze, which incorporated ASEAN agreements into national planning (Sulistowati 2011). The Plan was approved by the ASEAN Sub-Regional Ministerial Steering Committee, which regularly monitors Indonesia's progress against 'key performance indicators' (MoF n.d.). In 2009, the government also committed to reducing Indonesia's carbon dioxide emissions by twenty-six to forty-one per cent by 2020, largely through tackling forest fires and deforestation.

The implementation of the National Plan of Action has involved considerable transformation of subnational governance arrangements, realising the ADB's vision of a multilevel fire-suppression system linking villages to the regional level (see Figure 3.2). As the national 'focal point', the Ministry of the Environment (MoE) is directly inserted into a regional architecture and is tasked with coordinating national agencies to pursue regional plans. A ministerial-level coordinating committee has been created, chaired by the Coordinating Minister for the

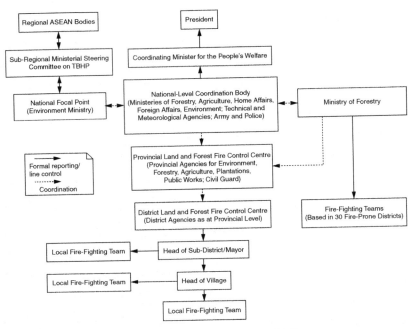

Figure 3.2 Indonesian Fire Control System (MoE 2011).

People's Welfare, with representatives from the ministries of forestry, agriculture, home affairs, foreign affairs and environment, technical meteorological agencies, the armed forces and the police.[2] During serious haze episodes, the National Disaster Management Board coordinates and finances fire-suppression efforts. Below the national level, the ADB's Fire Suppression Mobilisation Plans have been realised through establishing Land and Forest Fire Control Centres (LFCCs) in each province and district, coordinating various local government departments, while local 'Fire Awareness Communities' have been created in villages and towns. Fires are to be tackled at the local level, with action escalating to higher levels when local capacities are insufficient or fires cross district or provincial boundaries. The Ministry of Forestry (MoF) has also established Fire-Fighting Brigades (*Manggala Agni*) in thirty-two fire-prone districts, which it controls directly.

---

[2] This direct involvement of traditional security actors is also mirrored in Malaysia, where the National Security Council has oversight of the haze issue and directly monitors hotspot data (APFP 2010: 29).

However, the outputs of this complex, multilevel governance regime are highly uneven and meagre. From 2000 to 2010, the conversion of peatland into oil palm plantations almost tripled (Koh et al. 2011), while from 2000 to 2008, the area affected by fires more than doubled (Indrarto et al. 2012: 8). Accordingly, moderate transboundary haze recurs annually, with major episodes occurring in 2006, 2009 and 2013. Indeed, the 2013 fires created unprecedented, 'potentially life threatening' levels of pollution in Singapore (*Straits Times* 21 June 2013). Apart from 2006, regional fire-suppression mechanisms have largely been dormant. Despite numerous capacity-building interventions at the village level, with donors and NGOs seeking to cultivate alternatives to the use of fire, private-sector plantations – which satellite imagery suggests were responsible for around seventy per cent of fires (Varkkey 2013a: 13) – have been largely untouched.

Mainstream explanations for these lacklustre outcomes generally blame Southeast Asia's supposedly anachronistic attachment to sovereignty and non-interference in states' internal affairs, which has generated regional agreements 'containing the best of intentions, but severely lacking in effective sanctions and enforceability' (Tan 2005: 652; see also, for example, Tay 2002; Keyuan 2004: 349; Mayer 2006: 207). On this view, environmental insecurity persists because ASEAN has failed to acquire the supranational authority to 'intervene' in Indonesia (Jones 2006: 446). The Indonesian parliament's repeated refusal – until September 2014 – to ratify ASEAN's Agreement on Transboundary Haze Pollution (ATBHP) is frequently cited as blocking the emergence of such authority (Varkkey 2014). Liberal institutionalists also blame 'deficiencies in institutional capacity', Indonesia's muddled 'institutional structure' and poor institutional design (Jones 2006: 442; Tan 2005: 671; see also Luttrell et al. 2011; Qadri 2001: 161–2).

However, these explanations make little sense. As the foregoing illustrates, and as a senior Indonesian MoE official notes, 'even though there's no ratification [of the ATBHP], Indonesia has coordination with other ASEAN countries' and has reformed its fire and land management system, 'from the national... down to the local [level]' (Sulistowati 2011). An ASEAN Secretariat Official (2011) likewise reports that, despite non-ratification, 'Indonesia has been participating in... *all* the activities' promoted by ASEAN. The mistake here is to assume that regional security governance only occurs when power shifts in a zero-sum manner from states to supranational organisations. Instead, as this book argues, NTS issues are largely governed through state transformation – which is abundantly evident in this case. ASEAN's haze regime is not primarily designed to empower supranational institutions to 'intervene', but instead operates through regulatory regionalism, pursuing its goals by transforming and reshaping the operation of national and subnational institutions. As the ASEAN official states: 'we don't go to the ground . . . Our role is to coordinate . . . [ASEAN states] have to set up all the administrative, legal or other arrangements to comply' and 'cascade' regional regulations downwards (ASEAN Secretariat Official 2011). As a senior officer of the non-governmental Singapore Environment Council, which co-drafted the ATBHP, explains, its architects did not seek to create 'direct enforcement' powers, which 'would be akin to some kind of partial invasion', but rather to 'stimulate local government responsibility' (Shaw 2011). Explaining why the desired institutions have failed to emerge is also outside the scope of liberal institutionalist accounts, which merely end up demanding more political will or institutional reforms (e.g. Tan 2005: 668), or urging ASEAN to jettison non-interference. Fully explaining how Indonesia's rescaled forest governance institutions operate requires an analysis of the political economy and socio-political context in which struggles over governance rescaling have occurred.

The Indonesian context: plantations, patronage and decentralisation

Two aspects of the Indonesian setting are crucial for understanding governance outcomes in this NTS issue-area: the political economy of the forestry and plantation sectors, and government decentralisation since the late 1990s. The haze is predominantly caused by plantation operators burning land to clear it cheaply and therefore maximise their profits. They have a strong incentive to resist and deflect the rescaling of governance to perpetuate these practices, and their power and political connections enable them to do so. Furthermore, decentralisation has enabled new collusive relationships between plantation firms and district-level governments, entrenching resistance to meaningful governance transformation at the local level.

Fundamentally, the haze stems from the conversion of Indonesia's forests, which are first logged and then cleared for agriculture.

Indonesia's forests were a crucial patronage resource under Suharto's authoritarian New Order regime (1967–98). Suharto centralised control over forests and selectively dispensed logging permits to favoured military, political and business interests, thereby cementing the patronage networks underpinning state power. Corruption overwhelmed regulatory authorities, particularly in the powerful MoF, generating an uncontrolled timber boom and rapid deforestation (Ross 2001). From the 1980s, the timber industry declined as Indonesia's primary forests were exhausted. The Suharto regime – supported by the World Bank – therefore promoted the conversion of degraded forests into timber and oil palm plantations, and many politically connected logging firms moved into this sector.

This conversion often involves fire directly or indirectly. Fire has always been used to clear land in Indonesia by shifting cultivators and smallholders. However, since the 1980s, fire has been used to establish plantations on an industrial scale, with culprits enjoying impunity thanks to their corrupt relations with Indonesian state officials (ICG 2001). Clearing land using fire is far cheaper than using machinery, particularly on peatland, costing US$5 versus US$200 per hectare (Guyon and Simorangkir 2002; Varkkey 2013a: 3). Fire also saves businesses money because the resultant ash substitutes for fertiliser, which is particularly useful on low-fertility peat. The establishment of oil palm plantations is now the main driver of deforestation and fire. Since 2000, an average of 142,000 hectares has been cleared annually for palm oil, increasingly on peatland, and often by using fire (Koh et al. 2011). Companies also reportedly burn forests, or engage others to do so, in order to have them reclassified as 'degraded', thereby opening them up for plantation development (Sheil et al. 2009: 22). Today, although enhanced international surveillance may deter major firms from burning land directly, many still reportedly engage contractors or local communities to do so. Others acquire land via third-party companies, only incorporating them once they have burned the land. Agribusinesses' land-grabs also fuel the problem, because local people sometimes use fire to punish companies or reassert ownership over their land (Parish 2012; Saharjo 2011; Dennis et al. 2005).

Fires used to establish plantations directly cause transboundary haze pollution. In 1997/98, between forty-six and eighty per cent of fires were located on land designated for plantation development, three-quarters of which were for oil palm, and, of 176 firms identified by the Indonesian government as culprits, 133 were oil palm agribusinesses

(Wakker 2005: 21, 48). Although climatic conditions, notably the El Niño cycle, exacerbate the problem, an estimated ninety-eight per cent of the fires in 1997/98 were manmade (Tacconi 2003). Despite the government and plantation companies' efforts to present the fires as 'natural disasters' or to blame them on smallholders, they largely originated on state-sanctioned plantations (Dennis et al. 2005: 467). The serious 2006 haze also stemmed from the 'systematic burning' of vast tracts allocated for oil palm development amidst a boom in global crude palm oil (CPO) prices (McCarthy and Zen 2010: 155–6). WALHI, a leading Indonesian environmentalist NGO coalition, reported satellite data and ground surveys showing that eighty-one per cent of fires occurred on plantations (*Jakarta Post* 30 August 2006). In 2011, satellite data again showed that around seventy per cent of fires were on land designated for plantations (Varkkey 2013a: 13), and in 2013, satellite imagery pinpointed forty-seven per cent of fires on oil palm or timber plantations (Sizer et al. 2013).[3]

Curtailing the haze is now extremely difficult, since the palm oil sector has become one of Indonesia's most powerful industries. Indonesia overtook Malaysia as the world's largest producer of CPO in 2007; together, they produce eighty-eight per cent of the world's total (Teoh 2013: 20). Crude palm oil is Indonesia's second largest agricultural commodity after rice, and its leading agricultural export, driven by growing global, particularly Asian, demand (World Growth 2011: 4, 7). In 2010, crude palm oil exports totalled US$16.4 billion, comprising 9.3 per cent of Indonesia's exports and therefore generating significant customs revenue for the central government (*Quantum Indonesia Translogistic* 2011; UNCTADstat 2013). The industry is also a major employer. Agriculture comprises just fourteen per cent of Indonesia's GDP, but provides forty-one per cent of employment. The palm oil sector employs 1.7 to 2 million people directly, with a further 6 million benefiting indirectly (World Growth 2011: 4–5), making it important for Jakarta's poverty reduction goals. Accordingly, the government has set ambitious targets for oil palm expansion. The sector is also politically influential. It is dominated by ten large conglomerates and twenty

---

[3] The real figure is likely to be substantially higher. The World Resources Institute identifies the locations of fires by overlaying hotspot data on a MoF concession map. However, there is no nationally agreed map. As discussed below, corrupt local licensing has allowed many plantations to be established outside formal, MoF-recognised concession areas. Many fires located 'outside of concessions' are therefore probably linked to agribusinesses.

smaller groups – which, combined, operate over 1,000 subsidiaries – and organised into a powerful lobby group, GAPKI, which wields considerable influence over national parliamentarians, the MoF and the Ministry of Agriculture (MoA) (Jiwan 2013: 52; Varkkey 2013b: 683, 2014). Sixteen of Indonesia's top forty richest families, including twelve of the country's twenty-one US-dollar billionaires, made their fortunes from oil palm, alongside other commodities like coal (*Forbes Magazine* 2 December 2010). In a country dominated by money politics, but where the average annual income is under US$4,000, this gives oil palm oligarchs enormous heft.

Two recent transformations within the palm oil sector further complicate efforts to tackle the haze. First, the sector's changing structure has squeezed smallholders, diminishing alternatives to using fire. To offset agrarian unrest, the Suharto regime, supported by the World Bank and ADB, initially structured the oil palm sector around 'Nucleus Estate Schemes'. In exchange for free land and subsidies, plantation firms became the 'nucleus' for 'plasma' farms run by smallholders, who received government credit to purchase farming inputs (seeds, fertiliser, etc.), provided that they sold their oil palm fruits to the nucleus. This assured a steady supply of CPO for the processing mills, which the nucleus firms entirely monopolised. These arrangements allocated about seventy per cent of the land and half of the profits to smallholders. However, from the 1990s, the IFIs attacked these schemes, promoting market-based approaches. The Indonesian government withdrew its subsidies and credit facilities, introducing new 'partnership' schemes that reduced 'plasma' farms' shares to just twenty per cent of land and thirty per cent of profits (McCarthy et al. 2012). This ruined many smallholders, forcing them to sell their land to larger, state-linked companies. The remaining 'plasma' farms, and formally independent smallholders, now depend entirely on 'nucleus' firms to provide farming inputs on credit and to purchase, process and market their produce. The nucleus conglomerates collude to set high prices for inputs and low prices for fruit, thus reducing plasma farms' profit margins to a bare minimum (Achmad and Sawit Watch 2010). Accordingly, like other smallholders, plasma farmers cannot afford the machinery required to clear land without using fire (Sheil et al. 2009: 41–2). This differs from Thailand, for example, where the sector is dominated by smallholders with independent milling capacities, ensuring higher returns that can finance reasonable environmental management (Dallinger 2011).

As plasma farms declined, large conglomerates became increasingly dependent on third-party smallholders' produce, typically purchased through brokers, to fuel their gigantic CPO mills. Industry NGO Sawit Watch estimates that one-third of their input comes from independent smallholders (Tarigan 2011), though the figure for one major multinational is eighty-five per cent (Anonymous 2011a). The large firms' monopsony, and the profiteering of middlemen, means that, like plasma farmers, independent smallholders reap low returns and cannot afford land-clearing machinery. Although some nucleus estates use their machinery to clear plasma estates, none do so for third-party suppliers, and none regulate their supply chains. Their only interest is in ensuring a cheap supply of palm oil fruit for their mills. The sector's lopsided power relations thus fuel environmentally destructive practices that are increasingly outsourced to third parties, which large companies now conveniently blame for the haze (Tarigan 2011).

The Roundtable on Sustainable Palm Oil (RSPO) has sought to cultivate greater corporate social responsibility among major conglomerates through a certification scheme for sustainably produced palm oil (CSPO), thereby regulating the market at a global scale. The RSPO incorporated ASEAN's zero-burning policy into its assessment criteria and is seeking to adopt its peatland management guidelines too (Yacoob and Lee 2012). For environmentalist NGOs, the RSPO is an opportunity for politically useful scale-jumping. As one activist explains, they cannot ensure environmental laws are enforced domestically due to corporate influence; 'that's why we use the pressure from the outside... international pressure is more powerful' (Meridian 2011). Alongside international surveillance, NGO and investor scrutiny, a desire for RSPO certification has apparently helped deter some multinationals from directly conducting industrial-scale burning.

However, there are clear limits to the RSPO's influence. Crucially, the market for CSPO is tiny: by 2011 it attracted a premium of just US$0.30 per ton and accordingly, only 0.03 per cent of Indonesian plantations were certified (Harsono 2011: 24). Under a quarter of Indonesian exports go to the EU, the likeliest growth market for CSPO, while over half go to Asian markets that care little about sustainability (Sheil et al. 2009: 37). Unsurprisingly, therefore, 'ninety percent of the GAPKI membership aren't interested in doing good things through the RSPO' (Yacoob and Lee 2012). Even if the EU banned imports of non-sustainable palm oil, Indonesian exporters could simply shift to Asia, or segment their operations into compliant and noncompliant elements. The sector's structure actively facilitates this. For example, the conglomerate that takes eighty-five per cent of its inputs from third parties has RSPO certification for its nucleus and plasma estates, but does nothing to regulate its supply chain (Anonymous 2011a). Other certified firms are 'gaming the system' by acquiring land from firms, including subsidiaries, after they have cleared it using fire (Lawson 2011). Such practices allow firms to flaunt their 'green' credentials while effectively outsourcing environmental destruction to others. However, even this weak regulation was too much for GAPKI. In a clear instance of governance rescaling from the global to the national level, GAPKI left the RSPO in 2011, protesting the influence of environmentalist NGOs and the growing focus on peatland conservation. It instead colluded with government officials to create a nationally based certification scheme, focused on defending the sector's international competitiveness and adopting far weaker sustainability criteria (Tarigan 2011; Harsono 2011; Yacoob and Lee 2012).

The second important development in the sector is its transnationalisation. After the Asian financial crisis, several leading Indonesian agribusinesses went bankrupt, and the IMF forced Indonesia to open the sector to full foreign ownership rather than merely joint ventures. This facilitated massive land acquisitions by firms based in Singapore and especially Malaysia, which now reportedly control two-thirds of Indonesian plantations through sole ownership or joint ventures (Varkkey 2012: 315). These acquisitions were driven by land shortages in Malaysia, coupled with Malaysian government commitments to protect the country's remaining forests. They thus reflect the widespread outsourcing of environmental degradation to more poorly regulated jurisdictions (see Copeland 2008). Importantly, the major foreign investors are government-linked corporations, such as Sime Darby and Golden Hope, or vast conglomerates whose owners enjoy close ties to Malaysia and Singapore's ruling regimes, like Kuala Lumpur Kepong (KLK) and Wilmar International. Retired state officials often sit on their boards, and their mergers and acquisitions have been actively facilitated by their governments. These domestic patronage ties have been easily replicated in Indonesia, with firms co-opting retired military, police and ministry officials onto their boards and putting parliamentarians on their payrolls (Varkkey 2012: 315–22).

Accordingly, foreign firms – including RSPO-certified ones – are now widely implicated in the illegal acquisition of land for plantations, including peatland, and fires are frequently observed on their holdings (Greenpeace 2008; FoE 2008; Varkkey 2012: 318–19). Malaysian interests are highly organised within the Association of Palm Oil Investors in Indonesia (APIMI), a state-backed lobby group enjoying direct access to senior Malaysian and Indonesian officials (Varkkey 2013b: 389–90). Furthermore, the Asian crisis prompted many Suharto-era oligarchs to flee and relocate their companies to Singapore to escape possible repercussions under the new democratic government. Consequently, many of the most environmentally destructive conglomerates operating oil palm plantations in Indonesia, as well as timber and pulp and paper firms, which are also frequently linked to fires, are now headquartered in Singapore. These include Sinar Mas, Asia-Pacific Resources International Limited (APRIL) and their subsidiaries (Matthew and van Gelder 2002; Jikalahari 2008, 2009). As in Malaysia, leading politicians and retired officials sit on the boards of such firms, providing them significant political cover (Ellis 2013). Singaporean banks have also provided the finance for many mergers and acquisitions in the sector, and the city-state is also home to the world's largest biodiesel plant, which generates huge demand for palm oil (Teoh 2013: 33–4).

This transnationalisation means that although Malaysia and Singapore are the primary 'victims' of transboundary haze pollution, powerful interests based there are also among its primary drivers. The 2013 haze, for instance, was directly attributed to subsidiaries of firms like Sime Darby, KLK and APRIL (Foo 2013; Sizer et al. 2013). Yet their intimate relations with ruling elites renders them 'almost untouchable' (Varkkey 2012: 320). While the Malaysian and Singaporean environment ministries have promoted the rescaling of Indonesian governance, other state agencies provided cover for their corporate allies – attributing the haze to natural causes, slash-and-burn peasant farmers or even Australian bush fires – and taking little corrective action (Varkkey 2013b: 383, 390–93). This severely constrains how far the Malaysian and Singaporean governments can realistically promote meaningful governance rescaling in Indonesia, not least because Jakarta can always point to the involvement of, and threaten to prosecute, foreign firms – as it has done since 1997. An example of this restraint is that it took until 2014 for Singapore to enact laws to punish firms engaged in burning land in Indonesia. Even then, the prescribed penalties are meagre – a maximum of US$1.6 million – and the likelihood of successful prosecution miniscule, not least because local Indonesian actors' cooperation will be required to prove culpability (Ewing 2014).

The post-Suharto decentralisation of the Indonesian government also had important implications for haze governance. After Suharto's fall in 1998, the international financial institutions and some senior Indonesian technocrats promoted decentralisation to enhance accountability and produce 'good governance' by bringing power closer to the people (see Grindle 2007; Hadiz 2010). Owing to fears of regional separatism, authority was mostly delegated to the most local level of government, the district, with little power assigned to provinces. Districts now have elected local governments headed by mayors or regents, known as *bupatis*. However, the neoliberal technocrats promoting decentralisation failed to anticipate that second- and third-tier New Order elites and other predatory groups would be best-placed in struggles to control this new level of government. Posing as democratic leaders or defenders of local, particularist interests, they used their connections and wealth, plus violence and intimidation, to capture district governments, using them for their own purposes and thereby localising and exacerbating corruption and predation (Hadiz 2010). The Suharto-centred national patronage structure, which generated loyalty to the central government and facilitated its considerable control over local governance, thereby fragmented (Sidel 2004: 61). Local elites' interests are now often disconnected from or clash with those at the national level. This has created an intense form of territorial politics, with different levels of government contesting control over issue-areas and budgets useful for establishing patronage networks (Hadiz 2004). The stakes in this competition are extremely high: without access to resources, local politicians typically face electoral defeat and even personal financial ruin.

Land has been central to these inter-scalar conflicts. In 1999, districts were empowered to issue permits for small-scale timber concessions and agricultural plantations to promote local development and raise revenue, and assigned responsibility for plantation and environmental regulation. Countless *bupatis* swiftly exploited their new powers, corruptly issuing logging permits to themselves and their allies on a massive scale, generating a huge, unregulated logging boom enriching local politico-business elites and Malaysian investors (Barr et al. 2006:

43–44, 79–83, 118; Casson and Obidinski 2002). The horrified MoF
tried to grab back this vital patronage resource, issuing regulations that
reasserted its authority. However, many *bupatis* simply ignored this
and a lengthy struggle ensued (Yasmi et al. 2006; Bullinger and Haug
2012). To strengthen its hand, the MoF supported international governance rescaling and capacity-building projects. This resulted in the
MoF's significant internationalisation, with overseas donor agencies'
officials being incorporated directly into its executive units (Sarsito
2011). The MoF found engagement with projects like FLEGT useful to help 'resettle . . . internal power structures' after decentralisation
(van Heeswijk 2010: 102). Haze-related projects also helped the MoF
to extend its authority by coordinating local forestry offices and creating the *Manggala Agni* units. Combined with prosecutions for some
bupatis, the MoF's actions drove many districts out of logging. However, this only exacerbated the conversion of forests into plantations,
over which *bupatis* retained licensing power (Barr et al. 2006: 103–
6). The timber boom had degraded many forests, as well as drained
peatland via canals dug to transport logs, opening up land for conversion. Although the MoF is technically required to certify that a forest
is sufficiently degraded prior to its conversion for agriculture, *bupatis*
typically ignored this or misrepresented the forest's condition, issuing 'special' permits and bypassing legally mandated environmental
impact assessments in exchange for kickbacks and shares in plantation companies (Wakker 2005: 27; Varkkey 2013c: 681–5). The 2004
Plantations Act further authorised local governments to issue permits
for plantations up to 1,000 hectares in size. A massive expansion of
oil palm plantations ensued, often using fire.

These inter-scalar land conflicts feed directly into the politics of haze
governance rescaling. Rather than representing 'good' central authorities combating 'bad' local ones, these struggles are actually about
power and control over resource rents. National-level elites, including in the MoF, frequently issue 'special' permits and provide political
cover for their own clients (Varkkey 2013c: 685, 687–8). Accordingly, the MoF has only supported internationally driven governance
rescaling insofar as it strengthens its power against the districts, not to
the extent that its own patronage powers would be weakened. Meanwhile, decentralisation has afforded local politico-business networks
an opportunity to resist rescaling by keeping land and environmental

governance local, and by marginalising and weakening local regulatory agencies.

Haze governance in practice

This subsection shows how the political economy context of this NTS issue shapes the dynamics of governance rescaling and the practical operation of rescaled apparatuses. We first explore resistance to rescaling at the national level, showing how state–business networks have activated the state's 'scale management' functions to curtail external involvement in haze prevention and suppression, and undermined the implementation of regional regulations. We then show how local resistance, enabled by decentralisation, has kept transformed governance apparatuses weak and corrupted the operation of even regional apparatuses, facilitating the continued use of fire. The discussion focuses in detail on Riau and Jambi provinces, in Sumatra, which cause most of the haze pollution affecting Singapore and Malaysia.

The continued collusion of agribusiness interests and state officials at the national level means that regional regulations, despite being incorporated into Indonesian law, are rarely enforced in practice. Despite an official ban on agricultural development on deep peat, and a moratorium on all peatland development since 2011, permits continue to be granted and regulations bent or violated, including by the MoF. Consequently, twenty to twenty-five per cent of existing plantations and half of new ones are illegally established on peat (FoE 2008: 45). Moreover, despite abundant evidence of plantations' illegal use of fire, including by large conglomerates, only a tiny handful of cases have ever been prosecuted, and only two individuals convicted (Varkkey 2013a: 11–13; Greenpeace 2008; Saharjo 2011). Environmentalist NGOs attribute this to the corruption of state officials, including the police and judiciary, by agribusinesses. In practice, only those caught red-handed setting fire to land are likely to be prosecuted (Tanpidau 2011), which is highly unlikely given the extensive collusion between local police and plantation operators.

The palm oil sector's transnationalisation has also constrained rescaling by facilitating national-level resistance. GAPKI, the MoF and allied parliamentarians have exploited the involvement of Singaporean and Malaysian firms in land-burning to blame the haze on foreigners and refuse to cooperate until Malaysia and Singapore's governments take action, thereby blocking ratification of the ATBHP until September 2014 (Varkkey 2014).[4] This deployment of the state's 'scale management' function has not entirely negated governance rescaling, as we have seen. However, it doubtless constrains meaningful domestic action by signalling support for the plantations sector. Non-ratification also permits 'scale management' during haze episodes. When neighbouring governments urge the activation of regional institutions, MoF and MoA officials can protect their corporate allies from scrutiny by insisting, 'we don't have to, we are not obliged to' (ASEAN Secretariat Official 2011). This explains why regional fire-suppression capabilities have been so rarely deployed, and why the PoE has not been activated since 2006, despite the ASMC's hotspot thresholds being repeatedly breached. The haze regime is also undermined by a deal struck between APIMI and the Indonesian government, whereby fires detected on Malaysian plantations are reported to APIMI, which then takes no real action, rather than national law-enforcement or regional surveillance bodies (Varkkey 2013b: 393).

Decentralisation has also severely weakened national agencies that are critical to ASEAN's haze regime. The MoE's task as the ASEAN regime's 'national focal point' would always have been difficult, since its enthusiasm for regional environmental regulation is not shared by more powerful ministries like the MoF and MoA (Varkkey 2014). However, decentralisation has further undermined the MoE by reassigning environmental regulation to district *Dinas* (government departments), over which the MoE no longer exercises line control. Reflecting the broader shift towards regulatory statehood, the MoE has been transformed into a mere 'coordinator', setting regulatory criteria and standards for other agencies but lacking direct control and enforcement capacities (Mayer 2006: 212; Barr et al. 2006: 41–3). As a senior MoE bureaucrat complains, 'we don't have any authority to order directly to the local government', which creates 'many barriers' to policy implementation (Sulistowati 2011). The MoA also lost control over local agricultural *Dinas*, retreating to developing norms, criteria and guidelines for others but lacking the means to ensure

---

[4] They also criticise Singapore's refusal to extradite leading Suharto-era oligarchs and both states' lack of meaningful cooperation over the smuggling of illegal logs from Indonesia. Whilst somewhat tangential to the haze issue, these criticisms are valid.

compliance. Having lost control of agricultural permits to the districts, the MoA refuses to take responsibility for fires, passing the responsibility on to *bupatis* and failing to develop any independent fire-suppression capacities (Hidayat 2011). The MoF is the only national-level agency to have extended its territorial and functional reach through rescaling, by establishing tighter coordination of local forestry offices and the *Manggala Agni* brigades. However, its remit (and budget) does not formally encompass land designated for agricultural use, where around eighty per cent of fires occur (Hidayat 2011).

Given these national-level weaknesses, the haze governance regime's outcomes are strongly determined by local government behaviour. This explains why ASEAN and donors' capacity-building efforts have deliberately targeted this level, trying to direct local institutions to follow regional guidelines and build local capacity. However, although these interventions created Land and Forest Fire Control Centres (LFCCs) at the provincial and district levels, many regional and local officials interviewed remain in denial about the causes of fire, indicating their reluctance to confront corporate offenders. The Vice-Governor of Riau province, for example, who chairs the provincial LFCC, echoes plantation company rhetoric, claiming that most fires have natural causes, that private-sector firms always clear land mechanically and that any fires on their land must therefore be accidental (Mit 2011). Accordingly, the Centres and the agencies staffing them are kept too weak and marginal to seriously challenge local land-clearance rackets. Thus, according to the head of Riau province's environmental agency, the provincial LFCC is *ad hoc* and underfunded. His agency receives just 0.08 per cent of the provincial budget with resources instead diverted to economic and infrastructure development (Labay 2011).

Similarly, at the district level, *bupatis* systematically underfund their agricultural and environmental *Dinas*, allocating them an average of just four and one per cent of their budgets, respectively (McCarthy et al. 2012: 557). Moreover, they typically assign the authority to rescind firms' operating licenses to *Dinas* for trade and industry, thereby elevating business concerns over environmental ones (McCarthy and Zen 2010: 159). They confront a far more powerful constellation of forces in the form of the so-called 'TP3K', *ad hoc*, subdistrict committees of local political bosses, police and armed forces, and 'SATGAS', groupings of village elders, both of which are directed to persuade and intimidate local communities to accept palm oil development, and are frequently bankrolled by plantation companies (Jiwan 2013: 59). Unsurprisingly, a local plantations official laments, 'we are faced with an impossible situation... underpowered and unable to play our role. If we try and take things further... a senior official... will put pressure on us to back off' (McCarthy et al. 2012: 561). Since local plantation firms also frequently contribute financially to *bupatis'* election campaigns, or are even owned by *bupatis*, their families or allies, local officials are more likely to protect than to regulate them. Environmentalist NGOs investigating plantation fires claim they are often physically impeded by private security guards and 'gangsters' backed by the police (Mubarok and Rudiansyah 2011), while local protests are often violently suppressed (Jiwan 2013: 70). When NGOs, junior civil investigators or forestry officials report the use of fire, local agriculture offices typically react with indifference or hostility (Varkkey 2013a: 9; Sumarjo 2011). A WWF-Riau activist laments: 'it is very hard for the forestry institutions in Riau, because the government and companies are very close... For companies there is protection from the government... [and] the law enforcers... Corruption has become a disease' (Mahyuddin 2011). Another NGO leader observes that regulation is subordinated to economic calculations: 'law enforcement never happens... They don't dare to take strict action against the companies... the company would remove their investment' (Usman 2011). Even a provincial forestry official concurs: 'it's easy for companies to avoid prosecution... if we treated companies strictly... it would endanger the business climate in Indonesia. That's why the government still applies not very strong law enforcement' (Tanpidau 2011). Fear of deterring investment has only been heightened by decentralisation, since many districts have little to tempt investors besides unregulated access to land. Given elites' desperate need for resources to maintain electoral power, only where alternative revenues are available can local governments exert some autonomy from agricultural interests (McCarthy et al. 2012).

Accordingly, fire-control apparatuses within the LFCCs are generally kept weak and subordinated to politico-business interests. For example, Tebo district, in Jambi province, is one of Indonesia's most fire-prone. Despite covering 646,000 hectares – four times the size of Greater London – its Forestry Office has just fifteen staff, only two of whom are trained fire-fighters; its annual budget is Rp200 million (around US$17,800); and its equipment is limited to one manual water pump, three portable hoses, two uniforms, ten helmets and twenty-seven beating tools (Sumarjo 2011). The office head blames this situation on the district parliament, whose budget prioritises infrastructure projects (Sumarjo 2011). Similarly, while the MoF has established Fire Awareness Communities in thirty-two villages in Jambi, *bupatis* fail to pay or equip them, rendering them ineffective at suppressing fires (Tanpidau 2011; Rahardjo 2011; Handoyo 2011). The situation is similar elsewhere: Sambas district in Kalimantan has allocated just US$5,400 annually to supervise thirty-five oil palm plantations and many other agribusinesses (Colchester et al. 2013: 31). Although many *bupatis* cite insufficient resources, in reality, the timber and oil palm booms have yielded windfall tax revenues (Yasmi et al. 2006: 173–4). They choose to prioritise infrastructure projects over environmental protection because, according to a Greenpeace official, the former 'are ordered by companies, and ordered by governors or *bupatis* for their cronies... When the money is spent on environmental issues, the cronies cannot get something' (Zulfahmi 2011).

Consequently, districts generally depend either on plantation operators or the MoF's *Manggala Agni* brigades to suppress fires. However, although national laws require plantation firms to maintain adequate fire-fighting capacities, a 2009 review found their preparations in Jambi province to be grossly insufficient, with only one exception. The review's author explains that operators with local licences 'don't face the same legality checks from the forest service or the agricultural service' as nationally regulated firms; 'basically, no particular regulations are followed' (Sanders 2012). A MoF official admits that, although national laws hold concessionaries responsible for fires on their land, in practice, 'they can avoid [accountability] by reasoning that they tried to stop the fire', even if their fire-fighting capacities are inadequate (Rahardjo 2011). Meanwhile, *Manggala Agni* has just four outposts, 253 personnel and a budget of Rp13 billion (US$1.15 million) across Jambi province, which covers five million hectares (Rahardjo 2011). Moreover, their primary mission is forest conservation. Given the MoF's remit, *Manggala Agni* cannot access agricultural land without permission and funding from the concessionary. Although the MoF reports hotspots detected on plantations to their operators, they often 'don't care', only requesting help when it is convenient to them (Hidayat 2011). Nonetheless, the review of Jambi's fire-fighting arrangements found that *Manggala Agni* are frequently diverted to work on plantations, being 'most often used in oil palm areas. They're ... used politically' (Sanders 2012). Politico-business interests are thus able to divert the operation of rescaled institutions at the local level to suit themselves.

Local power relations have even constrained the operation of regional institutions within the haze regime, notably the ASEAN PoE. ASEAN officials hoped that empowering technical experts to assess fire sites and recommend ameliorative action would depoliticise decision-making during haze episodes, thereby neutralising Jakarta's tendency to resist international assistance. The Panel deployed three times to Indonesia during the severe 2006 haze. Its potential was displayed on its first deployment: the Singaporean and Malaysian members arrived without warning, before the Indonesians, and the Panel's recommen-dations, submitted to the MoE, were essentially followed, with MoF fire-fighters deployed and the fire suppressed, despite obstruction from local officials (Saharjo 2011). However, on another deployment, in Kalimantan, the PoE found that around 1,000 hectares of land were being burned to create an agricultural plantation. The Panel found that, while the local authorities 'ha[d] the capability to extinguish it, they [didn't] want to' until the land was converted. The provincial governor pressured the Panel 'not [to] send people to extinguish the fire yet' (Zukarnian 2012).

The PoE was also constrained by key ministries' interests. With the exception of one agricultural academic, all the experts nominated to staff the Panel are technocrats attached to particular national min-istries, whose interests distorted their work. Professor Saharjo (2011), the sole independent expert member, states: 'the real experts, we will say everything true, based on scientific knowledge. But sometimes this information is not so good for politicians or officials', who instead demanded a 'compromise statement' that shielded their ministries from blame. When Saharjo told the media the full story, he was reprimanded by the MoE. His personal experience reflects the very limited empow-erment of forestry and land management experts in land and haze management. Saharjo has investigated several fire sites to help the MoE prosecute plantation companies. He and his family received death threats, and whilst in the field he must be guarded by armed police. Despite assembling ample scientific evidence of companies' guilt, con-victions have rarely been secured (Saharjo 2011).

The pervasive power of plantation companies has consistently deflected the rescaling of land and forest governance away from corporate interests and towards poorer and weaker social groups, particularly village farmers. As noted earlier, villagers and smallholders do use fire to clear land. However, given that their plots are small, these fires do not contribute significantly to the haze unless they spread into other areas like plantations or forests, where concessionaries and forestry officials are legally responsible for fire control. However, as we have seen, they rarely take the action required, and instead unfairly seek to blame local communities entirely (Murdiyarso and Adiningsih 2007). Despite small-scale farmers' very limited contribution to haze, district and provincial environmental agencies devote much of their time and limited budgets to them, conducting small-scale 'socialisation' activities to 'educate' supposedly 'ignorant' villagers about the dangers of using fire, claiming that this is 'all we can do' (Oktavia and Suryono 2011; also Labay 2011). Similarly, local forestry officials focus on establishing village Fire Awareness Communities (FACs), often in league with local plantation firms. However, as we have seen, FACs are ineffective in tackling fire. Numerous interviewees report that villagers only attend the initial meetings to establish FACs because they receive an honorarium, treating it as 'a "project" to make money, a kind of trick' (Mubarok and Rudiansyah 2011; also Hasyim 2011; Kurniawan 2011). Because they receive neither equipment nor recurrent funding, they rarely mobilise to suppress fires. Villagers' cynicism is exacerbated by the fact that, when they report fires, 'there is no response if the culprit is a company'. This makes the community become more apathetic . . . they say, 'the big companies do the burning, so why shouldn't I do that?' (Mubarok and Rudiansyah 2011). The lack of government help to establish alternative livelihoods or land-clearing methods also leaves villagers feeling apathetic. Consequently, when asked to help suppress fires, 'they just ignore it' (Thamrin 2011). Unsurprisingly, a review of forty donor projects, which all tend to focus on local practices, treating small fires as a problem to be suppressed rather than an intrinsic and indispensable part of poor people's livelihoods, found that they were largely ineffective or even harmful (Tacconi et al. 2007).

The legal framework and law enforcement system also unevenly target the relatively weak and marginal. Given their poverty, villagers and smallholders lack any means to clear land apart from fire. ASEAN's Controlled Burning Guidelines recognised this problem, authorising them to burn small areas in a regulated way. In response to pressure from farmers, Riau province enacted these guidelines into local legislation in 2009, for areas up to two hectares. However, this was overruled by the MoF, which apparently feared that plantation companies would exploit this loophole to burn land more widely, for which the MoF would be blamed (Riau Forestry Official 2011; Sarsito 2011). Consequently, the nationwide zero-burning policy has been upheld. However, large companies and their agents are hardly ever prosecuted for violating this law. Instead, most of those fined or imprisoned for land-burning are 'local people... in Riau province, [if] you burn one... [or] two hectares, you will be put in jail. But sometimes, even if the smoke is in front of your eyes, you know it's a company, but [the law is not enforced]' (Saharjo 2011). As Greenpeace campaigner Zulfahmi (2011) observes, 'the police usually just attack the community – but... we don't have companies being punished'. Even some officials lament that this is not only pointless – since villagers lack any alternatives to fire – but also counter-productive, since fear of prosecution causes villagers to flee the site of fires, rather than remain to control them in a traditional manner, making fires more likely to spread to adjacent areas (Tanpidau 2011). This irrational approach does not simply stem from flawed public policies or misguided institutions. Rather, it reflects the broader political economy of natural resources in Indonesia, where law enforcement officials frequently attack 'easy' targets but ignore 'politically privileged and protected elites' (Magrath 2010). Environmentalist NGOs in Riau and Jambi provinces all concur that 'the police and law enforcers have been influenced by the power and the investment of the companies' (Mahyuddin 2011). 'The companies can pay everyone – they can pay the government, the police, soldiers, to back them up' (Kurniawan 2011). Compared to these entrenched interests, 'it is much easier to blame the local community because they are powerless... there is nothing to lose by blaming them' (Thamrin 2011).

Local governance interventions in Riau and Jambi

The constraints on local-level haze governance rescaling are further illustrated by the district-based interventions of the Singaporean and

Malaysian environment ministries. Following the 2006 haze, these agencies launched projects in Indonesia's Jambi and Riau provinces to spur the embedding of regional regulatory standards in local land management and fire control. Singaporean and Malaysian officials deployed to several Indonesian districts, providing equipment, training, capacity-building and policy guidance, alongside local and international NGOs, academic experts and corporate actors (NEA 2009; DoE 2009). The existing literature generally ignores this, perhaps because it upsets established tropes about 'non-interference'. In ASEAN meetings, however, Malaysian and Singaporean ministers boasted that their projects had successfully caused a decline in hotspots in Riau and Jambi. In reality, their projects faced identical constraints to Indonesia's domestic efforts and other donor interventions, and were also shaped by specific Singaporean and Malaysian economic interests. Consequently, their outcomes were similarly unimpressive.

Both projects aimed to hasten the transformation of local Indonesian land and fire governance along regional guidelines and to insert local institutions more firmly into the regional haze management regime. Each had two basic components. First, they installed surveillance and monitoring apparatuses to measure air quality, manned by *Dinas* staff but sending data directly to the Singaporean and Malaysian environmental agencies, and thence to the ASMC, thereby strengthening the regional early-warning system. This enabled Singaporean and Malaysian officials to monitor Indonesian territory directly and pressure district officials to take action, bypassing Jakarta entirely if necessary (Anonymous 2011b; MNRE Official 2012). Second, the projects sought to embed regional land management and fire control standards at the local level and build local governance capacity. In Riau this involved translating and disseminating ASEAN's Zero Burning Guidelines, with Malaysian officials partnering with the GEC and a local environmental NGO, Jikalahari, to provide training in zero-burning techniques and alternative livelihoods, fire risk assessment, fire-fighting and peatland rehabilitation. Local fire patrols were also established, with training and some equipment provided by Malaysia's Fire and Rescue Service (DoE 2009: 4–5, 10; Jikalahari 2010: 3; Zukarnian 2012). In Jambi, Singapore's National Environment Agency also sponsored APRIL's safety manager to review the province's fire-prevention arrangements, and academic experts from the National University of Singapore to issue recommendations on peatland planning and management (Sanders 2012; Lee 2011). Singaporean officials then drafted a provincial and district Master Plan that was 'implemented by the Jambi authorities' (NEA 2009: 7). APRIL's safety manager, technical experts, PINSE, a local environmental NGO, and Singapore Food Industries were also engaged to promote zero-burning, peatland management techniques and alternative livelihoods to local communities (NEA 2009: 9, 11, 18, 21; Thamrin 2011; Sanders 2012). Although the projects focused intensively on two districts, both were intended to be 'scaled up' by local governments.

However, these projects intervened into extremely difficult political economy contexts where Malaysian and Singaporean interests were themselves embedded. Riau province is a major centre of illegal logging and deforestation, having lost two-thirds of its forest cover since the 1980s. The pulp and paper industry controls a quarter of Riau's land and is blamed for widespread environmental destruction. The sector is dominated by subsidiaries of APRIL and Sinar Mas, both headquartered in Singapore (WWF 2008: 3, 11; Jikalahari 2008: 6). Following a major boom after decentralisation, Riau also has the largest palm oil sector of any Indonesian province, with at least forty Malaysian firms, including government-linked companies like Sime Darby, and their subsidiaries operating there, some of which were accused of burning land as recently as 2013 (Nagata and Arai 2013: 76, 81; Harahap 2013). Around forty per cent of Riau is peatland, which is rapidly being converted into plantations. Although many local officials have been implicated in corruptly facilitating this activity, few have been prosecuted. The situation is similar in Jambi province. By 2010 it hosted over 500,000 hectares of oil palm plantations, with plans for 500,000 more, plus 650,000 hectares of rubber plantations (Afrizal 2012). APRIL and Sinar Mas subsidiaries are again a major presence, as is the Singaporean palm oil giant Wilmar, which has allegedly hired local police to facilitate violent land grabs (Colchester et al. 2011).

Unsurprisingly, this context steered the Malaysian and Singaporean projects down a path of least resistance, away from – or even directly benefiting – corporate interests, and towards local farmers, mirroring the broader pattern of haze governance rescaling. Malaysia's Riau project hardly engaged the corporate sector at all. As the executive director of WALHI Riau comments, the project avoided the crucial issue of law enforcement for plantation firms because 'there are so many Malaysian palm oil companies in Indonesia, and many hotspots appear in their concession areas – so if it is brought to law enforcement, it will ruin their image' (Usman 2011). Corporate engagement was limited to the locating of a zero-burning and peatland rehabilitation demonstration plot alongside a Malaysian palm oil plantation and the solicitation of corporate donations to finance local fire patrols (Parish 2012). Even Jikalahari viewed this as 'greenwash', commenting that 'fire is not about fire but politics and the economy. Some of the companies here are Malaysian. They want to help some of their companies' (Muslim 2011). A senior Malaysian environmental official also reported that avoiding antagonising the District authorities was essential. Even with permission from a local mayor, Malaysian officials exploring voluntary carbon markets in Aceh province had earlier encountered harassment and threats of arrest (Abdul 2012).

Singaporean officials, meanwhile, actively collaborated with major corporations. They engaged APRIL as an 'expert' in fire-prevention and land management, tacitly accepting its claims of environmental sustainability and its blaming of fires on local communities. Training events for locals were also held on premises owned by oil palm company PT Wira Karya Sakti, a Sinar Mas subsidiary regarded by local NGOs as 'the worst company in Jambi' for its environmental and social record (Mubarok and Rudiansyah 2011). Even Singaporean officials became concerned that they were facilitating 'greenwashing', eventually cutting ties with Sinar Mas (Anonymous 2011b). Furthermore, the executive director of Singapore's local NGO partner says his organisation was selected over WALHI and WARSI, which are linked to international NGO campaigns, because it is 'more acceptable to companies... [they] are not very afraid of the existence of PINSE' (Thamrin 2011). Even then, local political leaders steered the project firmly away from locally licensed firms. As APRIL's safety manager recalls: 'you're completely regulated or dependent upon what your hosts allow you to have access to. They facilitated access to certain specific communities that were of interest to those government officials and certain specific companies... [But] they're not going to open up the black box' (Sanders 2012). Consequently, Singapore's project also avoided addressing law enforcement or corporate governance. Accordingly, 'there is no improvement to fix the problem... [because] there is [still] no law enforcement' (Muslim 2011).

Unsurprisingly, the projects were instead deflected towards village farmers, replicating previous initiatives. Although ASEAN's Controlled Burning Guidelines were supposed to be disseminated, in practice, the projects focused almost exclusively on *zero*-burning (Sanders

2012). In Riau, Jikalahari embraced zero-burning, fearing 'that if controlled burning is allowed, the companies will use the community to burn their concession area' (Muslim 2011), underscoring the constraints imposed by corporate impunity. In Jambi, however, even the NGO organising the training saw this focus as irrational, since 'if local communities are not provided with an alternative way of clearing the land, it will be almost impossible to get zero burning' (Thamrin 2011). APRIL's Brad Sanders (2012) concurs: 'I don't think that anything came out of that workshop that was completely applicable or usable to the people in the field'. Similarly, the fire-management and peatland rehabilitation measures established, although successful for the projects' duration (Parish 2012), later fell into disrepair. Because fire patrols were established in identical conditions to FACs, local communities simply treated them similarly, as a 'project' to earn money, discontinuing them when funding ended (Muslim 2011; Usman 2011; Thamrin 2011). In Riau, the peatland canals blocked to raise the water table have been re-opened, since they are essential transport routes. The fish pools introduced to help villagers earn income from maintaining water levels failed, because the species introduced were unsuitable and the fish died (Labay 2011). Pineapple cultivation is the only alternative livelihood project that has survived, because it alone is economically remunerative (Thamrin 2011; Parish 2012). Hopes that these projects would be 'scaled up' and replicated elsewhere proved unfounded (Labay 2011; Muslim 2011).

The capacity-building and training of local officials also produced meagre results, since key agencies remain weak, marginalised and under-resourced. The surveillance systems installed in both provinces broke down by 2011, with local environmental agencies lacking the resources to repair them (Hartati et al. 2011; MNRE Official 2012). Even when they were functioning, Riau's provincial environmental agency apparently did not act on the data received (Oktavia and Suryono 2011), confirming the general impression that sending hotspot data to Indonesia is like 'giving it to a black hole' (Anonymous 2011b). Jambi's environment officials were particularly cynical about the surveillance equipment, commenting that 'Singapore wants the data to spy on Jambi . . . to keep the air in Singapore clear . . . They don't want to help us, just themselves' (Hartati et al. 2011). They saw the equipment as a 'millstone', costly to maintain and unsuited to local needs, and would have preferred to receive fire-fighting equipment. They also complained of 'mismanagement' by their superiors, who dispensed the training placements provided in Singapore as patronage for favoured individuals instead of sending the most suitable personnel. The three officials were 'trained to be trainers', with the intention that they would impart what they learned to colleagues. In fact, they performed no training. 'They just went shopping in Singapore and brought back photos of themselves in front of Universal Studios and Orchard Plaza and put them on Facebook', lamented one of their colleagues. One 'trainer' was also reassigned elsewhere (Hartati et al. 2011). Capacity-building around land planning and management was also fruitless. A Singaporean expert engaged to help the Jambi authorities develop land governance master plans found little scope to contribute, since sound regulations on peatland development and management already existed, but were simply not being enforced. Enforcement, he suggested, was technically 'easy'; however, because the authorities lacked 'political willingness', 'they don't . . . really commit the resources to it' (Lee 2011). Similarly, the review of and recommendations on Jambi's land and fire governance have been ignored; accordingly, 'the area [targeted] still exists as a degraded peatland . . . There's been no real change' (Sanders 2012).

Finally, the projects were constrained by the politics of scale, particularly in Riau. Although they were initially established via intergovernmental memoranda, the Indonesian national government was subsequently bypassed, with Malaysian and Singaporean agencies working directly with provincial and district governments. This caused considerable disquiet in Jakarta (Hidayat 2011). At the time, the central government was engaged in a severe struggle against Riau's provincial and district governments by backing an unusually reformist police chief's investigations into local forestry corruption. As with other international rescaling efforts, the central government sought to harness the Malaysian project for its own ends, trying to control district-level activities and cut out the provincial governorate. According to the GEC, the province therefore played a spoiling role, directing the district environmental office to obstruct the project. The local *bupati* exploited this tension during a ministerial visit, directing attention away from the project, and thereby marginalised it. The provincial governor also opposed the project's extension, reducing a planned five-year intervention to just nine months, wholly insufficient to achieve lasting results (Parish 2012). Furthermore, Malaysian and Singaporean officials complain that their offers of new projects are being blocked in Jakarta. It appears that central government agencies are unwilling to support interventions that do not bolster the territorial reach of their own authority.

The Malaysian and Singaporean interventions thus essentially replicated over forty other donor projects in Indonesia, which have almost uniformly focused on local farmers' activities – fire suppression and technical capacity-building – without addressing the political and economic roots of the haze problem (Dennis 1999; Tacconi et al. 2007). This replication is no accident: it reflects external agencies taking the path of least resistance, working around local power relations and sensitivities and selecting the easiest, weakest targets. The lacklustre outcomes of such projects are an important corrective to poststructuralist accounts of aid and development interventions. These often imply that aid agencies have significant power to foster 'governmentalities' among target populations, producing self-regulating agents, and typically only see resistance in terms of competing local discourses. Here, however, governance interventions produced very slight changes, which dissipated rapidly after the material resources supporting them were withdrawn. They were unable to overcome – but were instead profoundly shaped by – entrenched local power relations that deflected rescaling away from politico-business interests and towards village farmers, thereby replicating many flawed efforts to improve land and fire governance.

Conclusion

Environmental degradation has been identified as a security threat on regional and global scales in recent decades. The perspectives of environmental advocates and Malthusian-realist policymakers have converged around the notion that achieving environmental security requires that the internal governance of 'at-risk' states be transformed to improve their 'resilience' and reduce 'spillover' from environmental crises. Environmental security is therefore pursued, not only through efforts to reach global climate change agreements, but also through a host of aid and governance interventions in developing countries.

This approach is visible in responses to Southeast Asia's haze problem. Existing accounts typically bemoan ASEAN's failure to establish supranational powers so that it can 'intervene' directly in Indonesia.

These views misunderstand the intentions of the regime's architects, who did not seek to create supranational authority. They instead promoted the internal transformation of Indonesia's land and fire governance, and its networking into subregional and regional frameworks, so that domestic institutions would operate according to regional environmental regulations and priorities. This considerably transformed and rescaled Indonesian environmental governance, despite parliament's refusal to ratify the ATBHP until very recently. However, powerful constraints emanating from the state–business networks in the forestry and plantations sectors have constrained rescaling, and the operation of transformed state and regional apparatuses and international interventions. Consequently, despite some improvements, the haze seems set to continue for years to come. Indeed, as deforestation, land degradation and agribusiness accelerate elsewhere in Southeast Asia – notably Indochina and Myanmar – its worsening is virtually assured.[5]

[5] ASMC data show sharp increases in 'hotspots' in these areas, sometimes exceeding those in Indonesia.

4 Governing infectious disease: H5N1 avian influenza in Southeast Asia

Infectious disease is as old as life itself, with devastating pandemics and plagues recurring throughout history. More novel though, is the tendency to depict infectious disease as a serious security threat on a global scale. The identification of health with security was practically unheard of until the early 1990s (Elbe 2009; Fidler 2003b). Even the infamous 1918–19 Spanish Influenza, which caused millions of deaths worldwide, only started to be invoked as the epitome of a disastrous pandemic that must be prevented at all costs decades later. At the time, it was seen as part of the general misery associated with the First World War and its aftermath (Alcabes 2009: 6). Now, however, for some of the world's most powerful governments and international organisations, notably the World Health Organization (WHO), rapidly spreading infectious diseases have come to be seen as 'pressing existential threats that require urgent and extraordinary international policy responses', thus 'abandoning the decades-old convention of equating security with the absence of armed conflict between states' (Elbe 2009: 2).

A burgeoning literature examining this securitisation of global health has considerably improved our understanding of the kinds of public health issues being discursively securitised – almost invariably, rapidly spreading infectious diseases – and who the securitising actors are. However, very few scholars have yet sought to systematically examine and explain how these diseases are managed in practice. Most scholars focus solely on the outcomes of interstate diplomacy, arguing that securitising infectious disease has generated a narrow, self-interested emphasis on 'national security', particularly among dominant Western states, rather than a cosmopolitan and just form of global health governance (Davies 2010; Elbe 2009, 2010b). However, this supposed dichotomy between national security and governance overlooks the fact that, given the transboundary nature of infectious diseases, the practices associated with national security – preparedness against pandemics – have been fundamentally transformed. It is now seen to largely depend on interventions to reconfigure domestic health governance within other states so that they function as part of coordinated regional or global surveillance and containment efforts (see Calain 2007). Given the health security literature's fixation on interstate diplomacy, it typically misses this crucial dynamic, and thereby fails to explore the factors shaping the actual implementation of international efforts to manage infectious disease (Curley and Herington 2011).

To transcend this limitation, this chapter employs the State Transformation Approach (STA) to examine the governance of Highly Pathogenic Avian Influenza (HPAI) H5N1 in Southeast Asia. Popularly known as 'bird flu', H5N1 is a highly pathogenic variant of the influenza virus, typically found in poultry, but with the capacity to infect and kill humans through zoonotic (cross-species) transmission. Southeast Asia was the epicentre of the H5N1 outbreak, which occurred in the middle of the last decade. Bird-to-human, and possibly rare human-to-human, transmissions caused very high levels of mortality: 379 deaths in 638 confirmed cases as of January 2014, including in Indonesia, Thailand, Cambodia, Laos, Vietnam and Myanmar (WHO n.d.a). Public health officials' main fear – that H5N1 would evolve to become rapidly transmissible among humans, creating a global pandemic – has not yet played out (Elbe 2010a: 49; Davis 2005: 9–19)

Nonetheless, few infectious diseases have been discursively securitised by governments and international organisations as much and as often as H5N1. At the height of the panic, estimates of global deaths, if the virus were to mutate, ranged from 50 to 350 million people (Davis 2005). During 2006, international donors pledged nearly US$2.4 billion towards managing the avian influenza threat. While much of this funding was dedicated to developing and purchasing H5N1 vaccines, substantial funds were earmarked for programmes of disease surveillance, capacity-building and response at the disease's points of origin (Scoones and Forster 2010). From 2009, the sense of urgency has declined as H5N1 has not spread to new countries and human infections have decreased, leading to funding cuts for these programmes. However, H5N1 remains an important part of worldwide pandemic preparedness frameworks.

For Copenhagen School adherents, Southeast Asia's response to the H5N1 outbreaks seems puzzling. H5N1 was consistently 'securitised' by regional governments and in official ASEAN communiqués (ASEAN 2004b, 2007b). However, there was little concerted action to tackle the disease and no indication that it was elevated to the top of the political agenda within Southeast Asian states (Caballero-Anthony 2008; Haacke and Williams 2008: 802–4). As chapter one showed, there is little in the Copenhagen toolkit to account for this unexpected paradox. Caballero-Anthony (2008) thus ends up urging a shift from the 'securitisation' of infectious disease to the 'institutionalisation' of a real regional response, without being able to explain why it has not already occurred.

This chapter transcends these limitations to explain the response to H5N1 in two key Southeast Asian states, Thailand and Indonesia. As the world's worst-affected territory, Indonesia received the most international funding for H5N1-related programmes: US$175 million from 2006 to 2010 (Forster 2010: 131; Forster and Charnoz 2013: z). Thailand also suffered serious outbreaks. However, while in Thailand reported outbreaks of H5N1 in poultry are now sporadic and no human cases have emerged since 2006, in Indonesia the disease remains endemic in poultry and new human infections still occur, despite falling from fifty-five to nine cases annually between 2006 and 2012 (WHO n.d.a). Clearly, governance outcomes vary markedly, despite the fact Indonesia received the most foreign assistance. Much of this divergence is attributable to differences in the political economy of the poultry industry. In both countries, the industry had considerable influence over the scale at which the disease was managed and the effects of programmes developed to manage H5N1 in poultry.

In Thailand, much of the commercial poultry sector at the time of the first outbreak was industrialised, vertically integrated, export-oriented and politically connected. Consequently, the Thaksin government, in which industry-affiliated politicians were strongly represented, moved quickly to reassure export markets of the safety of Thai poultry. This involved centralising the response to H5N1 in the hands of the Thai national government, which stringently imposed international regulatory standards, but without involving international agencies directly. This response clearly favoured large-scale, export-oriented commercial interests: while it eventually restored their export markets, the high costs imposed on smallholders drove most out of business, further concentrating ownership in the hands of large-scale conglomerates (Safman 2010).

Indonesia, conversely, was subject to far greater, internationally driven rescaling efforts from the WHO and the UN Food and Agriculture Organization (FAO). Their programmes attempted to build up human and animal health services at the local level that empowered technical experts dedicated to implementing international guidelines, and to insert these into internationalised, multilevel governance mechanisms. These programmes attracted support from actors within Indonesia's central government as a means of attracting funding and restoring some authority lost during decentralisation. However, the implementation and efficacy of these governance institutions was also shaped by economic actors. Alongside a large 'backyard' sector – poor villagers cultivating chickens for household consumption or income – Indonesia's commercial poultry sector was far more segmented than in Thailand, and almost entirely domestically oriented (Leboeuf 2009: 49; Sumiarto and Arifin 2008). It mainly comprised large, often transnational, corporations providing farming inputs on credit to thousands of small farms, which raised chickens, selling them to the corporations at set prices. Because corporations do not pay smallholders for dead chickens and have no export markets to lose, they were disinterested in tackling H5N1, and all sectors vigorously resisted culling (Charnoz and Forster 2011). Commercial interests used their local and national political connections to resist thoroughgoing governance rescaling, deflecting it towards the 'backyard' sector instead. While outcomes in the 'backyard' sector are hailed as an 'iconic success' for health security governance (Perry et al. 2009: 26), within the commercial sector they are negligible (Forster and Charnoz 2013: ap).

The chapter proceeds as follows. The first section examines the securitisation of infectious disease and the rescaling of governance mechanisms for managing pandemic risk. The second then discusses the governance of H5N1 in Thailand and Indonesia in two subsections, respectively.

The securitisation of infectious disease

Infectious diseases and attempts to mitigate their effects are as old as human civilisation (Alcabes 2009). However, since the early 1990s, infectious disease has increasingly been defined as a *security* problem

(Fidler 2003b; McInnes and Lee 2006; Elbe 2009; see WHO and Heymann 2007). The burgeoning literature on health security is divisible into two main camps, as described in chapter one. The first, adopting a realist ontology, sees the securitisation of public health as reflecting the growing threat posed by existing and new pathogens. This literature argues that the undesirable side effects of globalisation, particularly the growing encroachment of humans on natural habitats, intensive industrial livestock farming practices, and climate change, along with the hypermobility that air travel provides for pathogens, have considerably heightened the risk of devastating pandemics (Garrett 1995; Dupont 2001: 212–27; Fidler 2003a; Elbe 2008).

However, there is simply no necessary correlation between the objective scale of a threat and the governance response to it. The infamous 'Spanish flu' of 1918–19 killed more people than World War I, without eliciting the kinds of discursive and governance responses observable today (Wraith and Stephenson 2009; Alcabes 2009). Indeed, it generated no major revisions to the International Sanitary Regulations (ISRs), the international treaty dedicated to managing infectious disease. Conversely, viral outbreaks like SARS and H5N1 were used to promote revisions in the International Health Regulations (IHRs) – the successor to the ISRs – making the regime far more intrusive and regulatory. This is despite the fact that HPAI and SARS were only ever *potential* pandemics: in reality, they killed only hundreds of victims, while the Spanish flu killed tens of millions. Spanish flu claimed an estimated 4.3 million lives on the Indonesian island of Java alone (Chandra 2013). While H5N1 has killed fewer than 170 people across the entire Indonesian archipelago, it was subjected to vast and intrusive international intervention unimaginable in 1919.

The second camp within health security adopts the Copenhagen School approach, depicting the securitisation of infectious diseases as consequence of successful securitising moves rather than a changing threat environment. As in other subfields, scholars here have largely focused on applying the CS framework to this particular issue-area and on describing specific securitisations, identifying the actors, their discourses of threat and referent objects (e.g. Enemark 2009; Kelle 2007; Elbe 2009). This approach has been applied to the HPAI outbreaks. Elbe (2010b), for example, shows medical professionals first securitised the disease as a political strategy to attract attention and resources to prevent a potentially devastating pandemic and to assist health systems in developing countries that had been devastated by decades of structural adjustment (also Davies 2010). To make their case, they underscored the risk of a global pandemic, with some experts warning of up to 350 million deaths, although the WHO estimated 50 million (Davis 2005).

This strategy clearly succeeded: few other pathogens have been described in starker terms by important governments and international organisations. In 2005, then US Senator, later President, Barack Obama wrote in the *New York Times* with fellow Senator Richard Lugar:

[W]hen we think of the major threats to our national security the first to come to mind are nuclear proliferation, rogue states and global terrorism. But another kind of threat lurks beyond our shores, one from nature, not humans – an avian influenza pandemic. An outbreak could cause millions of deaths, destabilize South-East Asia (its likely place of origin), and threaten the security of governments around the world (Elbe 2010a: 47).

Announcing the establishment of the International Partnership on Avian and Pandemic Influenza (IPAPI) at the 2005 UN High-Level Plenary Meeting, then US President George W. Bush said: 'It is essential we work together . . . to protect our citizens' (White House 2005). The British Civil Contingencies Secretariat claimed that avian influenza is 'as serious a threat as terrorism' (Lean 2005), and the disease still ranks highly on the UK's National Risk Register (Cabinet Office 2013: 7, 12). The WHO (2007: 45) described H5N1 as 'the most feared security threat', while the World Bank (2008: 10) warned that 'the virus remains a substantial threat to global public health security'. In 2006, a World Economic Forum report stated that 'the global risk most preoccupying global business and political leaders is the H5N1 avian flu virus' (WEF 2006: 2).

This discursive identification of an existential threat also translated into substantial monetary commitments, apparently confirming the CS's expectation that successful securitisation would attract emergency responses (Elbe 2010b). In 2005, the US government allocated US$3.8 billion in emergency funding to manage the threat of emerging and re-emerging infectious disease domestically and internationally. A total of US$334 million was earmarked for overseas programmes to combat H5N1 (State Department 2006). The justification given for this expenditure was that, 'since pandemics are diseases without borders,

the influenza virus will not respect political or geographic boundaries –
a threat against one nation is a threat against the entire world' (HHS
2005: H-60). These funds formed part of a total US$1.9 billion pledged
at an international donors' conference in Beijing in January 2006, US$1
billion of which was in grants. The European Commission pledged
US$100 million in aid grants and US$20 million for research, while
EU member-states individually contributed US$140 million in total
(EU 2006). At another meeting in Mali in December 2006, a further US$475.9 million was allocated to the global fight against avian
influenza, with the US making the biggest pledge (US$100 million),
followed by Canada (US$92.5 million), the European Commission
(US$88.2 million) and Japan (US$67 million) (Pellerin 2006). The
funds, according to the IPAPI plan, were to be used mainly for
surveillance and prevention; preparedness, planning and outreach; and
response and containment of avian influenza (HHS 2005: H-60). This
represents a very substantial commitment of resources to tackle a single disease, considering that the WHO's total annual operating budget
is typically just over US$1 billion.

Scholars exploring the securitisation of health have generated some
very useful insights. They highlight the highly uneven nature of the
securitisation of public health, which they attribute to the agendas
and interests of governments in the global North (Davies 2008, 2010;
McInnes and Lee 2006; Rushton 2011; Kelle 2007). Although concepts
such as 'global health security' have gained traction within the WHO
and elsewhere (e.g. WHO and Heymann 2007), the diseases identified
as security threats are almost exclusively those with pandemic potential, especially those capable of 'jumping scales' rapidly, that is, moving from a local scale – typically in developing countries – to become
global epidemics affecting wealthy states (Ali and Keil 2009: 195; see
Rushton 2011: 780). The UN Secretary-General's High Level Panel on
Threats, Challenges and Change (2004: 19) claims, for example, that
infectious diseases should be considered a security concern because of
their potentially unlimited reach, appealing to the 'enlightened self-
interest' of Western governments: 'the security of the most affluent
State can be held hostage to the ability of the poorest State to contain
an emerging disease'. However, endemic health problems, which kill
millions of poor people within developing countries, such as malaria,
dengue fever and tuberculosis, have generally not been securitised, nor
allocated funding commensurate with the challenge.

As this book demonstrates, the argument that because new security problems easily cross borders they should concern governments and people far from their origins is not unique to infectious disease but common to all NTS issues. However, rather than recognising this commonality, health security scholars have incorrectly assumed that their field is unique and thus we are witnessing the 'medicalisation' of international security (Elbe 2010a). Instead of probing this commonality for insights into security governance more broadly, they have preferred instead to evaluate normatively the advantages and drawbacks of securitisation as a political strategy (e.g. Elbe 2006, 2010b; Davies 2010; Enemark 2010). This again reflects the broader limitations of the CS, with its long-standing preoccupation with the merits of securitisation and desecuritisation (see Wæver 1995, 2011; McDonald 2008). The CS emphasis on 'speech acts' has also led to an overwhelming focus on the intergovernmental level, where public pronouncements abound, rather than on how disease is governed in practice. Yet, discourse is frequently misleading; the language of 'national security' and 'sovereignty' is sometimes deployed even as extensive international intervention in domestic health governance is underway (Hameiri 2014). What such interventions involve is missed when scholars confine themselves to, for example, judging that the securitisation of diseases like HIV/AIDS or H5N1 is negative because it reinforces 'national security' perspectives and thus zero-sum, combative logics rather than cooperation (Elbe 2006, 2010b).

Rescaling the governance of infectious disease

Fundamentally, what is missed is that because 'national security' in the global North is now taken to require the containment of diseases in the global South, security governance is acquiring an increasingly *post*-national form, involving efforts to rescale human and animal health governance where diseases originate and to integrate them within transnational regulatory frameworks for managing infectious disease. This shift, which Fidler (2007) describes as a transition from *international* to *global* health governance, is reflected in the development of broad risk-management platforms for pandemic disease preparedness, such as the revised IHRs and the Pandemic Influenza Preparedness (PIP) framework, which the WHO coordinates.

It is also reflected in specific attempts to contain particularly dangerous pathogens like SARS and H5N1.

The shift is clearly expressed in the evolving ISRs/IHRs (Fidler 2005). The first ISRs were created in 1851, following the 1830 and 1847 cholera outbreaks in Europe. Later revisions, like those issued in 1969, maintained an early focus on the management of *international* contact points – airports, border-crossings and ports – and only required governments to notify the WHO of outbreaks of six infectious diseases: cholera, plague, relapsing fever, smallpox, typhus and yellow fever (Fidler 2005). The WHO relied entirely on official information submitted by governments. However, the 2003 SARS outbreak proved an important catalyst for change. China's initial attempt to conceal the outbreaks and subsequent refusal to cooperate with the WHO for two months was widely seen to have enabled SARS to spread (Fidler 2003a; Abraham 2007; Stevenson and Cooper 2009). The international emergency response saw the WHO assume new coordinating functions vis-à-vis governments, and it unprecedentedly issued unilateral travel warnings (Kamradt-Scott 2011). The World Health Assembly (WHA) subsequently demanded that the 'inadequate' IHRs be revised to more clearly specify the roles of governments and the WHO (Davies 2012: 593). Accordingly, the 2005 IHRs focused attention on ensuring domestic health systems had the capacity to manage infectious diseases locally to protect health security globally. They specified the competences states must develop, including establishing disease-surveillance networks and reporting mechanisms, and installing laboratories and other core infrastructure. The revised IHRs, which are not confined to a specified list of pathogens, also authorise the WHO to obtain information from non-governmental sources and declare a Public Health Emergency of International Concern, triggering trade and travel warnings (Kamradt-Scott 2011). Justified as necessary to manage the risks arising from transboundary disease, the WHO's new role is described as 'further developing and maintaining an effective international system that is able to continuously assess the *global context of public health risks* and is prepared to respond rapidly to *unexpected, internationally-spreading events* and to contain specific public health threats' (WHO n.d.b, emphasis added).

Crucially, this does not denote the WHO's emergence as a supranational authority, subordinating states to its will. Governments retain the right to reject WHO interventions if they wish, as some observers lament (Kamradt-Scott 2011). Instead the WHO has become a locus of regulatory 'meta-governance', providing pandemic preparedness guidelines and standards for states to adopt in their domestic health systems, as well as a repository of public health expertise for states to draw upon when implementing the IHRs (Fidler 2007).

Indeed, far from developing autonomous supranational power, as constructivists might expect, the WHO's new role is substantially directed by powerful state interests. The new IHRs are not supported by additional funding to develop poor countries' internal capacities (Bhattacharya 2007). Rather, the WHO's core funding has declined steadily since the 1970s as donors like the US and the UK have shifted to funding specific projects on a case-by-case basis. Consequently, donors now control around eighty per cent of the WHO's total budget, as opposed to its rather meagre operating budget, deliberately bypassing the WHA, where Northern governments are outnumbered by poor developing states (Butler 2013; Davies 2010: 34–5; Chorev 2012). Donors have thereby redirected the WHO to focus on specific diseases that they find threatening to their security.

A further aspect of the rescaling of health security governance has been its expansion into hitherto disconnected policy areas, bringing in new agents and potential sources of contestation. This has partly been driven by the enhanced role of technical experts – in this case, public health experts, virologists and epidemiologists – in defining the nature of 'threats' within regulatory regimes. These experts are particularly concerned by zoonotic diseases, said to have comprised sixty per cent of all emerging infectious diseases from 1940 to 2004 (Scoones 2010: 3). They include SARS, H5N1, H1N1 ('swine flu') and the Ebola, Nipah and Hendra viruses. Expert concern over this linkage between animal and human health has helped broaden health security to encompass the governance of animals, which is inevitably associated with agriculture and economic development. Since pandemic prevention and containment is now seen to require surveillance and response in wild, domestic and livestock animal populations, and because zoonosis is thought to be influenced by climate change and deforestation, the scope of 'domestic health governance' has expanded dramatically (see Coker et al. 2011). Commensurately, a bewildering array of governmental and non-governmental agencies and actors are increasingly incorporated into disease control systems, while the WHO itself cooperates with a wide range of agencies, such as the FAO, the World Organisation for Animal Health (OIE) and the World Bank, through the 'One World, One Health' agenda (FAO et al. 2008). This expansion of health governance has also given powerful interests associated with livestock and other agribusiness industries a strong, and often decisive, stake in the way that some infectious diseases are managed, as our cases studies now demonstrate (Vu 2011).

The governance of H5N1 in Thailand and Indonesia

Southeast Asia was the centre of the last decade's H5N1 outbreaks. This densely populated, relatively impoverished region is often seen by scientists as one of the world's worst hotspots for infectious disease outbreaks. Rising human encroachment on natural habitats and the often close proximity between humans and domestic animals are said to greatly increase the risk of zoonotic diseases. Indeed, in late 2005, the WHO declared Southeast Asia would become the 'next ground zero' if the H5N1 pandemic were to materialise (Caballero-Anthony 2008: 508; also Thomas 2006: 930). Southeast Asian governments appeared to agree that H5N1 posed a serious threat. In 2004, ASEAN leaders identified avian flu as one of the region's 'key challenges' (ASEAN 2004b). In 2007, they labelled it one of the top three transnational threats to regional security, stability and peace (ASEAN 2007b).

However, several commentators have noted a yawning gap between this urgent rhetoric and the actual response to the H5N1 outbreaks, which appeared lacklustre. They have emphasised the region's infamous attachment to national sovereignty – centrepiece of the so-called 'ASEAN Way' (Acharya 2009a) – as rendering it unable to formulate an adequate response to H5N1, as with other transboundary problems (Caballero-Anthony 2008; Haacke and Williams 2008; Maier-Knapp 2011). This is fundamentally unpersuasive. As we demonstrate, deep international interventions did occur in Southeast Asia to rescale domestic health governance as part of the broader international effort to manage the disease, usually with the active support of national government ministries (Scoones and Forster 2010; Hameiri 2014).

This section provides two in-depth case studies of the response to H5N1 in Thailand and Indonesia, which managed the same disease in starkly different ways and generated divergent outcomes. The securitisation of H5N1 by international organisations and donor governments was used by central governments, in different ways and with varying degrees of success, to justify particular policy responses, as well as to legitimise their uneven consequences for different societal groups. The political economy of poultry production, and the poultry industry's relationship with governments at various levels, was the principal factor shaping these trajectories. In Thailand, the dominance of an export-oriented, highly industrialised poultry industry drove a centralised policy of tight biosecurity, which rendered small farms unviable and concentrated industry ownership in conglomerate hands. The Thai government's response was apparently effective, as no new human cases have been recorded since 2006 (WHO n.d.a). Conversely, in Indonesia, a more disaggregated and domestically focused poultry industry has perverse incentives to avoid regulation. Consequently, despite extensive externally driven governance rescaling, absent in Thailand's case, the governance response is ineffective because it was deflected towards the weakest group: poor villagers raising 'backyard' poultry, which were actually the victims of the disease circulating in commercial farms (Forster and Charnoz 2013). Consequently H5N1 remains endemic among Indonesian poultry, although human infections have declined since 2006 (Forster 2010).

Thailand

The Thai response to H5N1 had two important features. First, while international experts were occasionally consulted and international regulatory standards were often invoked, Thailand's central government did not permit the direct involvement of international organisations and other agencies in the management of H5N1 outbreaks but instead monopolised its governance. It thus retained discretion over the manner in, and the extent to which, 'best-practice' guidelines from OIE, FAO and WHO were brought to bear on different stakeholders. Second, this discretion, particularly with regards to animal health, clearly favoured the interests of Thailand's large-scale, industrialised, export-oriented and vertically integrated poultry producers, at the expense of small producers and other interests groups, like cock-fighting enthusiasts and backyard poultry holders, spurring the sector's further industrialisation and concentration (Safman 2010).[1]

---

[1] This outcome is also found in other cases, such as Egypt (Bingham and Hinchliffe 2008).

Thailand's apparent success in containing H5N1 in humans, with no new cases since 2006, is often explained by the alignment between the medical imperative of reducing contact between humans and diseased poultry and major producers' production methods, since their large-scale, integrated farms require only limited human–poultry contact. However, though little information is available on the circulation of H5N1 in commercial farms, the persistence of localised periodic outbreaks in poultry suggests it has shifted to an endemic pattern of infection (Meyer and Preechajarn 2006; Safman 2010: 179; Thomas 2006). Indeed, contrary to industry claims and the assumptions inherent in the FAO's classification of poultry farming sectors, some evidence suggests that large-scale farms incubate disease, which then spreads to wild birds and backyard poultry (Davis 2005; Bingham and Hinchliffe 2008: 189; Forster and Charnoz 2013).

The Thai case demonstrates clearly that the rescaling of governance is a strategic move privileging particular societal interests over others. It also demonstrates that, despite the relativisation of scale associated with transnational security problems, governments retain an important role as 'scale managers', determining the kinds of international interventions permitted and the interests affected by them. Rather than reflecting a die-hard commitment to 'sovereignty', however, how this capacity is used is determined by particular contexts of state–society relations. To understand the context here, we must examine the political economy of the most affected industry.

The political economy of poultry production in Thailand

By the time H5N1 emerged in 2003, Thailand's poultry sector had become both heavily industrialised and politically well connected, defining the basic social power relations that subsequently shaped H5N1 governance.

Thailand's poultry sector had undergone significant transformation since the 1970s. Initially it largely comprised small companies raising chickens from local stock for domestic consumption. Charoen Pokphand (CP) – then a small animal feed producer – began importing breeding stock and selling day-old chicks (DOCs) to Thai farmers, who were contracted to raise them and sell back at an agreed price, before they were marketed to consumers. As production costs fell, large-scale producers like CP became competitive in export markets. By 2003, annual Thai poultry exports reached nearly US$1 billion and the sector contributed approximately four per cent of total agricultural GDP (Safman 2010: 182). Independent smallholders were increasingly replaced by contract farmers, who were themselves later dispensed with as the large corporations brought production in-house, with their share of output growing from thirty-three to fifty-seven per cent from 1993 to 2003 (NaRanong 2006).

These vertically integrated farms are typically very large facilities housing over 10,000 birds. All production and processing is handled in-house, giving the company total control over cost and quality. Because production typically occurs in biologically isolated and highly mechanised environments, it is often argued – not uncontroversially (Davis 2005; Bingham and Hinchliffe 2008: 189) – that these facilities better address biosecurity concerns than other forms of poultry production (Safman 2010: 205). Indeed, the emergence and dominance of these mega-farms were driven not only by concern to achieve economies of scale, but also by stringent regulatory standards demanded by important export markets like Japan and the EU, which were more achievable in vertically integrated facilities (Delgado et al. 2003). In 1995, for example, the EU had threatened to ban Thai poultry imports following the discovery of banned additives in chickens raised by contract farmers (Burgos et al. 2008). This was particularly critical given exporters' shift to pre-cooked chicken products to realise higher profits. By 2003, such products comprised around a third of poultry export revenues; after the outbreak, they became exporters' main commodity (Safman 2010: 185).

The poultry industry's growth and consolidation was accompanied by enhanced political influence. The major poultry producers are very well organised, fronting highly professional lobby groups like the Thai Broiler Processing Exporters Association. The industry's power at the time of the outbreak was also enhanced by political circumstances. The administration then in office, led by billionaire businessman Thaksin Shinawatra, was highly sympathetic to the interests of the Thai bourgeoisie, particularly in export-oriented industries. Thaksin's *Thai Rak Thai* party came to power in 2001 on the back of popular anger over IMF-imposed austerity following the Asian financial crisis of 1997–8. Thaksin developed a populist mix of pro-business and pro-poor policies, and Thai business elites were heavily represented in his government (Pasuk and Baker 2004). This included the powerful poultry industry: Thaksin's Commerce Minister, Watana Muangsook, is the son-in-law of CP founder and chief executive officer, Dhanin Chearavanont, who *Forbes Magazine* (2 December 2010) identifies as Thailand's wealthiest person.

Consequently it is unsurprising that '[a]t numerous points during the epidemic, decisions taken by Thai officialdom clearly reflected direct input from and/or collaboration with the industry lobby' (Safman 2010: 182). Indeed:

> While it is self-evident that any country with such a large and economically vibrant industrial poultry sector would go to great lengths to preserve and protect that sector's interests, it is not clear that Thailand's effort need have been implemented in a manner that was so costly to the smaller producers who, while economically less influential, were (and are) nevertheless quite numerous . . . the Thai government consistently and almost unilaterally sided with the large-scale producers, making only token concessions . . . to small-scale commercial and non-commercial interests (Safman 2010: 201).

As we shall see, the tight state–industry relationship profoundly shaped the governance of H5N1 as a non-traditional security issue.

Thailand's governance response to H5N1

The Thai government's response was principally shaped by the desire to defend the export markets of the politically and economically powerful large-scale poultry producers. In pursuit of this goal, the government mobilised international regulatory standards, but concentrated power in state hands rather than permitting extensive governance rescaling through the direct involvement of international actors. This isolated opponents of the government's response from external allies who may have been more sympathetic to their plight, benefiting the large producers.

Although H5N1 first appeared in Thailand in late 2003, the Thai government officially admitted this only in January 2004, as the outbreaks became widespread and the first human victims died (Thomas 2006: 924–5). The government was immediately accused, both by domestic political rivals and internationally, of attempting to conceal the disease to protect Thailand's poultry exports. This was not unwarranted, since the EU and Japan – Thai poultry's biggest export markets – plus Hong Kong, the Philippines, Singapore, Myanmar and Cambodia immediately imposed import bans (*Bangkok Post* 24 January 2004). These were maintained for raw meat until 2008, but even cooked meat products were given only limited access to European and Japanese markets from late 2005 (Safman 2010: 175).

Following the revelation, the Thai government took swift, decisive action to eliminate H5N1, vigorously publicising these efforts to reassure domestic and international consumers. Although its response resembled the emergency measures that CS adherents expect, it actually involved the ruthless application of international regulatory guidelines provided by the FAO, WHO and OIE, again illustrating how security governance has become more internationalised, bureaucratised and technical. The measures taken included: comprehensively culling poultry from all farms within a five-kilometre radius of confirmed outbreaks, disinfecting affected facilities, and restricting movement within a fifty-kilometre radius of outbreak sites. Importantly, however, this application of international 'best practice' was not simply neutral, but was rather enabled by and reflected the interests of the large-scale, export-oriented segment of the poultry industry. The culling policy immediately imposed a disproportionate burden on small- to medium-sized farms, where most of the sixty-two million birds culled were located (Safman 2010: 175). Similarly, the Thai government's follow-up measures to regularise its response to H5N1 and develop better surveillance and outbreak preparedness favoured industrial players. Three new regulatory requirements were introduced: a ban on vaccinations, controls on the movement of poultry, and the compartmentalisation of facilities. While most of Thailand's mega-farms already complied with these rules, the adjustment cost for small farmers was often unbearable. Many thus 'decided to close down their operations entirely, making the period from 2005 to 2006 a period of significant consolidation and restructuring within the Thai poultry sector' (Safman 2010: 180).

The vaccine ban is an area of major difference between the Thai and Indonesian cases; while Indonesia promoted vaccinations, the Thai government refused to permit the vaccination of birds, even of fighting cocks – a popular sport in the country. This decision was justified by invoking the OIE Manual, which recommended mass culling and disinfection rather than vaccination (Scoones and Forster 2010: 26–7). The more pressing reason was that the EU and Japan had banned imports of vaccinated chicken products (Leboeuf 2009: 51). The decision prompted outrage among small-scale farmers and fighting cock owners. To manage this, the government formed a national committee to investigate the viability of vaccination in July 2004, between the first and second waves of H5N1 infection. However, again citing scientific evidence and best practice, the committee maintained the policy, claiming that vaccination, particularly if incomplete, would only spur H5N1's evolution into a more dangerous pathogen. Government and industry representatives then used these findings, along with OIE standards, to justify the vaccination ban (Safman 2010: 187). Despite the appearance of neutral, technical rationality, this again reflected big producers' interests. Many large-scale farms were reportedly using the same vaccines to immunise hens used to produce eggs – which are marketed domestically, not exported – but no government ban was imposed here (McSherry and Preechajarn 2005).

Poultry movement controls and their uneven implementation also showed how the same powerful interests shaped the design and operation of the governance regime. Again invoking OIE regulations, a June 2004 law specified that no susceptible animals could be transported from or through an area within ten kilometres of any H5N1 outbreak for ninety days without special permission from local animal health authorities. The burden of this new regulation fell heavily on small farms and cock-fighting enthusiasts since, as the mega-farms were increasingly vertically integrated, with all stages of production colocated, their need for movement was low (Safman 2010: 189). When movement was needed, their resources and clout meant they could more easily acquire permits than small farms and fighting cock owners, who endured long waiting periods. Cock-fighters were reduced to bribing local officials to smuggle birds through quarantine zones, though eventually a compromise was found in the form of travel 'passports' for their birds (Safman 2010: 194).

Finally, the concept of compartmentalisation also advanced the interests of large-scale producers. First introduced by the OIE in the mid 1990s, compartmentalisation allows the recognition and certification of different sectors based on distinctive production circumstances. It allowed for producers that met biosecurity and handling standards to be certified as fit to export, while denying certification to others. Pushing this approach suited large-scale producers, since they had been segmenting the poultry sector since the 1990s. To pursue this approach, the Thai government permitted a modest degree of governance rescaling, allowing the OIE to independently regulate Thai regulators from the Ministry of Agriculture. Japan and the EU accepted this approach in 2007 and 2008, respectively, and certificates were swiftly issued to CP and one other major corporation, although no raw meat has yet been sold under this scheme (Meyer and Preechajarn 2006; Safman 2010: 190; Ratananakorn and Wilson 2011).

Thailand's response to the security threat of H5N1 was thus clearly shaped by powerful economic interests. The Thaksin government's primary goal was the defence of the politically connected industrial sector's export markets, and all other sectors' interests were subordinated to this. Had the large-scale producers' interests been different, the application of international regulatory standards would arguably have been far less stringent – as the case of Indonesia clearly suggests.

Indonesia

Indonesia has been hit harder by H5N1 than any other country, with the highest number of human deaths and the greatest amount of international assistance to combat the disease. Unlike Thailand, where the government largely excluded international actors while selectively implementing international regulatory standards, in Indonesia, the FAO, WHO, other UN agencies and bilateral donors have been heavily involved in designing, funding and implementing large-scale programmes of surveillance, culling, vaccination and risk communication, together with national government agencies (Lowe 2010). The most significant and best-funded development has been the rescaling of local animal and human health agencies to provide permanent grassroots surveillance of H5N1 outbreaks and to respond where necessary. Initiatives like the Participatory Disease Surveillance and Response (PDSR) project in animal health and the District Surveillance Officers (DSO) project in human health often created local health services and established new governance networks across the local and national scales in Indonesia, which were hitherto frequently weak or non-existent. International agencies also improved laboratories' diagnostic facilities and the capacity of hospitals across Indonesia to treat avian flu patients. Nevertheless, although the incidence of human infections declined from its peak in 2006, people continue to be infected every year to 2013, and the disease remains endemic among poultry in Indonesia's most populous islands, Java, Sumatra, Bali and Sulawesi, with sporadic outbreaks reported elsewhere (Forster 2010: 131). To understand both why Indonesia's reaction to the exact same NTS threat diverged so much from Thailand's and why it was so ineffective, we must understand the specific power relations shaping the governance response, notably the very different relationship between local and national political scales and the political economy of its poultry industry.

The political economy of poultry production in Indonesia
In Indonesia, a poultry industry, which produces exclusively for domestic consumption and in which the big and dominant conglomerates profit from selling production inputs to small, independent farmers, has had little interest in applying costly international standards of biosecurity and disease eradication. Meanwhile, government decentralisation has enabled powerful players in the poultry industry to keep the governance of animal health at the local level and in the hands of industry-friendly officials.

The decentralisation of the Indonesian state, described in detail in chapter three, had two major implications for infectious disease management. First, international donors concerned with managing H5N1 have had to develop multilevel governance approaches that engaged directly with local-level governments, since significant authority had been delegated to them. This has spawned new governance networks designed to connect particular government agencies across various scales, with donors acting as coordinators. The second implication of decentralisation is that proponents and opponents of rescaling have clustered around the national and local governmental levels, respectively. Those trying to resist the international regulation associated with rescaling have sought to keep governance at the district or provincial level and in the hands of local livestock services officials (Charnoz and Forster 2011). Conversely, central government ministries have selectively embraced international rescaling to benefit from additional funding and bolster the territorial and functional reach of their diminished authority (Hameiri 2014; Forster and Charnoz 2013). They also seek to blame decentralisation for their failures in managing H5N1. Indonesia's former health minister, Dr Siti Fadilah Supari, for example, argued:

Vietnam, as a centralised socialist country, can get high compliance on national policies and so has succeeded, for example, in implementing rapid culling of birds... In contrast, Indonesia is in transition towards a decentralized democracy after three decades of authoritarian national rule.

We are still on a learning curve, and compliance of the relatively independent regional authorities with national policies is often poor (Butler 2007).

Decentralisation has also shaped the political economy of Indonesia's poultry industry. Chicken is Indonesia's favourite meat and is a very important source of protein, particularly for poorer people (Sumiarto and Arifin 2008: 7). The poultry sector is also very significant economically. The livestock sector as a whole, of which the poultry industry is by far the biggest component, contributes about 1.8 per cent of total GDP in Indonesia and it grew at an average rate of 4.47 per cent per annum between 2001 and 2006, the period immediately before and during the H5N1 outbreaks. Poultry farms are also the largest employers within the livestock sector, which collectively employs three million people, around three per cent of the national workforce (Sumiarto and Arifin 2008: 6).

Beyond these headline figures, however, Indonesia's industry is organised very differently to that of Thailand, and this has critically shaped the governance response to H5N1. Ostensibly, Indonesia's sector is also highly concentrated, with the ten largest poultry producers controlling all industrial production and eighty per cent of total output (Charnoz and Forster 2011: 21). The largest three producers, of which the Indonesian subsidiary of Thai multinational CP is the biggest, have a combined market share of seventy per cent (Sumiarto and Arifin 2008: 10). However, unlike Thailand, where production now largely occurs in vertically integrated mega-farms, Indonesia's situation is closer to Thailand in the 1970s and 1980s. The large-scale companies dominate the supply of farming inputs, but production is almost entirely outsourced to thousands of small and medium farms – the 'nucleus–plasma' arrangement also found in palm oil (see chapter three). Essentially, the 'nucleus' companies provide inputs on credit to the 'plasma' farms – or 'Sector Three' – which raise the chickens for 28 days, then sell them back to the 'nucleus' at pre-agreed prices. The large companies then market the chickens solely to domestic consumers. This structure was introduced to the sector in 1996, ostensibly to assist small, local agricultural businesses to develop. In reality, it was highly advantageous to powerful interests associated with the Suharto regime, which dominated the nucleus companies, and it helped expand centre-dominated patronage relations (see McCarthy 2006 in the palm oil context). The arrangement also allows the nuclei to extract enormous profits, up to ninety per cent of which come not from retailing chickens, but rather the oligopolistic sale of inputs – primarily DOCs and feed – to Sector Three farmers, who lack alternative sources of credit to purchase them from elsewhere (USAID 2009: 19–20; Charnoz and Forster 2011: 32). Sector Three farmers are thus forced into permanent dependence on the large companies and operate on tiny profit margins.

This highly exploitative structure carries significant implications for the incidence and management of H5N1. Sector Three farms, where most production actually occurs, are usually very small, basic facilities. They typically house between 500 and 5,000 birds and cannot afford the hi-tech methods and biosecurity measures deployed by Thailand's mega-farms. Many lack adequate walls to separate chickens from the surrounding environment, protective gear for farmers, or showers they can use upon entering and exiting the facility (Sumiarto and Arifin 2008; USAID 2009). Furthermore, under standard industry contracts, farmers are not paid for dead chickens. The large corporations consequently have little exposure to the risk of poultry deaths as a result of diseases like avian influenza – barring a mass consumer boycott, which has not happened to date – and are thus likely to be indifferent about it. Adding to the large corporations' complacency is the fact that despite the outbreaks and mass chicken deaths, because of sharply rising demand for poultry products among Indonesians, Indonesia's poultry population actually grew by seven to fifteen per cent annually at the height of the H5N1 scare between 2006 and 2008, while industrial production as a whole has grown by nearly tenfold over the decade to 2009 (Forster and Charnoz 2013: z). Conversely, hard-pressed farmers have every incentive to conceal outbreaks and even sell dead, diseased chickens via brokers. Due to widespread poverty, Indonesia has a thriving market for chickens that died of unnatural causes, which are sold at discounted prices (Brum 2011). These perverse incentives clearly impede the management of H5N1 (see also McLeod 2010).

This might change if the industry became vertically integrated, as in Thailand, but a government–business pact apparently precludes this. For the central government, vertical integration is not politically palatable because, by killing off smaller farms, it would generate significant unemployment (Forster and Charnoz 2013; Delima 2011; McGrane 2011). The government has thus apparently struck a bargain with the larger firms, who agreed not to vertically integrate their operations in exchange for continued protectionist measures against imports of agricultural inputs and chicken meat (Mulyanto 2011). Indeed, only 0.28 per cent of the poultry products consumed in Indonesia are imported (Sumiarto and Arifin 2008: 6), and no chicken meat has been imported into Indonesia since 2000. Imported meat would be significantly cheaper than domestic produce, because sophisticated production technologies used in countries like Thailand reduce costs, whilst the massive profit margins extracted by Indonesia's conglomerates on farming inputs inflates them. As Ministry of Agriculture (MoA) officials put it, imports 'are cheaper. If it comes in, the market will collapse' (Azhar and Noeri 2011).

Accordingly, the large corporations are disinterested in either changing the industry's structure or improving biosecurity measures to help tackle H5N1, while Sector Three farmers are simply unable to do so. When the 'nucleus' firms were engaged by the USAID-funded Community-Based Avian Influenza Control (CBAIC), one of very few international projects to directly target the private sector, their representatives acknowledged biosecurity needed improving in Sector Three, but made few commitments to fund this. CBAIC instead focused on training farmers in basic biosecurity – washing hands, disinfecting coops – as if the main problem was the ignorance of farmers. Far more important is the fact that Sector Three farmers lack the capital to invest in biosecurity and cannot obtain loans from banks, the large corporations or the government for this purpose. The president of the Indonesian Poultry Farmers Association and Information Centre, which represents Sector Three farmers, insists:

We can control [avian influenza]. Sector Three's problem is only money ... Farmers can't make the investment – why [doesn't] the government give us money? ... We want soft loans. It is very hard to get credit from banks to invest in biosecurity ... It is very expensive: to build a fence around ten hectares – 100,000 square metres – is one billion rupiah [$91,000] (Hartono 2011).

The FAO's Eric Brum (2011) adds: 'We would've expected the commercial sector to be more willing to allocate resources to ultimately control the disease, but ... it's really become an industry that's built around mitigating losses from disease, as opposed to properly controlling and eliminating diseases which decrease production'.

Together, the structural environment of decentralisation and the industry's political economy have underpinned a radically different response to managing H5N1 in Indonesia to that in Thailand. The large corporations' lack of exposure to the risks of disease and their ability to evade regulatory intervention through the decentralised health governance system has meant that the commercial sector has managed to avoid scrutiny, while poor owners of 'backyard' poultry bore the brunt of the regulatory response.

Indonesia's governance response to H5N1

Avian influenza was never a high priority for the Indonesian government, but with international pressure mounting and with large amounts of donor funding in the offing, the government developed a national disease mitigation plan and established governance mechanisms dedicated to this. The political economy context just described allows us to make sense of the objectives of international rescaling efforts and their highly uneven outcomes. Although some rescaling of health governance has been permitted, largely to improve central oversight of local governments, the Indonesian government nonetheless sought to deflect attention from the commercial sector, towards 'backyard' poultry, which was in fact a victim of the disease's circulation in farms (Forster and Charnoz 2013).

The Indonesian government's response to H5N1 reflected the industry's interests from the outset. It initially sought to conceal the emergence of H5N1 in Indonesian poultry in late 2003, apparently under pressure from major industry players, who were afraid it would hit sales (Sipress 2005). Chicken deaths were instead attributed to Newcastle disease, which has similar symptoms as H5N1 in poultry but no zoonotic capacity. The presence of H5N1 was only admitted in January 2004, but MoA officials initially maintained that the Indonesian strain was incapable of zoonotic transmission. The central government also attempted to pass the responsibility for managing the disease to local governments (Curley and Herington 2011: 156–7). However, after a spike in human cases in 2005, international and domestic pressure on the national government to act became overwhelming. Indonesian government officials and international consultants thus crafted the H5N1 National Strategic Work Plan (NSWP) 2006–8. This identified nine core objectives for H5N1 eradication, highlighting 'backyard' poultry – 'Sector Four' – as a particularly important vector for the disease's spread and zoonotic transmission (Perry et al. 2009). Although the plan mentioned restructuring the commercial sector, this was not identified as a priority or allocated any resources. The NSWP thus embedded industry interests and the state–business pact described above.

However, the governance structures subsequently established created new networks between many national governmental agencies and funding requirements provided an entry point for international actors. A National Committee for Avian Influenza Control and Pandemic Influenza (Komnas FBPI in the Bahasa Indonesia acronym) was established to implement the NSWP. Led by the Coordinating Ministry for People's Welfare, Komnas FBPI included the ministers for health, agriculture, forestry, national planning and industry, the Coordinating Minister for Economics, the commander of the armed forces, the police chief and the chair of the Indonesian Red Cross. It had a secretariat and six task forces containing scientists and other experts, which were to provide direction on research and development, animal health, human health, vaccines, anti-viral medicines, mass communications and public information (Forster 2010: 145). The NSWP specified that US$322 million would be needed over three years to manage H5N1, part of which would be provided by donors (Charnoz and Forster 2011: 72). International contributions were thus sought at the aforementioned Beijing meeting in January 2006. However, because operating budgets remained with relevant government bodies, it was through them that international agencies became involved.

Despite this apparent securitisation and emergency response, it is clear that the H5N1 agenda was largely driven by external rather than domestic interests, reflecting the broader orientation of 'global health security' towards defending societies in richer countries from disease outbreaks in the global South (Rushton 2011). That H5N1 was not a domestic priority is suggested by the fact that only US$57 million, or 1.7 per cent of the national health budget, was allocated to controlling the disease at the peak of the crisis in 2006–7 (Curley and Herington 2011: 157). Similar disinterest is reflected in the bizarre claim that H5N1 was not actually zoonotic, made by Indonesia's then health minister, who stated: 'there's no relationship between human virus and chicken virus. There's no possibility of human to human transmission because it is very different' (Siti 2011). Such nonsense aside, clearly H5N1 was just one problem among many facing this impoverished country. As one high-ranking Ministry of Health (MoH) bureaucrat (Anonymous 2011c) says, 'we have so many diseases – all of the diseases are a priority'. The focus on H5N1 was donor driven, the health minister's special advisor explained (Indriyono 2011). This is underscored by the government's growing disinterest in the disease after international pressure and assistance waned from 2009. Dr Emil Agustiono (Emil 2011), who heads Komnas Zoonosis, which succeeded Komnas FBPI and now seeks to replicate its work across all existing and potential zoonoses, observes: 'the previous one [had] a lot of assistance from donors. The current one [Komnas] has no donor funding... Compared with a couple of years ago, national priority is not there'. Indeed, in July 2011, more than a year after it was established, Komnas Zoonosis was entirely unfunded. Emil laments: 'I wish the pandemic will come again so we are able to exercise our plan!... We don't have enough vaccines. We don't have enough capacity.' The real reason why the national government embraced global health security interventions was apparently an instrumental one: to help strengthen its hand against local governments. H5N1 donor programmes helped forge new governance networks both horizontally and vertically. A senior MoH official argues this helped Indonesia's health system by networking the MoH with other ministries through Komnas FBPI and in particular facilitating better collaboration with the MoA, creating direct links at the directorate-general level and collaboration in the field, with joint investigations of suspected outbreaks (Anonymous 2011c). However, far from merely yielding technical improvements, international funding also empowered national-level agencies, relative to their local counterparts. As the minister of health's special advisor recalls, donor interventions to improve 'pandemic preparedness... helped the centre have a bit more control over provinces and districts, particularly if we have the money... We can advocate and convince them... Resources are always a problem at the local level' (Indriyono 2011). Similar efforts to use international funding to help recentralise authority occurred within the MoA, although the ministry also invoked local governments' resistance to explain both the policies adopted and implementation difficulties. For example, Delima Azahari (Delima 2011), Director-General of Agricultural Quarantine and Manager of the Emergency Centre for Transnational and Asymmetric Threats at the time of the initial outbreaks, argued: 'Local governments were a problem. We can't do anything without the help of local governments.'

Notwithstanding this instrumental support for governance rescaling from national-level agencies, in practice, the regimes that emerged were heavily conditioned by the political economy of poultry production and resistance to rescaling at the local level. We can illustrate this by examining one programme in detail.

Rescaling local health governance: the PDSR project

The implementation of international programmes for managing H5N1 in Indonesia reflects the political economy context of poultry production and state–industry relations that also shaped the NSWP. While 'backyard' poultry was subjected to considerable rescaling, through large-scale surveillance, response and public education campaigns, the commercial industry was left almost entirely untouched and its involvement in H5N1 eradication has so far been wholly voluntary.

The two most significant, internationally funded projects to manage H5N1 in Indonesia were the FAO-managed PDSR and the WHO-managed DSO, with the PDSR's perceived success heavily influencing the DSO's design (see Figures 4.1 and 4.2). This section focuses mainly on PDSR since it was much bigger, with a budget of approximately US$30 million between 2005 and 2012, provided mostly by USAID and the Australian Agency of International Development (AusAID), and it clearly reveals the forces shaping the governance of this NTS threat. The PDSR and DSO both sought to shift local health governance 'upwards', to the regional and national levels, and 'sideways', into the hands of like-minded experts who would implement international regulations. This created a complex, multilevel governance system that was substantially internationalised, with rescaling occurring at multiple levels simultaneously.

At the *local* level, the PDSR and DSO programmes often created health governance systems where none had hitherto existed. These programmes essentially involved training and empowering veterinarians and health officials to conduct local surveillance to detect H5N1 outbreaks and educate local populations on the risks of transmission. Although PDSR officers were officially employed by local *Dinas* (local government departments), until late 2011 their salaries were funded by the FAO, with local governments supposed to assume responsibility from 2012. The PDSR's scale at the local level was vast:

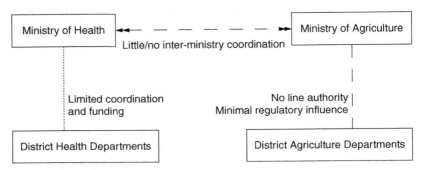

Figure 4.1 Indonesian health governance before the PDSR intervention.

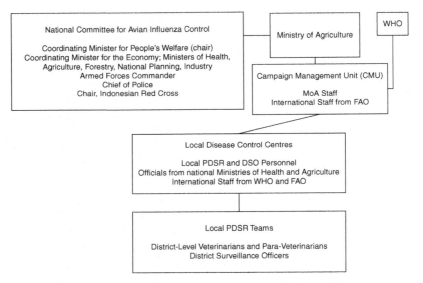

Figure 4.2 Indonesian health governance following the PDSR intervention.

From January 2006 to September 2008, PDSR teams, comprising over 2000 trained veterinarians and para-veterinarians, conducted over 177300 surveillance visits, detected 6011 outbreaks of avian influenza in 324 districts, and met with over two million poultry farmers and community members ... In May 2009, there were fifteen international and sixty national staff/consultants employed by FAO, with a majority of them supporting the PDSR programme (Charnoz and Forster 2011: 69).

At the *provincial* level, Local Disease Control Centres were established. District-level PDSR staff reported suspected outbreaks to these centres, which brought local PDSR and DSO personnel together with national officials from the MoH and MoA, plus international officials from the FAO and WHO. The centres mobilised rapid response teams to investigate reported outbreaks and respond as required. They also rapidly reported their findings to the FAO and WHO. At the *national* level, the PDSR system was coordinated by a Campaign Management Unit (CMU) within the MoA's Directorate-General of Livestock Services, which FAO consultants helped design and staff. The CMU was meant to coordinate its activities with Komnas FBPI.

This multilevel design, with donors working with and coordinating both local- and national-level agencies, was necessitated by decentralisation. As an FAO official explained: 'The central government has little or no outreach. We therefore work though *Dinas* locally' (McGrane 2011). Another FAO advisor puts it more bluntly: 'the national government has no authority to do anything . . . We couldn't get the national government to tell [district and provincial governments] to do it, so we had to go to the local level' (Brum 2011). CMU officers concurred: 'The functional link between central, provincial and district governments was previously constrained during the decentralisation era. We can bridge the gaps' (Azhar and Noeri 2011). Consequently, the PDSR 'has been active in facilitating the relationship between national and local government' (Brum 2011), spawning new functional networks linking Indonesia's various levels of government in the management of H5N1. This was particularly important in agriculture, where since decentralisation there was little coordination between the MoA and local *Dinas*.

Crucially, the PDSR also sought to shift authority 'sideways' to empower veterinarians over other local officials. Enhancing veterinary authority was seen as essential for embedding OIE and FAO standards in local governance. Such attempts to empower technical experts are a common aspect of NTS rescaling, aimed at quarantining policymaking areas from political control. However, empowering veterinarians proved very difficult. There are few trained veterinarians in Indonesia and at every level of government they have worked under managers with backgrounds in animal husbandry or agricultural economics, who are typically more concerned with commercial aspects of livestock services than with animal health. Within the MoA, for example, animal health was until recently only a Directorate within the Directorate-General of Livestock Services. Its powerlessness within the MoA was exemplified by a turnover of four directors in three years, as the government developed its response to H5N1.

The difficulty encountered in changing this situation clearly stemmed in part from political economy constraints. One director of animal health who left the MoA was reportedly dismissed because she wanted to implement widespread culling in H5N1 outbreak areas, the OIE-sanctioned procedure for managing the disease's spread in poultry, rather than the industry's preferred vaccination policy (Charnoz and Forster 2011: 91; Lowe 2010). Unlike in Thailand, Indonesia's big industry players preferred vaccination since, because they did not export chicken, they did not have to worry about meeting EU and Japanese regulations. Moreover, alongside pharmaceutical companies, they could actually increase their profits by producing and selling vaccines. At one point, Indonesia had thirty-five to forty poultry vaccine manufacturers, and the industry was very poorly regulated, with some farmers being sold H5N2 instead of H5N1 vaccines, for example (Suwandono 2011; Heru 2011). Vaccinating chickens is also notoriously difficult: every chicken must be vaccinated three times to acquire immunity and whole flocks must be vaccinated six times each year. It is practically impossible to vaccinate broiler chickens since they are grown for only twenty-eight days. Smaller farmers and villagers also opposed culling, since they do not receive income for dead chickens and meagre government compensation was provided infrequently. Consequently, no one supported culling apart from some government veterinarians, who were swiftly overruled.

The weakness of veterinarians was exacerbated by the absence of structures linking animal health practitioners across different levels of government. In human health, despite the localisation of about eighty per cent of the budget to the district level under decentralisation, the pre-existing line structure linking the MoH to local *Dinas Kesehatan* (human health departments) was largely maintained. However, this was not the case in animal health, for which there was no dedicated *Dinas* in almost every province and district. Animal health services were generally under departments of agricultural services (*Dinas Pertanian*) or livestock services (*Dinas Peternakan*). Furthermore, in some cases wild animals are managed by the forestry *Dinas*, fish by the fisheries *Dinas* and domestic animals by the agriculture *Dinas*. Generally these departments do not have veterinarian leadership, or even input. Funding for local animal health services is currently entirely at the discretion of the *bupati* (district regent) or mayor, who tend to view it as a dispensable service, and often there is only one vet to serve an entire district (Normile 2007; Andri and Riana 2011). This fragmentation and marginalisation of animal health reflects the fact that, unlike human health, agriculture is a very important source of rents and patronage resources. In the context of growing electoral competition at all levels, control of key industries has become essential to attaining and keeping political power in most Indonesian jurisdictions. Reflecting this wider pattern of inter-scalar conflict in post-decentralisation Indonesia (Hadiz 2010), *bupatis* have sought to grab control of agriculture and isolate its governance from both interference by veterinarians and the national authorities in order to capture these resources for themselves. As Professor Wiku Adisasmito (2011), a former member of Komnas FBPI, explains: 'human health is more integrated vertically but in animal health this is not the case because of local economic structures'.

Like national-level officials, Indonesian veterinarians tried to exploit the rescaling of H5N1 governance to enhance their power. The Indonesian Veterinary Medical Association (IVMA) in 2004 launched a campaign to re-establish veterinary authority over livestock services across all levels of government. Veterinarians have long resented being managed by officials with no concern for animal health who forced them to support animal production services instead of regulating them. Vets typically consider themselves as 'professional' and 'independent', unlike animal husbandry experts who are seen as 'political' or 'entrepreneurs' (Charnoz and Forster 2011: 49, 51). They also perceive themselves as part of a transnational professional community working to implement international guidelines for the public good. As one insisted, 'we need authority to implement the norms of OIE' (Charnoz and Forster 2011: 47). The IVMA thus used high-profile issues like H5N1 to demand greater autonomy (Wiwiek 2011). The IVMA's vice president explained its objectives in terms often used by those advocating the rescaling of governance: 'Disease knows no borders. That's why the Vet Association fights over . . . the animal health system, to make it at least the same as the health system . . . We want to be able to issue regulations from the centre [that] they [the districts] will have to work with' (Heru 2011). Similarly, other veterinarians working with international projects demanded that 'farmers . . . should be forced to report' outbreaks to enable veterinary intervention (Andri and Riana 2011).

This campaign had some success, but in practice veterinary authority remains limited. After decades of wrangling, IVMA's efforts, combined with the threat of H5N1, finally spurred parliament to pass National Law 18/2009 on Animal Husbandry and Veterinary Hygiene in May 2009. Whilst still not up to OIE standards, the legislation transformed the DGLS into the Directorate-General of Livestock Services *and* Animal Health, and mandated the establishment of animal health *Dinas* countrywide, to be linked and coordinated nationally. The IVMA contested the law in the Constitutional Court, arguing that ambiguity in Article 68 still subjected veterinarians to discretionary control by the Minister of Agriculture. The Court ruled in its favour, deleting the ambiguity (Charnoz and Forster 2011: 52). This was seen as a major victory for veterinarians. However, the law's implementation has been very slow. No implementing regulations have been issued, no funding allocated and no central veterinary authority has been created. The head of the DLGS, who was, for the first time in many years, a veterinarian, was sacked for supposed 'incompetence' in mid 2011 after just six months in post. Meanwhile, local governments retain considerable autonomy over animal health and, since the mandated new *Dinas* rely on local funding, they are at liberty to underfund them. Thus, as IVMA President Dr Wiwiek (2011) observes: 'in law, we are strong enough, but to have the law really implemented and in line with OIE guidelines, we need political will'.

However, political will to support veterinary authority has not been entirely absent; rather, it has been exercised very unevenly, reflecting the political economy context. On the one hand, government vets are still not even allowed to enter commercial premises without the owner's permission, rendering the industrial sector essentially immune from scrutiny (Andri and Riana 2011). Conversely, veterinary authority in managing outbreaks of disease in *backyard* poultry has been accepted by governments at all levels. Similarly, while mass culling was rejected in favour of poultry vaccination, vaccination was only made compulsory for backyard poultry (Wiku 2011). Clearly, the empowerment of veterinarians within the transformed governance structures has been deflected away from powerful interests towards relatively powerless villagers. As Agus Suwandono (2011), a prominent Indonesian scientist and former Komnas FBPI member, observes: 'regulation is regulation, but money is money'.

This outcome reflects the broader direction taken in the management of this NTS threat. As mentioned above, the NSWP had focused on backyard poultry as the source of H5N1 in Indonesia, deflecting scrutiny from the commercial sector. While the Indonesian government was clearly concerned with shifting attention away from the commercial sector, and the big players in the industry also actively sought to reassure consumers by publicly claiming H5N1 affected mostly 'native' birds in villages (Forster and Charnoz 2013: an), the focus on the 'backyard' sector also reflected the common wisdom among international experts at the time, as well as international donors' usual preference for working with the rural and urban poor and reluctance to take on big business (Perry et al. 2009: 26–7; Forster and Charnoz 2013). Thus, 'international organisations . . . initially exercised their influence where they could – which was not in the commercial sector, nor in the [live poultry] markets' (Charnoz and Forster 2011: 90). Indeed, as long as the PDSR remained focused on Sector Four, its implementation was very smooth. In fact, it was described as an 'iconic success in HPAI detection' (Perry et al. 2009: 26).

However, when the PDSR began to be partially redirected toward the commercial sector, the results were modest at best, reflecting how scientific expertise was marginalised when it clashed with commercial interests. This reorientation began in late 2008, as evidence accumulated of H5N1 circulating in Sector Three farms. As CMU officials reported, research showed 'most sources of infection are in small-scale Sector Three – they have less biosecurity and vaccination and when they get cases they don't want to lose money so they sell [dead chickens] to traders – that's our challenge' (Azhar and Noeri 2011). Heru (2011) goes further to claim that H5N1 already circulates in the breeding farms, and can be found in DOCs sold by nucleus firms to Sector Three farms, though the industry's extreme secrecy makes it very difficult to verify this. Nonetheless, action to tackle infections in the commercial sector has certainly been very limited. The PDSR launched a Commercial Poultry Veterinary Program to develop cost-effective biosecurity measures and encourage farmers to allow veterinarians to visit during H5N1 outbreaks. However, this was a small pilot conducted in only six Sector Three layer farms, participation was entirely voluntary, and farmers were disinterested for the reasons outlined earlier. On the whole, lower-level officials remain fixated on the myth that the problem is Sector Four. For example, health officials in Banten Province, near to Jakarta and home to many poultry farms – insisted that ignorant backyard farmers are to blame: 'They keep the poultry beside the house; they don't separate it. We have regulations for Sector Four – they have to make a cage' (Wahyu and Ritanugraini 2011).

Importantly, it is not simply that local governments are powerless vis-à-vis private interests; rather, reflecting their tight interrelations, they have sometimes actively disrupted efforts to transform or regulate industry. Consider the attempts to alter poultry marketing in the Jakarta Metropolitan Region. Around eighty per cent of poultry in Jakarta is sold live and butchered in open markets. In 2007, with FAO assistance, the Jakarta Provincial Government issued Province Act 4/2007. This effectively banned Jakartans from raising chickens by insisting that poultry be kept at least twenty-five metres from human dwellings – impossible in the crowded capital – and that poultry owners must register biannually with the *Dinas* and allow inspections (Charnoz and Forster 2011). The Act also sought to close the city's 2,000 informal slaughterhouses, replacing them with twenty-five shelters and five massive slaughterhouses – four owned by the Jakarta government – which adhere to the highest biosecurity standards (Dwazil 2011). The FAO helped fund the transition and the training of inspectors, while FAO consultants liaised between local government and industry stakeholders, and attempted to persuade Jakarta businesses that buying chickens from registered slaughterhouses would help their reputation and create 'a "win–win" situation' (McGrane 2011). Nevertheless, the Act's implementation was delayed in April 2010 and again in December 2010, and there is currently no clear indication when, if ever, it will be properly implemented. The main stumbling block is the same provincial government that passed the Act. FAO's James McGrane (2011) elaborates: 'the pushback occurred last year from the Assistant [sic – Deputy] Governor for Economic Affairs. [It] has meant that we weren't as successful as we might've been'. Currently, FAO provides only limited assistance with market hygiene and sanitation capacity-building with more meaningful plans for market reform scrapped. While the precise constellation of industry–government interests underlying the Deputy Governor's intervention is murky, it is nonetheless significant and telling that the official responsible for economic issues was able to override the Jakarta public health and livestock *Dinas* and completely halt the programme's implementation.

A different approach was taken by USAID's Strategies Against Flu Emergence (SAFE) project, a follow-up to CBAIC, which was uniquely focused on the commercial sector. Like many USAID-funded programmes, SAFE bypassed government altogether, attempting instead to persuade nucleus and Sector Three operators that better biosecurity was in their material interests. SAFE also sought to convince 'nucleus' corporations to include biosecurity-related standards and bonuses in their contracts with small farmers. However, as explained earlier, current practices provide nucleus firms with gargantuan profits with minimal economic risk from disease, while Sector Three farms cannot afford biosecurity measures. Consequently, SAFE's efforts were both naive and fruitless. As one poultry market expert argues, the private sector is solely concerned with profit: 'decision-making is about economic imperatives, not public health – public health people can't get that' (Anonymous 2011d).

Thus, reflecting the political economy context, despite the supposedly urgent securitisation of H5N1 in Indonesia, the industry's involvement has remained voluntary or, where regulation was announced, as in Jakarta, it has not been implemented. Industry players only engaged with the PDSR on their terms (Forster and Charnoz 2013: ap). For example, in August 2011, the CMU helped negotiate the establishment of a national committee on poultry health. It has twenty-six representatives from industry, MoA and universities and it is meant as a forum for discussing problems in the sector and possible solutions. Industry representatives only agreed to participate on the condition that discussions remained confidential. The only part of the NSWP that potentially threatened industry interests, the proposals for vertical integration, was essentially ignored because the state–business pact that underpins the existing nucleus-plasma structure remains intact. As the director of the MoH's Zoonotic Diseases Division observes, 'restructuring the poultry industry is the only part of the national avian influenza strategy not yet done' (Misryiah 2011).

The decentralisation and political economy context in Indonesia has thus profoundly shaped the governance of H5N1, producing a highly uneven and largely ineffective governance regime. PDSR, the biggest international H5N1 project, did considerably rescale the management of H5N1, but only among backyard poultry owned by poor, relatively powerless villagers. Conversely, few inroads were made in the commercial sector. Local government resistance to efforts to establish strong animal health systems and the central government's indifference to the disease's spread in the commercial sector meant that the new, multilevel governance systems affected only the weakest societal group. Even this attenuated regime now seems in decline as donor interest wanes. Although the CMU has expanded its focus to zoonoses more broadly, at the time of writing it appeared the unit would be disbanded. The situation is worse at the provincial and district levels, where local governments were supposed to take ownership of donor projects. But given local power relations, as FAO's Eric Brum (2011) observes, 'there is no advocate [for these issues] at the local level' (also Normile 2007). Consequently, local governments show little willingness to adequately fund the agencies established by donors. Local health officials in Banten, for example, already complain that their Local Disease Control Centre is ineffective, because 'there's no . . . personnel budget, no support from national government' (Wahyu and Ritanugraini 2011). While poststructuralists often suggest that donors cultivate a 'governmentality' that outlasts their interventions, these findings show, as in the case of haze (chapter three), that governance arrangements tend to revert to local power relations when international pressure and resources are withdrawn.

Conclusion

Infectious disease is now frequently portrayed as a dangerous security threat on a global scale. Securitisation scholars have usefully shown that the public health issues that are securitised are almost invariably rapidly spreading infectious diseases that are seen to emerge in poorer countries and have the potential ability to proliferate around the world, threatening the populations of Northern states and the global economy. But, like other Copenhagen School adherents, these scholars have not examined the factors shaping how these health security issues are managed on the ground in the countries in which they are seen to originate, instead focusing on the 'speech acts' of international health diplomacy. Yet, as our case studies and others show, there is often a large gap between the rhetoric of securitisation and the governance response. Copenhagen scholars can only lament this gap, blaming it on the reluctance of Southeast Asian states to relinquish their sovereignty. This argument is clearly incorrect. In our cases, Thailand was the most resistant to international intervention, yet stringently implemented international biosecurity protocols; Indonesia accepted the most intervention of any country on Earth, yet the governance regime produced was weak and uneven. It is only when attempts to govern NTS issues are analysed, via the STA, as contestation over rescaling, situated within concrete state–society and political economy contexts, that real-world outcomes can be adequately understood.

In Thailand's case, an export-oriented, politically powerful poultry sector pushed for strong and immediate action on H5N1 when it lost its export markets overnight. The Thai government then simultaneously prevented direct international involvement in the management of the disease, while selectively rescaling H5N1 governance by applying international regulatory standards to legitimise policies that favoured the conglomerates but highly disadvantaged small producers. This spurred the further centralisation and consolidation of the poultry sector, but within highly mechanised and technologically sophisticated farms, which has apparently helped curb H5N1 infections among humans significantly. In Indonesia, decentralisation and a poultry sector with a very different political economy have generated a dissimilar and uneven pattern of rescaling. On the one hand, poor villagers were subjected to considerable international intervention and surveillance through the large-scale, multilevel programmes of PDSR and DSO. On the other, the powerful commercial sector, where the disease largely circulates, was left almost entirely exempt from regulation. The critical difference made by different *local* contexts of NTS governance is clearly illustrated by the practice of multinational poultry industry behemoth CP, which operates in both countries. In Thailand, it endorsed stringent international regulatory standards, since its profits depended on reassuring export markets; in Indonesia, it persisted with a nucleus–plasma arrangement that actively fosters avian influenza, because its profits are best safeguarded that way.

5 | Governing transnational crime: securitisation and the global anti-money laundering regime

Since the late 1990s, international regulations aiming to curb money laundering and, after the September 11, 2001 terrorist attacks, the financing of terrorism, have gone from near-obscurity to be adopted by every country on the planet except Iran. This makes the international anti-money laundering/combating the financing of terrorism (AML/CFT, from hereon AML) regime a remarkable global governance success, at least in terms of governments' adoption of the recommendations produced by the Financial Action Task Force (FATF) – the intergovernmental organisation responsible for developing and promoting global AML rules. This is particularly notable because the FATF Recommendations are very comprehensive, specifying not only legal changes, but a range of institutions and governance processes governments must establish. Indeed, to be implemented, the FATF Recommendations require considerable internal transformation and rescaling of state apparatuses, including the creation of a dedicated Financial Intelligence Unit (FIU) to investigate suspected money laundering cases, closely networked with other parts of the state and the private sector in its jurisdiction and internationally with peers and relevant international organisations.

A contested term, money laundering broadly refers to the attempt to disguise the origins of criminal proceeds to allow them to be freely enjoyed and used, including to fund future legal and illegal activities (Sharman 2011a: 15; Naylor 2004: 137). As old as money itself, money laundering was first criminalised only in 1986, by the US as part of its 'war on drugs', and in 1989 the FATF was established by the G7 governments, under American pressure (Hülsse 2007: 166). The criminalisation of money laundering was based on the assumption that preventing criminals profiting from criminal proceeds would reduce the incentives for criminality, and hence crime itself. Later, global AML activities expanded to combat the financing of terrorism. The

AML regime is therefore an attempt to simultaneously tackle, via the indirect means of state transformation and rescaling, a broad range of non-traditional security (NTS) threats associated with transnational crime and violence by non-state actors.

The AML agenda rose to prominence in the late 1990s alongside two other major international financial governance initiatives – the Financial Stability Forum (FSF), which focuses on the soundness of financial institutions, and the Organisation for Economic Co-operation and Development's (OECD) action on 'harmful tax competition' from offshore tax havens (Rawlings 2007). Observers generally agree that the AML regime is the most successful of these in attaining compliance because of the *securitisation* of money laundering. Even before September 11, the organised criminal groups engaged in money laundering, particularly those from the former Soviet Union, were often portrayed as a major global security threat. Then US Senator John Kerry, for example, argued: 'Organized crime is the new communism, the new monolithic threat' (in Naylor 2004: 13). After September 11, the securitisation of money laundering intensified, and with it the pressure on jurisdictions to adopt FATF's modified AML regulations (see Winer and Roule 2002; Unger and Rawlings 2008: 336). Furthermore, unlike traditional money laundering, funds used to finance terrorists may have legitimate origins, and so the AML agenda has widened in scope, becoming more pre-emptive (Sharman 2011a: 31), seeking to minimise risk by improving financial regulation, particularly the transparency of financial institutions and the transactions they facilitate (Sharman 2009). The securitisation of money laundering has thereby morphed into a securitisation of financial secrecy in general. As Sharman (2009: 727) observes: 'The moral resonance of rhetoric about fighting terrorism has been a powerful tool for rebutting or silencing those who would restrict governments' access to personal financial data . . . financial institutions are generally reluctant to complain about the costs of the AML/CFT regulations for fear of being portrayed as "soft on terrorism"'.

Where scholars disagree is on whether the impressive worldwide spread of the FATF's AML regulations reflects the capacity of powerful states, notably the US and the EU, to enforce global rules (e.g. Drezner 2007), or the FATF's capacity to elicit compliance by socialising bureaucrats into new norms and inflicting reputational damage on dissenters (e.g. Sharman 2011a).

However, a commonly neglected prior question is why adoption has been so widespread in the case of AML compared to other NTS issues. As chapters three and four demonstrate, attempts to manage other NTS problems have often been highly fragmented and contested, generating quite different modes of governance worldwide, and even within a single country. Addressing this question requires transcending the tired debate on international organisation (IO) versus state power to examine the political economy of state rescaling associated with the AML regime. We argue that the worldwide formal adoption of FATF rules largely reflects the highly mobile and transnational nature of financial capital flows, and investors' strong desire to protect their assets, whether derived legally or illegally. Investors are generally very risk-sensitive, but particularly so when allegations of money laundering or terrorist financing emerge, because of the securitisation of this issue. Under these circumstances, jurisdictions that openly flaunt international AML rules, particularly those on the periphery of global financial markets, are punished severely as they are cut off from global financial circulation, either indirectly, through 'blacklisting' by other governments, which leads to financial market players adjusting their risk profiles for blacklisted jurisdictions, or directly, as investors withdraw their money, fearing the devaluation or confiscation of their assets. This dynamic severely hampers the capacity of societal interests for whom this transformation of domestic financial governance is deleterious to entirely resist rescaling and keep AML governance local, therefore creating widespread *formal* adoption of the FATF's regime.

Nevertheless, the actual implementation of FATF Recommendations in particular jurisdictions has still undoubtedly been shaped by resistance from contending social and political forces. These forces have been unable to substantially affect the form of rescaled AML governance mechanisms, which is largely predetermined by FATF Recommendations, but they have managed to affect their practical efficacy. Ultimately, AML governance still warps around powerful societal interests, sometimes reflecting another case of 'mock compliance' (Walter 2008).

To demonstrate this claim, we present two very different case studies – Vanuatu and Myanmar – both of which appear highly inhospitable to AML rules but have nevertheless adopted them. Vanuatu is a small Southwest Pacific tax haven, operating an offshore financial centre (OFC) since the early 1970s. Tax havens have become closely identified with money laundering and terrorist financing, because the secrecy that they provide to foreign investors, an essential aspect of their 'product', is often said to increase the risk of these activities (Shaxson 2011; Sharman 2009: 717; Rider 2004: 72). Threatened with blacklisting, Vanuatu adopted FATF's Recommendations in 2000. The AML agenda was also boosted from 2006 when Australia's Project Wickenby began targeting Australians' tax evasion via Vanuatu. Linking this to money laundering, Australian agencies pressured Vanuatu's government and regulatory agencies to permit greater access to information held by private financial institutions there.

Despite these pressures, the AML regime's implementation in Vanuatu has been lacklustre, largely due to efforts to spare OFC interests. So far, there have been no criminal convictions for money laundering charges in Vanuatu and there are no pending criminal investigations. However, repeated Australian attacks have considerably damaged its OFC's reputation, seriously curtailing its growth and causing Vanuatu-based offshore operators to attempt to shift to new markets and services. This has displaced, not terminated, the money laundering problem.

Our second case study, Myanmar, was until recently an international pariah state, where the military-dominated government or its clients were often alleged to be involved in drug production and trafficking. Despite the regime's ostensible rejection of many other international norms, after being blacklisted in 2001, Myanmar embedded FATF guidelines in domestic legislation the following year. Domestic institutions were reshaped to meet international standards and intrusive FATF inspections were accepted, apparently rescaling the governance of financial crime to the international level. By 2006, Myanmar had been de-blacklisted and admitted to the Asia Pacific Group on Money Laundering (APG). These remarkable developments reflected Myanmar's concern to avoid further alienation from financial markets in the context of Western economic sanctions. But they also expressed, more importantly, the then-military government's determination to tackle drug-trafficking groups associated with ethnic-minority resistance organisations. Rescaling and securitising money laundering governance via FATF gave the regime an additional weapon against these groups. Commensurately, however, the regime carefully constrained the degree of rescaling to enable the law to be used flexibly, sparing its own allies. Consequently, despite the international-standard governance system now in place, the number of prosecutions and degree of general compliance remains relatively low, while drug production and trafficking remain entrenched practices.

The following section briefly discusses the nature and evolution of FATF's AML regime and examines its worldwide spread, focusing on the significance of its securitisation. We also critically evaluate contending explanations for its near-universal adoption. The next section offers an alternative analysis based on the STA, examining the rescaling of AML governance in Vanuatu and Myanmar and the effects of contestation over its implementation and the functioning of rescaled apparatuses.

Securitisation and the global anti-money laundering regime

This section describes the key features of the evolving global AML regulatory regime centred upon the Financial Action Task Force (FATF). This is not an exhaustive survey; Sharman's (2011a) seminal book *The Money Laundry* does this job admirably. Rather, we aim to show that, as with other efforts at managing transnational NTS issues, the AML regime is essentially a drive to rescale parts of states' apparatuses including, in this case, the establishing of a designated national FIU to regulate private financial institutions within these countries. Private sector actors' active participation is thus integral to this regulatory governance system, as is the internal and cross-border networking of agencies ranging from financial supervision to law enforcement and criminal justice systems. FATF and affiliated regional organisations like the APG also evaluate the regime's implementation within national jurisdictions and prescribe steps for improving AML governance. We also demonstrate that AML regulation has been justified as essential for mitigating serious security risks, such as organised crime and terrorism, which money laundering purportedly enables. Money laundering thereby came to be seen, and managed, as a significant NTS issue in itself.

We then evaluate the two main explanations provided for the spread of AML regulation to almost every country: the realist view that it reflects the will and capacity of great powers and the constructivist view that it reflects how FATF's normative authority generates a capacity to coerce and socialise states, thus transforming their behaviour. We argue that these approaches cannot explain the wide adoption of the FATF's Recommendations when the governance of other NTS problems remains typically fragmented and uneven. Existing approaches also struggle to explain the yawning gap between the formal adoption of rules and practical governance outputs (see Sharman 2011a, 2011b) and variation in the actual functioning of AML regulation in different countries.

The global anti-money laundering regulatory regime and the rescaling of states

'Money laundering' typically denotes the process whereby illicitly derived money is made to appear as if it was legally earned (Sharman 2011a: 15). Accordingly, money is considered truly 'laundered' only when it can be used openly (Naylor 2004: 137). Like many other NTS threats, money laundering is certainly not a new issue. For centuries, criminals have sought to obscure the illegal origins of their money, so that they could enjoy their ill-gotten gains or invest them in other legal or illegal ventures (Sharman 2011a: 15–16).

What is new is the development, and remarkable spread in the past two decades, of an expansive international regulatory regime directed at curbing money laundering. As the following section elaborates, this was directly related to the securitisation of what was previously seen as a domestic problem of criminality. Until the late 1980s, money laundering was barely visible on the international policy agenda or even domestically. In 1986, the US became the first country to criminalise concealing and laundering criminal proceeds as part of the Reagan administration's 'war on drugs'. This was underpinned by a logic that remains the dominant rationalisation for contemporary AML action: 'if most crime is profit driven, then lowering the profits will lower the incidence of crime' (Sharman 2011a: 20). Curbing money laundering is intended to reduce the profits realised from crime, thereby disincentivising criminal activities, and to deprive criminals of funds to support further such activities. Thus, the ultimate objective of AML, and later of CFT, regulation is not the reduction of money laundering itself, but of the preceding (predicate) crimes or future terrorist acts supposedly enabled by laundered funds (Sharman 2011a: 21).

After criminalising money laundering domestically, the US government pressured its G7 counterparts for coordinated international action, arguing it was a transnational problem that could not be solved by individual states. Because financial flows, particularly in the post-1970s era of financial deregulation, are highly transnational and fast-moving, AML regulators believe that the global financial system is only as sound as its weakest link (Hülsse 2007: 168). Consequently, the FATF was established in July 1989. The FATF is a small organisation of thirty-six member-states, roughly coinciding with OECD membership. Its main role, as stated on its website as of 11 July 2011, is to 'set standards and promote effective implementation of legal, regulatory and operational measures for combating money laundering, terrorist financing and other related threats to the integrity of the international financial system'. In practice, this has occurred through the internal transformation and rescaling of states' domestic governance apparatuses dealing with AML, including those of non-FATF members.

There are two main dimensions to this rescaling. First, the FATF developed a list of recommendations, initially issued in 1990 then revised in 1996, 2001, 2003 and 2012. The FATF's 40 Recommendations specify both the legal changes countries should make to curb money laundering and the regulatory institutions and processes they must establish to comply with internationally agreed best practice. For example, the Recommendations' core legal requirement is that countries criminalise money laundering. This is far from trivial, because, as mentioned, no state had done this before 1986. In terms of institutional requirements, the Recommendations direct countries to create a Financial Intelligence Unit (FIU) as the main focal point of AML activities and the interface between other domestic agencies and private financial institutions, as well as the wider regional and international regulatory apparatus. The Recommendations further outline the procedures private financial institutions should follow to detect, prevent and report suspected money laundering, and direct regulatory agencies to monitor private-sector compliance. Finally, FATF's Recommendations delineate how law and justice agencies should respond to money laundering, specifying the confiscation of criminal or terrorist assets.

The FATF's Recommendations have evolved over time. Responding to the September 11 attacks, in 2001 and 2003 terrorist financing was added as a concern and nine special CFT recommendations were developed. Combating the financing of terrorism required the adjustment of pre-existing regulations and a conceptual tweaking of AML regulation. Whereas in traditional forms of money laundering a predicate offence is generally required, terrorist financing could, and often does, come from legal sources (Sharman 2011a: 31; Winer and Roule 2002). Combating terrorist financing is thus 'future-focused', requiring risk-based evaluations of customers and transactions. The most recent revisions cemented a wholesale shift to risk management, with focus shifting from the monitoring of technical compliance towards jurisdiction-specific assessments of the main risks and capacities (FATF 2012). Proving a predicate crime is now no longer a requirement for launching money laundering investigations. Rather, money laundering is assumed to occur whenever the origins of funds and/or the identity of the beneficiaries are obscure (Sharman 2009).

Indeed, the main stated objective of AML action has always been making financial systems more transparent, so as to distinguish illegal or otherwise risky flows from legal ones. Accordingly, the main principle underpinning FATF Recommendations is 'Know Your Customer' (KYC). The KYC principle refers to the requirement for banks and other financial institutions to 'establish and record' their customers' identity (Sharman 2011a: 11). The FATF Recommendations also require financial institutions to report suspicious transactions or activities to the local FIU. Commensurately, private organisations, such as banks, accounting and law firms, real estate agents, remittance-wiring services and even casinos, are integral to the worldwide governance of money laundering, since if they do not file Suspicious Transaction Reports (STRs) money laundering is almost impossible to identify.

The second dimension of governance rescaling is the incorporation of newly mandated domestic institutions into regional and global regulatory and surveillance networks designed to ensure FATF Recommendations are implemented. These networks conduct 'peer-review' assessments of jurisdictions in their areas. Where implementation is deemed unsatisfactory against FATF benchmarks, governments must respond to the findings, and subsequent reviews assess improvement against these earlier results and objectives. The FATF is currently on its fourth round of mutual evaluation. This evaluation process is the 'stick' FATF wields to ensure compliance with its Recommendations.

In February 2000, FATF published a list of Non-Cooperative Countries and Territories (NCCT), 'blacklisting' countries refusing to implement their rules. Although formal blacklisting was dropped in 2006, with the final NCCT report published in October 2007, peer-review reports still identify incomplete compliance with FATF Recommendations.

Peer review is typically delegated to FATF-style regional bodies (FSRBs), such as the APG, established to monitor compliance with the Recommendations. Unlike FATF, FSRBs encompass practically every country in the world. The APG, for example, currently has forty-one member-states, ranging from Pakistan to small Pacific island states. The FSRBs also coordinate AML technical assistance among members, conduct research into money laundering and terrorist financing in their regions and contribute to policy development as FATF observers.

Other intergovernmental organisations are also involved supporting the FATF-centred regulatory network. The UN, regional organisations, and the international financial institutions (IFIs) have all started to support AML activities in the last two decades, and many have observer status in FATF or FSRB meetings. The APG's observers, for instance, include the UN, the International Monetary Fund (IMF), World Bank, the ASEAN Secretariat, and the Pacific Islands Forum (PIF) Secretariat. Like the FATF and the FSRBs, the chief aim of these bodies has also been the rescaling of domestic governance. For example, the IFIs have linked compliance with FATF Recommendations to broader programmes promoting good governance, corruption eradication and financial system integrity; incorporated assessments of compliance with the Recommendations into their regular economic scrutiny of developing countries; and made loans conditional upon conformity.

The advent of international AML regulation has also spawned the Egmont Group, an informal global network of 130 national FIUs that facilitates inter-FIU cooperation, information exchange and training. Also notable is the Wolfsberg Group, a network of eleven major global banks that develops and disseminates voluntary AML standards for the financial sector.

Anti-money laundering regulation has thus rapidly developed into a complex, multilevel, regulatory governance regime linking intergovernmental, governmental and private organisations in a range of new relationships and regulatory activities – both within states and transnationally – with the FATF as the main standard-setting and coordinating body. The main focus of AML regulation is the transformation and rescaling of the domestic governance apparatuses dealing with this issue. This includes specified legal, institutional and procedural changes and international/transnational relationships. AML governance thus resembles other attempts to manage transnational NTS problems examined in this book.

The securitisation of money laundering

From the outset, the criminalisation of money laundering and the creation of regulatory apparatuses to tackle it were rationalised as a security imperative. The specific security rationale has shifted over time, from fighting drug trafficking to organised criminal gangs, terrorism and more recently to preventing financial calamity following the global financial crisis. This securitisation has led to the FATF's AML regulation being far more widely implemented, particularly in OFCs, than other attempts to regulate global finance, like FSF and the 'harmful tax competition' initiative (Palan et al. 2010: 205). Securitisation transformed Money laundering from a domestic law-and-order concern to a global governance problem, and, as with other NTS issues, it also underpinned the drive to rescale domestic state apparatuses, described above.

Crucially, money laundering and terrorist financing have been securitised not as direct threats in their own right, but indirectly, because they are viewed as enabling other serious NTS challenges. Therefore, their securitisation necessarily involves the prior and ongoing securitisation of the problems that money laundering supposedly exacerbates, predominantly drug trafficking, crime and terrorism. The aim of AML regulation is not stopping money laundering or terrorist financing *per se*, but mitigating the security problems they are alleged to enable and exacerbate (Sharman 2011a: 21). It is essentially a case of 'situational risk management', aiming to produce governance environments less likely to generate security risks (Clapton 2009).

The origins of AML policy in the US reflected the Reagan administration's intensifying 'war on drugs', and the attendant securitisation of the long-running problem of domestic drug abuse (Sharman 2011a: 21). National Security Decision Directive 221, issued in April 1986, identified drug production and trafficking as a national security threat. The 1986 Anti-Drug Abuse Act contained forerunners of AML regulation, creating a certification process for Latin American countries that evaluated their support for US drug eradication efforts. In Europe too, AML provisions began appearing in the 1980s, initially as part of anti-drug legislation (Sharman 2011a: 23).

This securitisation of drug trafficking spurred the creation of the FATF; consequently, AML activities initially focused solely on the laundering of profits from the drug trade. During the 1990s, however, the FATF's scope broadened to organised crime groups more generally and to any crimes involving money laundering. Particularly after the Soviet Union's implosion, 'organised crime' – itself a vexed category (Naylor 2004) – became viewed as a serious transnational menace, challenging states' capacity to protect their citizens, and even threatening democracy (Hülsse 2007: 172–3). Thereby, 'what was formerly a criminological challenge has become a national security threat' (Naylor 2004: 14).

Yet, although the language of national security was often invoked, a crucial dimension of the securitisation of drug trafficking and organised crime was the perception that criminal groups were globalising their operations. In the 1990s, reports abounded of summit meetings between criminal masterminds from around the world, and of criminal organisations 'so dripping with wealth as to threaten the integrity of entire national economies as well as the international financial system itself' (Naylor 2004: 13). In one example, former US Senator, now Secretary of State, John Kerry's book, *The New War: The Web of Crime that Threatens America's Security*, argued that crime had become globalised, identifying a 'global criminal axis' preying on America's freedoms and ultimately threatening to destroy its way of life (Sharman 2011a: 24). Similarly, the deputy director of Britain's National Crime Intelligence Service claimed: 'there is little point in collectively having won the Cold War, when you are going to lose the war to another tyranny' (in Naylor 2004: 14). Claire Stirling, author of the influential *Thieves' World*, which highlighted the transnationalisation of crime, argued that funds once used to fight the Cold War should be redirected to fighting organised crime, declaring 'we have no time to waste – the enemy has already broken through the gate' (in Brandt 1995). Similarly, the director of the UN's International Drug Control Program warned trafficking had reached a 'scale . . . unimaginable a generation ago . . . the power of international drug trafficking organisations threatens to corrupt and destabilise the institutions of government' (in Dupont 1999: 434). This alarmism was echoed by scholars.

Yui (2010b: 50) warns transnational criminal gangs are now strong enough to 'attack institutions of governance . . . a poor, weak state . . . can literally be taken over and destroyed' (see also Yui 2010a; Dupont 1999: 447, 449–50). EU official William Gilmore (1995: 24) summarised the emerging consensus, stating that transnational criminal groups were 'now universally recognised as a global problem requiring a global solution'.

This perceived global security threat from transnationalised crime supported two assumptions subsequently embedded into the emerging AML regime. First, if organised crime groups operated like transnational corporations, then targeting the profitability of crime would weaken them and limit their capacity to execute future criminal activities. Second, because money could be moved around the world rapidly, 'the chain was only as strong as its weakest link' (Sharman 2011a: 24). It was therefore pointless to tighten money laundering controls in some countries, but not elsewhere: all countries must adopt similar regulations, laws and standards.

A key problem, however, was distinguishing criminal money from other financial flows. With global financial transactions totalling trillions of dollars daily, and vast sums changing hands through property deals, gambling, informal money transfers and other 'at risk' activities, illicit flows are difficult to identify (Naylor 2004: 134). Consequently, AML regulators perceive the transparency of financial institutions, reflected in the KYC principle, as a crucial precondition for effective action, and financial opacity as a security risk in its own right – 'privacy as roguery' (Sharman 2009). The view that financial privacy increases the risk of malfeasance put particular pressure on tax havens, which trade heavily on their capacity to provide this to clients. Indeed, some regulators now see these jurisdictions as a security problem, not merely a challenge for national tax authorities.

Following September 11, the securitisation of money laundering accelerated. While 'welding terrorist financing concerns into the existing AML framework caused relatively little substantive regulatory redesign, politically and rhetorically it made an important difference' (Sharman 2011a: 30). September 11 galvanised action by many agencies within and beyond the US in a way that the slow-burning war on drugs and organised crime had not. The 2001 USA PATRIOT Act expanded the AML regime and intensified pressure on non-compliant jurisdictions and financial institutions by empowering the US Treasury

Secretary to prohibit US financial institutions from transacting with jurisdictions of 'primary money laundering concern' (Palan et al. 2010: 208–9). Having hitherto resisted such pressures, the IFIs were now compelled to include AML compliance in their purview. Nearly all developing countries rushed to adopt counter-terrorism measures, including AML regulations (Sharman 2011a: 30–31).

This pressure on non-Western states to embrace the AML agenda is clearly visible in the regions from which we draw our case studies. Southeast Asian states began securitising the issue in 1994, when they issued the Manila Declaration on the Prevention and Control of Transnational Crime (ASEAN 1998). They warned that 'transnational crime undermines civil society, distorts legitimate markets and destabilizes States'. Reflecting the 'weak link' thesis, it called for tighter international cooperation because 'criminal groups are . . . establishing alliances in the region and in other parts of the globe by taking advantage of gaps and weaknesses in international cooperation in criminal matters' (ASEAN 1998). Following September 11 and Southeast Asia's depiction as the 'second front' in the 'war on terror', money laundering and terrorist financing became key agenda items. ASEAN (2007b) declared terrorism a 'grave danger . . . to innocent lives, infrastructure and the environment, regional and international peace and stability as well as to economic development . . . a profound threat to international peace and security'. Analysts and policymakers asserted a strong link between crime, terrorism and money laundering. Abuza (2003: 172), for example, observed that 'Southeast Asia has long been a centre for transnational crime activities such as drug and gun-running, money laundering, people smuggling and document forging . . . terrorists require the same [economic] infrastructure as organised crime. Southeast Asia, thus, becomes an important area of operations [for them]'. ASEAN (2005a) identified the 'growing challenges of terrorism and other transnational crimes, including . . . money laundering' as a combined threat. Declaring that 'money laundering and terrorism financing issues have been considered as the backbone of most transnational crimes activities [sic]', it initiated a Plan of Action to Combat Transnational crime (ASEAN 2011). ASEAN acquired observer status with the APG, endorsing its status as the main pan-regional AML body and thus supporting FATF's rescaling of governance. Asia-Pacific OFCs faced similar compliance pressures.

For example, in 2001, Nauru, which was openly flouting FATF demands to close over 400 shell banks, was linked with al Qaeda, and was eventually forced to comply through near-total commercial isolation (Sharman 2011a: 30–31; Larmour 2007: 6).

There were limits, however, to this drive to improve financial transparency through the securitisation of money laundering, even post September 11, which were rooted in powerful ideological and economic concerns in dominant Western states. For example, the conservative Bush administration remained ideologically committed to low taxation and hence the 'tax competition' OFCs purportedly offer, failing to even mention 'tax havens' in the PATRIOT Act. Indeed, historically, the US government's attitude towards tax havens has been ambivalent, as has Britain's. Some American states, like Delaware, operate OFCs, while New York and London – the world's biggest financial centres – are also arguably OFCs (Sharman 2010: 11; Shaxson 2011: Ch. 7). The OECD, led by Germany and France, whose governments have long opposed tax havens, has attempted to use tax havens' supposed link to money laundering to foster greater transparency on tax issues since 1998. However, given intra-Western divisions, this initiative barely modified how tax havens actually operate, as we shall see in Vanuatu's case (Palan et al. 2010: 206; Shaxson 2011: 212).

Contending explanations for the spread of FATF's regulatory regime

Virtually no international regulatory regime has been so widely adopted as the FATF Recommendations framework. By early 2015, only Iran was openly refusing to cooperate with the FATF. Despite this, very few studies of AML examine it as a form of global governance (Heng and McDonagh 2008: 556). The vast majority are specialist law or finance publications, not particularly concerned with the politics of defining and regulating this issue globally (e.g. Naylor 2004; Baker 2005). This section briefly examines the existing explanations of the development and spread of AML regulations and their weaknesses.

The realist view is that compliance with the FATF reflects the coercive capacity of the major powers, specifically the US and the EU, to force other countries to accept global rules (Drezner 2007). The constructivist argument is that it reflects the FATF's normative power, as an international organisation, to harness expert authority to define the problem, to compel countries to adopt the Recommendations by 'naming and shaming' recalcitrants and to 'socialise' national-level officials into its normative framework (Sharman 2011a). Both these approaches convincingly debunk liberal interpretations of global governance as rational, utility-maximising, functionalist responses to shared concerns which spread through 'policy diffusion' (e.g. Simmons 2000), so this alternative view need not concern us here. Finally, poststructuralists also consider the FATF to be a form of 'global governmentality' (Heng and McDonagh 2008).

Drezner (2007) explains the emergence and spread of international regulatory regimes as stemming from the agency and interests of great powers. Drezner (2007: 142) argues that financial regulations are 'club-derived standards'; they originated with the great powers, which have the world's most developed financial systems and wanted to design regulations advantageous to them. To facilitate this, they created 'club IGOs [intergovernmental organisations]' that they could dominate to enforce the rules, while marginalising universal-membership IGOs like the IFIs. Exploiting their economic power, the US and the EU threatened 'sanctions' – exclusion from access to their markets – to compel other states to comply. Thus, 'through club IGOs like the G-7 and FATF, great powers were able to cajole, coerce, and enforce a global anti-money-laundering standard into existence' (Drezner 2007: 145). Similarly, Sharman (2011b) observes that FATF rules are staunchly applied to small OFCs whilst more serious breaches in the US are ignored; indeed, it is easier to establish shell companies in the latter. Thus, inconsistently with his generally constructivist orientation, he emphasises 'the power of dominant states to impose rules on others that they do not follow themselves' (Sharman 2011b: 981). Other scholars also argue that the post-September 11 fusion of AML and CFT clearly reflects US pressure and thus powerful states' domination of the regime (Navias 2002; Shields 2005).

A constructivist interpretation is offered by Sharman's comprehensive and illuminating *The Money Laundry* (2011a). Here, he adopts Barnett and Finnemore's (2004: 7) constructivist framework, which emphasises how international organisations 'exercise power as they use their knowledge and authority not only to regulate what currently exists but also to constitute the world, creating new interests, actors and social activities. This can be understood as "social construction power" because IOs use their knowledge to help create social reality'. Hülsse (2007: 156) similarly argues that bodies like FATF 'not only make global policies but [also] global problems'. Sharman argues that FATF successfully promoted global AML regulation through a mix of normative coercion and the 'socialisation' of national officials through international regulatory networks. He demolishes liberal policy diffusion approaches, which see supranational governance regimes as driven by problem-solving and benefit-maximising rationales (see Slaughter 2004). By demonstrating the ease of violating AML regulations – by doing it himself – Sharman conclusively shows that the FATF regime has been adopted *despite* being ineffective in managing the problem. The FATF cannot sanction or otherwise punish uncooperative jurisdictions directly, but countries have nevertheless been coerced into compliance because of the FATF's ability to damage their reputations by listing them as NCCTs. This reputational damage is reinforced by the private sector's tendency to use compliance with FATF Recommendations as 'a proxy for the underlying risk' of conducting transactions with given states (Sharman 2011a: 8). This indirect coercive capacity is augmented, Sharman argues, by the extensive socialisation of regulators through meetings, workshops, capacity-building and training exercises, organised by international organisations like the FATF and the APG, to see the adoption of AML regulations as an important aspect of modern statecraft.

Finally, Foucauldian analysts Heng and McDonagh (2008: 558) also emphasise the indirect exercise of power entailed by the AML regime, focusing on the 'multiple sites and trajectories where power is exercised, which may or may not involve a hegemonic state'. They argue that the FATF works by cultivating a governmental rationality – 'governmentality' – among diverse actors, despite lacking formal, legal, state-based authority. This overlaps with Sharman's 'socialisation' mechanism but excludes discussion of the FATF's capacity to punish non-compliance via 'reputational damage'.

These approaches have many merits. It is clear, for example, that in the absence of support from Western policymakers and regulators, the FATF would not have been established. It is also true that threats of reputational damage concern policymakers and regulators in most countries that have implemented FATF rules, not least many tax havens. There are, however, two main weaknesses these approaches share. First, while scholars apparently concur that *because of securitisation* FATF Recommendations have attained far greater worldwide adoption than other attempts to regulate global finance, this logic struggles to explain FATF's success relative to efforts to manage other NTS issues. In different issue-areas, as our other chapters demonstrate, governance responses have been far more contested and fragmented, varying considerably across national boundaries and even between different sectors of a single industry in just one country. What accounts for the FATF's unusual success, when great-power coercion, normative power, and/or governmentality are also observable in other issue-areas? Second, existing approaches fail to explain the gap between AML regulatory ideals and reality in most jurisdictions. If FATF regulations are coercively imposed by very powerful states, are internalised as norms or imbued into officials' very consciousness as 'governmentality', this gap ought to be miniscule. Yet, as some of these authors admit, this is far from the case (see esp. Sharman 2011a). According to the IMF (2011), 'full compliance' with FATF rules is 'rare', and 'partial compliance' occurs in only a quarter of jurisdictions. We therefore need to explain why AML regulation is such a unique 'success story' in terms of near-universal adoption, but such a constrained success in terms of actual implementation.

The political economy of money laundering regulation

This book argues that the securitisation and governance of NTS issues is shaped by the political economy of the industry that rescaling the governance of the issue-area would affect. We also contend that how given NTS issues are governed in particular contexts depends on contestation between actors and coalitions over the extent and form of the rescaling of governance, and the practical operation of rescaled governance institutions. These coalitions' relative strength is, in turn, underpinned by broader state–society relations. This section briefly outlines our application of this approach to AML, then presents the case studies of Vanuatu and Myanmar. In both countries, the political economy context of global finance restricts the capacity of otherwise powerful local interests that could be harmed by rescaling to completely resist state transformation associated with the adoption of international AML regulations. Thus, contestation has tended to revolve around the extent to which FATF Recommendations are to be adopted and on how rescaled institutions actually operate. Indeed, our two quite different cases clearly illustrate the importance of local political economy and social power relations for how governance functions in practice.

A full explanation of the FATF's apparent success needs to encompass the political economy of the specific issue-area: global finance. Today, all states and most tradeable sectors rely to some extent on the international banking system and on global financial flows. Because banks use FATF blacklisting as a proxy measure of investment risk, blacklisting may prompt them to withdraw credit facilities, freeze accounts and generally block transactions with particular jurisdictions. This often raises the stakes of complete resistance to rescaling to unacceptable levels, even for economic and political elites in countries that are relatively isolated from economic globalisation processes, like Myanmar. For offshore financial centres (OFCs), the highly mobile nature of contemporary portfolio capital, upon which they largely depend, makes it especially difficult to resist FATF-promoted governance rescaling, because investors, whether investing legally or illegally derived funds, are reluctant to place their money in risky institutions and jurisdictions. The very purpose of money laundering is to make 'dirty' money 'clean' again. Consequently, the stability and reputation of the financial institutions and jurisdictions where funds are invested are equally important for criminals as for other investors. This is why the world's worst-regulated OFCs, like Tonga and Nauru, fail to attract large investments (Rawlings 2007; Sharman and Rawlings 2006; Palan et al. 2010: 160), while a reputation for stability and good management is essential to OFC success stories like the Cayman Islands and the British Virgin Islands. These jurisdictions, like the Channel Islands, benefit from being associated with Britain, which creates an appearance of good governance and political stability (van Fossen 2012: 27). Even in non-tax havens, investors want to know their money is safe.

As the Vanuatu case study demonstrates, it is this combination of investors' risk aversion, banks' use of FATF ratings as proxy risk indicators, the context of highly mobile global capital flows and the securitisation of money laundering that uniquely empowers FATF to inflict 'reputational damage' on non-compliant jurisdictions carrying substantial consequences. *Pace* Drezner, it is private sector actors that actually 'enforce' this 'reputational damage' by withdrawing their money, rather than powerful states imposing 'sanctions'. Regulators of OFCs understand that it is private sector investors they must 'persuade' of their sound 'reputation' (Sharman and Mistry 2008: 6). But, *pace* Sharman, it is this material action by financial institutions that grants FATF's normative assessments their political efficacy. This capacity to impose reputational damage with clear material consequences that compel national regulators and private sector actors to react very seriously, is highly specific to AML regulation, and not generalisable to other NTS issue-areas. Nonetheless, the Vanuatu case also shows how powerful local interests are still able to direct how AML governance operates in practice.

The case of Myanmar is rather different. Myanmar was ostensibly very inhospitable to international AML governance efforts, because the then-military regime had been actively facilitating domestic money laundering to co-opt drug traffickers and smugglers connected with ethnic-minority separatist groups. Furthermore, although defying FATF was not cost-free, Myanmar was less exposed than Vanuatu to 'reputational damage' because it was already marginalised from global financial markets in the context of Western sanctions to promote regime change, and even now the interests of financial capital remain weak. Surprisingly though, after being identified as an NCCT in 2001, Myanmar adopted FATF governance guidelines and was de-blacklisted in 2006. Nonetheless, the extent and form of this rescaling of domestic AML governance was shaped by the local socio-political context. Conformity with FATF Recommendations was tempered by loopholes to exclude powerful players, enabling the new governance system to be used selectively against anti-government groups, leaving regime supporters untouched.

The political economy of AML regulation in Vanuatu

Vanuatu, a small Southwest Pacific state, was the region's first OFC, and remains one of its largest, though it is tiny compared to those in the Caribbean (Sharman 2005; Sharman and Mistry 2008: 135; van Fossen 2012: 50–68). The FATF has focused considerable attention on tax havens like Vanuatu, relative to other states (Sharman 2009, 2010). The secrecy their OFCs provide to non-residents, which allows them to avoid taxes or regulations elsewhere, has become linked with the prevalence of money laundering and the transnational crimes it enables, increasing international pressure on them to improve financial transparency. As Shaxson (2011: 27) states: 'The drug smugglers, terrorists and other criminals use exactly the same offshore mechanisms and subterfuges – shell banks, trusts, dummy corporations – that corporations use.' From the late 1990s Vanuatu's OFC was thus attacked by the FATF, the OECD and FSF. It was never listed as an NCCT because, unlike several other Pacific tax havens, it reacted early to the impending threat of blacklisting, implementing FATF Recommendations from 2000. This is because Vanuatu recognised that, given investors' risk sensitivity and the highly competitive and fluid global OFC market, 'Failing to meet [FATF] standards is not an option, being tantamount to making an exit from that market' (Sharman and Mistry 2008: 164). Nonetheless, Vanuatu's actual implementation of the FATF Recommendations, though involving considerable state transformation and rescaling, has been shaped by powerful domestic interests from the OFC and has mostly amounted to 'mock compliance' (Walter 2008). Although continual reputational crises – exacerbated by Australia's Project Wickenby – have sent the OFC into steep decline, the main outcome of international regulation has not been to eliminate the NTS problem of money laundering, but rather to displace it to other secrecy jurisdictions abroad, and other sectors domestically.

The political economy of Vanuatu's offshore financial centre
Vanuatu's OFC was established pre-independence in 1971 (Rawlings 1999). Under the New Hebrides' unique British–French 'condominium', three legal systems – English common law, French civil law and indigenous law – coexisted, with residents allowed to choose which applied to them. This ambiguity, and a tradition of zero taxation for foreign residents, provided the basis for Britain to establish an OFC as a 'development' initiative to reduce dependence on London. From 1971 to 1975, overseas banks, trust funds, and accountants – particularly from Australia and New Zealand – flocked to the capital, Port Vila, generating a wider economic boom via construction and infrastructure development, enhancing indigenous employment opportunities (Rawlings 2005: 9–10, 15).

The OFC also had tremendous political implications. It became one of the main catalysts for Vanuatu's independence in 1980 by empowering pro-independence British officials and Australian and New Zealand financial interests over French colonists. The latter, who dominated the agricultural sector using land seized from indigenous peoples and were consequently fearful of post-independence land redistribution, preferred continued imperial rule (van Fossen 2002: 44–5). The OFC increased the British authorities' revenues to twice those of the French by 1976, strengthening their hand. Financiers also dispensed patronage to pro-independence, indigenous Anglophone politicians (van Fossen 2002: 45).

Consequently, Vanuatu's post-independence political elite has strongly supported the OFC. A revolving door also operated between the OFC and regulatory offices, notably the Reserve Bank of Vanuatu. Moreover, as elsewhere in the Pacific, OFC operators cultivated strongly laissez-faire ideologies among politicians and public officials. The OFC's peak body, the Financial Centre Association of Vanuatu (FCAV), typically faces minimal resistance from other domestic groups, and – despite the OFC's senior ranks being dominated by well-paid expatriates – has successfully associated challenges to the OFC with disloyal subservience to foreign governments (van Fossen 2012: 40, 60, 274). The OFC's political dominance has been further strengthened by the post-1980s fragmentation of Vanuatu's dominant one-party system. As elsewhere in Melanesia, intensified political competition in Vanuatu is non-ideological, with candidates' capacity to outspend one another locally determining electoral outcomes. Governing coalitions are likewise highly fluid, with 'money politics' providing the necessary, albeit temporary, cement. This has increased OFC interests' power, since no other economic sector (excluding booming real estate businesses, which are often also OFC-related) has equivalent resources to back political contenders. By the 1990s, Vanuatu was renowned for resisting international pressure on its OFC, notably the OECD's 'harmful tax competition' initiative. The Government of Vanuatu (GoV) has not only blocked the extradition of expatriates indicted overseas for money laundering, but one political elite even adopted one such individual – Robert Bohn – as his son, enabling him subsequently to become Vanuatu's first foreign-born parliamentarian (van Fossen 2012: 277).

The OFC's political dominance is underpinned by its economic importance. Vanuatu's import dependency makes it reliant on the OFC as a source of foreign currency; in 2006, the OFC's foreign exchange earnings were equivalent to sixty-two per cent of exports (van Fossen

2012: 62). Estimates of the OFC's contribution to the economy vary considerably, from the IMF's three per cent of gross domestic product (GDP) and less than two per cent of government revenue, to the PIF's five per cent of GDP and nine per cent of government revenue, to the OFC's own claims of over twelve per cent of GDP (IMF 2003; van Fossen 2012: 64–6; see also Sharman and Mistry 2008: 133). Its contribution is certainly miniscule relative to total OFC deposits: in 2005, for example, it yielded just US$127,000 in government revenues but held deposits of US$202.3 million (Sharman 2005). The sector's influence thus stems from close inter-elite connections, not its contribution to wider society.

Money laundering and the rescaling of financial governance in Vanuatu

Despite the OFC's dominance in Vanuatu, the GoV adopted FATF's Recommendations in 2000. The regime's implementation escalated after September 11, 2001; APG inspections occurred in 2000 and 2006, and AML governance was substantially rescaled. This is directly attributable to a series of reputational crises that threatened to marginalise Vanuatu from global financial markets.

Most serious was the spillover from the 'Russiagate' scandal. In 1999, journalists reported that Russians evading their country's financial crisis had laundered US$70 billion through shell banks in Nauru, another Pacific Island OFC. Panicked investors withdrew large sums from Nauru and other regional OFCs, including Vanuatu. Later that year, Ukraine's central bank identified Vanuatu as the world's fourth most popular OFC for Ukrainian capital flight. In November, four leading US banks suspended dollar transactions with Vanuatu, citing weak AML regulations. Popular media coverage disparagingly – and sometimes inaccurately – linked Nauru and Vanuatu, deepening the crisis (van Fossen 2012: 285). A Vanuatu delegation, led by senior OFC financier Thomas Bayer, met representatives of these banks, the US Federal Reserve, the State Department and the IMF, successfully persuading the banks to resume transactions in exchange for a State Department visit and APG evaluation in 2000. However, Vanuatu-based banks still struggled to transact with major international banks for a further eighteen months (van Fossen 2012: 278–82).

The 'Russiagate' fallout clearly compelled the GoV to adopt the FATF Recommendations and gradually transform and rescale its domestic AML governance apparatus. Its 2000 Financial Transactions Reporting Act (FTRA) established an FIU and imposed reporting requirements on the private sector. Although the FIU was initially neither staffed nor resourced, the appearance of action sufficed to preclude Vanuatu's inclusion in the 2000 NCCT list (Sharman and Mistry 2008: 143). However, Vanuatu was blacklisted in 2002, adding to US pressure following September 11 and the US PATRIOT Act, and a critical IMF report. In 2002, therefore, the GoV amended the FTRA and passed the International Banking Act, the Proceeds of Crime Act and the Mutual Assistance in Criminal Matters Act, all compliant with FATF guidelines, and formally joined the OECD's initiative on harmful tax practices. Specifically, the International Banking Act required all offshore banks to maintain staffed, in-country offices. This implicit assault on shell banks caused the number of offshore banks to fall from fifty-one in 2001 to fourteen in 2003, to just three by 2012. Accordingly, offshore banking assets declined from US$1.4 billion to just US$100 million from 2004 to 2010 (van Fossen 2012: 54–5). In trying to rescue the OFC, the GoV thus spurred its further decline.

Despite initially lacking substance, by the time of the APG's 2006 visit, Vanuatu's AML governance had been substantially rescaled in line with the FATF guidelines. The main agencies responsible for OFC regulation – the FIU, the Reserve Bank of Vanuatu (RBV), the Vanuatu Financial Services Commission (VFSC), the Vanuatu Police Force (VPF) and the Department of Public Prosecutions (DPP) – have been integrated into a transnational regulatory regime. The FIU, staffed since 2005, receives STRs from financial institutions and forwards them to the VPF where necessary. The FIU joined the Egmont Group and also receives technical assistance from the PIF Secretariat and Austrac, Australia's FIU. In 2003, responsibility for licensing and regulating offshore banks was transferred from the VFSC to a special department of the RBV. This department receives ongoing technical assistance from the IMF's Pacific Financial Technical Assistance Centre, which develops and disseminates regional banking supervision and regulatory standards. The VFSC is now mainly responsible for registering and levying fees on international firms, and licensing offshore insurance and trust companies. To satisfy FATF requirements and OECD demands, the VFSC established a dedicated supervision unit, which is directly networked with regional and global agencies, as well as the FIU and RBV.

On the enforcement side, the VPF investigates files submitted by the FIU, passing evidence to the DPP, which is responsible for prosecutions. Within the VPF, a Transnational Crime Unit (TCU) was established, largely for this purpose. This unit is co-funded – separately from the VPF – by the GoV and the Australian Federal Police (AFP). Via the AFP and the Pacific Plan (see Hameiri 2009b), the TCU is networked with regional counterparts and until May 2012 was regularly co-staffed by AFP officers. In May 2012, the AFP was expelled from Vanuatu, officially due to the mistreatment of Vanuatu's prime minister at Sydney airport, but more likely due to the arrest in Australia of his private secretary on tax fraud charges (*ABC* 10 May 2012). In early 2013, it was announced that the AFP would return, on a smaller scale (*ABC* 13 February 2013). In the interim, one of the present author's fieldwork observations underscored the TCU's reliance on AFP support: basic equipment like computers and photocopiers fell into disrepair and was not fixed, rendering staff largely unable to work. The DPP, on the other hand, has received relatively little international intervention and support beyond limited training from the UN Office on Drugs and Crime (UNODC).

The FATF's work in Vanuatu has been reinforced by Australian-dominated regional governance initiatives. Since 2003, the rescaling of formerly domestic Australian government agencies has powerfully defined and promoted regulatory regionalism designed to tackle many NTS issues in the Pacific (Hameiri 2009a, 2009b). Australia's government is primarily interested in AML because it is seen to enable domestic tax evasion. Unlike most jurisdictions, Australia identified tax evasion as a predicate offence when criminalising money laundering in the late 1980s; accordingly its FIU, Austrac, is housed in the Australian Taxation Office (ATO). Conversely, the FATF only adopted tax evasion as a predicate offence in 2012. Aside from the AFP's pivotal role in the Vanuatu TCU, Australia also supplies substantial funding and support to APG, which is housed in AFP-owned offices in Sydney, while Austrac and the Reserve Bank of Australia (RBA) have financed capacity-building, regional workshops and infrastructural upgrades for fellow FIUs and central banks. Indeed, the RBA has become the centre of a regional network, promoting tight-knit cooperation between central bank regulators that has survived inter-state political acrimony unscathed (Naiyaga 2012). The Australian Attorney-General's Department also helps its regional counterparts draft FATF-compliant legislation. Finally, Australian agencies have linked APG and PIF, convening annual meetings between them and technical assistance providers (FATF, UNODC, the World Bank and the IMF) to promote donor assistance for implementing FATF rules. Without this extensive Australian involvement, very little AML governance would likely occur in this region.

The operation of AML regulation in Vanuatu and the offshore financial sector

This extensive involvement by a regional hegemon, coupled with una-nimity among Vanuatu government, regulatory, and OFC actors that unless FATF Recommendations were followed the local OFC would be destroyed, has led to formal AML governance being significantly rescaled. The experience of Nauru, which resisted post-'Russiagate' regulatory pressure, provides a salutary tale: within a few years it was left with no financial institutions whatsoever (Sharman 2011a). Accordingly, Vanuatu's regulators sought to exploit international pres-sure and capital flight to enhance their funding and relative authority over other parts of the state and the financial sector, with some suc-cess. However, due to the entrenched power of OFC interests, the resultant regime, although apparently compliant with FATF stipula-tions and substantially rescaled, is still largely ineffective in catching and prosecuting money launderers. Although the attention focused on Vanuatu by Russiagate and Project Wickenby pushed the OFC into relative decline, this has largely displaced the problem of money laun-dering into new spaces and sectors, rather than suppressing this NTS problem.

Australia's success in promoting formal governance rescaling is, in important part, due to support from powerful domestic interests in Vanuatu. Government, regulators, and private-sector OFC opera-tors in Vanuatu all believe that improving the country's reputation is essential for surviving in a globally competitive offshore market and attracting more foreign investment, and see the establishment of AML legislation and supportive institutions as part of this. This reflects the uniquely fluid nature of global financial markets and the importance of reputation for tax havens. As the FIU's manager admits: 'We had a

bad reputation as a tax haven and accepted all sorts... The bad reputation was justified because the government was reluctant to make
[legal] amendments when it was necessary' (Mera 2012). Similarly, the
RBV's Noel Vari (2012) observes: 'For us, the reputation of our jurisdiction is very important. We [must] ensure that the legislation and
guidelines are stringent... [because] we live in a global environment
and experience has shown that when the wall [i.e., the international
regulatory environment] moves, you have to move'.

Similarly, although Vanuatu's offshore operators complain that they
are unfairly targeted relative to, say, US and UK institutions, they no
longer publicly insist on financial secrecy as a sovereign prerogative.
Instead, they seek to position themselves at the professional and 'legitimate' end of the offshore market, along with the Cayman and Channel
Islands. Offshore banking representatives have long sat on committees
designing the sector's legal regulation, for many years constraining the
development of AML regulation. Today, the FIU's manager suggests,
'they've come to realise that the world has changed and they have
to catch up... Now the Centre understands it has to commit itself in
order to survive.' It is keen to be seen as cooperating with the FIU (Mera
2012). Although OFC figures like FCAV chairman Mark Stafford still
insist that 'the propensity for money laundering is very, very, very,
small' in Vanuatu, he admits that 'the link [made] between money
laundering and tax havens has not been helpful' for the sector, being
'a strong dissuader' to investors. Conversely, 'by being a well-regulated
jurisdiction we should be able to enhance our reputation and capacity
to market ourselves in a better fashion... [in] the global marketplace'
(Stafford 2012). Thomas Bayer (2012), the longstanding public face of
Vanuatu's OFC, concurs that the offshore sector's survival depended
on restoring its 'reputation and the image that reputable people are
using it'.

This consensus among powerful groups enabled regulators, who
otherwise lack any meaningful domestic support base, to exploit the
crisis of investor confidence and international pressure to extend their
power and authority. Regulators have particularly sought to leverage
their integration within wider regulatory networks to enforce regulatory discipline within Vanuatu. The FIU gained its first staff member
prior to the first APG evaluation in 2005. With another inspection
scheduled for 2014, the FIU manager planned to 'use the external
assessment internally to push for more resources... we'll be in a good

bargaining position because we're up for review in 2014' (Mera 2012). Similarly, despite OFC resistance, the RBV – backed by IMF pressure – successfully promoted the International Banking Act (IBA), which substantially enhances the RBV's authority, because they could 'sell the law on the reputation of Vanuatu...the IBA helps our reputation' (Vari 2012).

Despite its apparent compliance with FATF Recommendations and the close integration of domestic regulatory agencies and the international AML regime, however, Vanuatu's AML regulation is clearly ineffective at catching money launderers. Vanuatu has *never* secured any successful money laundering convictions, despite criminalising money laundering as early as 1989 and subsequently enacting FATF-compliant legislation. As of late 2012, no cases were pending with the VPF or DPP (Banimataku 2012). During this time, however, several high-profile, Vanuatu-based operators were indicted or convicted overseas for money laundering and predicate offences – some of whom were, as mentioned above, then sheltered by the GoV, including Thomas Bayer and Robert Bohn.

The agencies comprising Vanuatu's AML regime clearly lack sufficient power to perform their required tasks. The FIU's manager observes that, whilst adequate legal and procedural arrangements are in place, monitoring private-sector compliance remains difficult, due to resource constraints and an inability to secure convictions, saying, 'we do have a stick to whack, but it's been cut shorter and shorter' (Mera 2012). Although the FIU has passed several cases to the TCU, no one has ever been charged, let alone successfully prosecuted, for money laundering. Despite the AFP's extraordinary support and involvement, the TCU's team leader blames this on a lack of resources and expertise (Banimataku 2012). Vanuatu's Director of Public Prosecutions reports that even if the DPP did receive case files from the TCU, it lacks the capacity to properly investigate and prosecute them (Tavoa 2012).

Public and private entities through which money may be laundered also appear disinterested in compliance. The head of Vanuatu's Investment Promotion Authority, which is responsible for approving foreign investment, confirms he has no means of assessing whether overseas investments come from criminal sources (Tebu 2012). This is despite the fact that money laundering often occurs through investment outside the financial sector, such as in real estate or small business ventures. In the private sector, the National Bank of Vanuatu's training manager said that, although his bank had established an AML compliance unit, it had never identified any suspicious transactions. Claiming that money laundering was more common through real estate and law firms, he expressed scepticism about capacity-building: 'It's good because it raises awareness ... But why do we need this training if we've never seen one [suspicious transaction]?' (Joes 2012). This indifference even extends to non-governmental groups. Transparency Vanuatu, the local branch of the international anti-corruption non-governmental organisation (NGO) Transparency International, has no interest in money laundering, or indeed in the relationship between the OFC and politicians, focusing instead on educating local people about the meaning of corruption and the abuse of public office (Taufa and Tamaru 2012). Transparency Vanuatu is managed by the expatriate wife of a leading OFC figure.

Ultimately, the weak *de facto* operating of rescaled AML regulatory institutions reflects the underlying reason why FATF Recommendations were adopted: the protection of interests bound up with the OFC. Vanuatu accepted the Recommendations to protect its financial centre from further reputational damage, not to tackle money laundering *per se*. Commensurately, the regime's actual implementation tends to accommodate the politico-economic interests being defended. The VFSC's Edmond Rengacki Toka (2012), for example, identifies his organisation's main role, in consultation with the OFC, as finding a path between satisfying FATF, so as restore the jurisdiction's reputation, and keeping Vanuatu competitive as an investment destination, which requires maintaining a degree of secrecy. This widespread orientation is not a recipe for meaningful enforcement of AML regulations.

Indeed, the OFC's continued decline has reinforced pressure to avoid prosecutions that might, ironically, further damage Vanuatu's reputation. Having adopted state-of-the-art, FATF-compliant legislation, Toka (2012) complains that Vanuatu's legal environment 'isn't as competitive' as some offshore competitors', and consequently it is losing business. Similarly, the OFC's Thomas Bayer (2012) complains that the FATF regime's net effect is that 'small centres are being squeezed out of business, while the big ones – New York, London – are thriving'. The Tax Justice Network reported that, from 2005 to 2012, total unreported wealth held in tax havens grew from US$11.5 trillion to an estimated US$21 to US$32 trillion (Henry 2012). Accordingly, some Pacific tax havens boomed. From 1999 to 2008, the number of international companies registered in Samoa, one of Vanuatu's key competitors, increased from 3,329 to 27,039, while bank liabilities towards Samoa rose from US$4.8 billion to US$7.3 billion. Similarly, assets held in the Marshall Islands grew from US$17 billion to over US$26 billion between 2007 and 2009. Conversely, in Vanuatu, the number of international firms slumped from 4,972 to 1,713 between 2006 and 2010; bank liabilities fell from US$915 million to US$484 million; total bank assets, already decimated by the International Banking Act, only grew from US$119 million to US$122 million between 2007 and 2009; and OFC foreign exchange earnings for 2006, at US$23 million, were lower than the US$25 million earned in 1990 (van Fossen 2012: 54, 59, 90; Sharman and Mistry 2008: 162–3). Similarly, while government revenues from OFCs in Barbados and Mauritius grew strongly after 2000, in Vanuatu, revenue from international companies stagnated and international bank fees had fallen by ninety-one per cent by 2008 (Sharman and Mistry 2008: 162–3).

Vanuatu's inability to halt its OFC's decline, despite its compliance with FATF, stems from the severity of its post-'Russiagate' reputational crisis, exacerbated by persistent attacks from Australia's Project Wickenby since 2006. Despite some setbacks, this multi-agency campaign against Australian tax cheats snared some major OFC players, notably Vanuatu-based Australian accountant Robert Agius, and other high-profile Australian tax evaders, charging sixty-nine people and convicting thirty by October 2012. ANZ Bank's Vanuatu subsidiary was also compelled by the Australian High Court to provide the ATO with details of thousands of accounts held by Australian citizens. This constant pressure caused capital flows from Australia – Vanuatu's main source of clientele since 1971 (van Fossen 2003) – to contract by over half from 2007–8 to July 2012 (Thomson 2012). Resentful OFC figures argue 'the Australian government is doing everything it can to close down the financial centre in Vanuatu' (Bayer 2012). Complaining about the 'myths' propagated by Project Wickenby, they assert:

The impact on Vanuatu's economy has been significant . . . a real decline in the number of international companies and the number and size of international banks compared to five years ago . . . we haven't grown. The pressure on the growth of new business from Australia and New Zealand has been significant . . . The media attack on Vanuatu is placing doubts in the heart of potential customers (Stafford 2012).

This pressure has generated conflict between regulators and the politico-economic interests behind the OFC. In May 2008, following Agius' shock arrest, VFSC Commissioner George Andrews announced that Vanuatu would overhaul its secretive tax provisions, effectively eliminating its tax-haven status. This caused uproar among financiers, prompting the finance minister to refute the suggestion and reaffirm the GoV would maintain secrecy provisions (*The Australian* 7 May 2008).

Despite this apparently 'successful' crack-down on Vanuatu's OFC, even in the absence of effective rescaled AML governance apparatus, the outcome is apparently the displacement, rather than suppression, of the NTS problem of money laundering. Bayer (2012) argues Australians are simply 'creating a more difficult task for themselves... If that money is going to London or New York it's much more difficult to find.' Following Samoa's lead, Vanuatu OFC players have also redirected their energies to Asia, where Australia's influence is far weaker. The OFC's plans include establishing offices in Hong Kong and marketing itself across Asia's main markets (Macdonald 2012). Declining revenues from portfolio investments have also led OFC players to look for economic opportunities in other sectors. Most importantly, they have partly redirected their activities into domestic real estate deals. Although foreigners cannot legally buy land in Vanuatu, OFC institutions have been mediating long-term leases that effectively amount to land-grabs for developers, since their termination requires landowners to compensate tenants for improvements they make, which most of them cannot afford. An estimated eighty per cent of coastal land on Vanuatu's main island has been alienated in this manner (Garrett 2011). Political elites are also involved. Former Minister of Land James Bule exploited his authority to resolve communal 'disputes' to effectively privatise large tracts of land (*Vanuatu Daily Digest* 8 January 2013). As regional tax expert Greg Rawlings (in Garrett 2011) observes, this development has been promoted by OFC actors who, increasingly crippled in traditional markets, have sought new ways to exploit the 'low-tax environment' that remains their main comparative advantage.

Although certainly attractive to OFC interests, land grabs may be creating new political contradictions. The attraction is that land is a non-portable asset: investors cannot simply relocate it elsewhere, as in highly fluid financial markets. Land speculation thus appears less vulnerable to reputational damage and capital flight, enabling its beneficiaries to keep its governance local, unlike financial regulation, where as we have seen the OFC has been unable to resist governance rescaling. However, although the OFC has faced no resistance to its off-shore financial activities, of which most Vanuatu citizens are ignorant, the situation with land is different. As noted earlier, land conflicts with French settlers were an important locus of national liberation struggles and remain a live political issue. When Vanuatu's prime minister resigned in March 2013 and a new government was formed, James Bule was ousted as land minister by Ralph Regenvanu, an outspoken critic of large-scale land leases. The OFC's entry into the domestic land market could therefore generate wider socio-political contestation of its role for the first time since independence.

The political economy of anti-money laundering regulation in Myanmar

Despite its vociferous rejection of many other international norms and regulations, Myanmar's then-military regime joined the FATF's global governance system in the early 2000s, leading to the considerable rescaling of Myanmar's domestic AML governance apparatus, in line with FATF Recommendations. After being blacklisted as an NCCT in 2001, the government adopted the FATF's Recommendations via its 2002 Control of Money Laundering Law (CMLL), established an FIU, joined the APG, underwent peer review, resulting in its removal from the blacklist in 2006, and still remains under enhanced international surveillance. This outcome, all the more remarkable given Myanmar's 'pariah' status, has been heralded as a great success for global governance and international cooperation (Wilson 2010; Sharman 2011a). In line with prevailing realist and constructivist explanations, this is typically depicted as a response either to post-September 11 US counter-terrorism pressure and threats of sanctions (Turnell 2003: 274–5; Wilson 2010: 305), or to a domestic banking crisis triggered by the blacklisting, which convinced the regime 'that it had to adopt the standard AML policy template and thereby hand control of important elements of its criminal justice and financial regulation systems to an outside body' (Sharman 2011a: 121). As demonstrated below, however, the evidence suggests otherwise. The adoption, scope and operation of Myanmar's AML regime have actually been shaped by the intimate relationship between money laundering, drug production and trafficking and centre–periphery struggles. Governance rescaling has not 'hand[ed] control . . . to an outside body' but has instead been harnessed by centralising forces to strengthen their hand against groups resisting unitary state power.

Money laundering, drugs and resistance in Myanmar

Unlike Vanuatu, where responses to FATF were shaped by its tax-haven status, money laundering in Myanmar is closely related to drug production and trafficking, which is in turn connected to long-running ethnic conflicts. Soon after decolonisation in 1948, Myanmar (then Burma) faced separatist insurgencies from ethnic-minority groups located in the country's borderlands, which resisted incorporation into a unitary state dominated by the ethnic-majority Bamar. They were later joined and partially united by the insurgent Communist Party of Burma (CPB). The situation deteriorated further with the retreat into Burma of a Guomindang army after the Chinese civil war. The Guomindang, backed by the CIA and Thai security officials as an anti-communist bulwark, set up a quasi-state in eastern Burma, growing and trafficking opium to finance military raids into China (McCoy 1972). After the Guomindang were forced to withdraw, Burma's indigenous rebel groups seized control of the opium trade, using it to finance their own insurgencies. Following a cessation of Chinese support, the CPB's militias also turned to opium, controlling fifty to eighty per cent of the trade by the late 1980s (Brown 1999: 244). A rearguard effort by the Maoist leadership to suppress opium trafficking sparked mutinies in 1989, with CPB forces splintering into ethnically based armed groups. The country's military regime, which seized power in 1988 following unconnected pro-democracy uprisings in central Burma, seized this opportunity to pacify the borderlands. Taking advantage of the war-weariness of resistance groups, and their leaders' desires to enjoy their ill-gotten gains in peace, the regime concluded fourteen ceasefires from 1988 to 1997, encompassing nearly all the major groups.

The challenge of money laundering in Myanmar stems from this pacification strategy. Under the ceasefire terms, ethnic-minority militias were permitted to continue controlling territory and border checkpoints and (for the time being) producing and trafficking drugs. Indeed, opium production nearly tripled from 1987 to 1995, and by 1996 the US estimated that drugs exports had reached US$900 million, equal to all legal exports (Meehan 2011: 382; Geopolitical Drug Watch 1997). In exchange for ceasefire groups demobilising and accepting an enhanced military and state presence in the borderlands, the regime offered development projects, welfare spending and business opportunities for their leaders – a process Woods (2011) calls 'ceasefire capitalism'. By co-opting these leaders into a centralised system of economic patronage, the regime hoped to neuter Myanmar's centrifugal forces and secure Myanmar's stability and territorial integrity (Jones 2014a). A vital means by which this was achieved was money laundering. Myanmar's leading drugs barons were encouraged to invest their proceeds in the central economy after paying a twenty-five per cent 'whitening tax' to the state. In exchange for mediating several ceasefires, the notorious drugs kingpin Lo Hsing Han was allowed to form AsiaWorld, Myanmar's largest conglomerate, and given lucrative government contracts and privileged access to foreign investment. Renowned drugs baron Khun Sa also became a leading businessman after his 1996 'surrender' to the government (Jones 2014b: 152–3). The country's emergent private banking system, dominated by Sino-Burmese tycoons linked to the drug-traffickers and smugglers that had financed Myanmar's insurgencies, became a key node for money laundering (Turnell 2009: 260–65). By the late 1990s, one analyst observed, 'the current Myanmar Business Directory of the Union of Myanmar Chamber of Commerce and Industry reads like a who's who in the drug trade' (Lintner 1998: 179). Indeed, alarmist observers suggested that Myanmar's state had been captured by drug lords (Dupont 1999). This situation intensified several NTS challenges for Myanmar's neighbours. Growing drug use contributed to a rising HIV/AIDS epidemic across mainland Southeast Asia and southwest China, whilst heroin, and later methamphetamine tablets, exported from Myanmar were identified as the primary threat to Thailand's national security by its army chief in 2000 (Jones 2012: 194). Although Myanmar was frequently lambasted for such problems, and for becoming the world's leading heroin exporter, the drugs trade was strongly driven by local and global market dynamics: poverty and a lack of alternatives for local farmers coupled with international demand in wealthier, mostly Western, countries (Paoli et al. 2009).

Moreover, despite rising international protest, the symbiotic domestic interests bound up with money laundering made it difficult for Myanmar's regime to tackle, despite the 1993 Narcotics Drugs and

Psychotropic Substances Law, which criminalised money laundering predicated on drug offences. Myanmar's relative peace and stability was underpinned by a *quid pro quo*: ceasefires in exchange for the toleration of illicit activities. As the then finance minister admits, 'the big insurgent groups...were money laundering. The laundered money was put into the business community here. For their surrender... we promised that...we wouldn't press charges against them' (Abel 2012). Moreover, Myanmar's investment-starved economy and emaciated state desperately needed sources of capital – a situation intensified by Western sanctions imposed on the military regime. In addition to yielding 'whitening tax' revenue, money laundering also benefited specific regime-linked groups, particularly military owned firms in joint ventures with emerging tycoons, senior generals with corrupt ties to former drug lords and well-connected individuals and state-owned enterprises which dominated borrowing from the newly established private banks (Bearnstein and Kean 1996; Lintner 1998: 175–80; Turnell 2009: 271–4; Mya Maung 1998: 200–201). This, then, was the situation prevailing in 2001 when the FATF listed Myanmar as an NCCT.

Rescaling governance: creating an anti-money laundering regime

Given the foregoing, Myanmar's adoption of the FATF Recommendations looks all the more surprising. As noted earlier, this has been attributed either to US pressure or the 'reputational damage' of FATF blacklisting causing a domestic banking crisis. Although Myanmar's elites were certainly not immune to global market pressures, neither explanation is fully compelling. US pressure on CFT certainly mounted after September 11, and in November 2003 the US Treasury Department listed Myanmar as a territory of 'primary money laundering concern', banning US financial institutions from dealing with two private banks, Asia Wealth and Myanmar Universal Bank, and barring Myanmar's financial institutions from access to US markets via correspondent banks (Turnell 2009: 306–7). US diplomatic cables also reveal that Washington sought to use the FATF to intensify pressure on Myanmar's regime and encourage its allies to support wider financial sanctions against it. However, this was motivated by a desire to 'reinforce...the 2003 Burma Freedom and Democracy Act' and contain Myanmar's sanctions-busting; Washington tried to instrumentalise the FATF, not for counter-terrorism purposes, but to further promote regime change (US Embassy 2003a). Furthermore, Myanmar's CMLL – which had already been enacted by this point – does not in fact encompass CFT. Indeed, by 2008, remarkably, Myanmar had still not even criminalised terrorism, let alone its financing (FATF 2008). Only in January 2014 did Myanmar's legislature begin considering an anti-terrorism bill. It therefore makes little sense to suggest that Myanmar's embrace of FATF regulations resulted from compliance with a US counter-terrorism drive.

The constructivist reliance on 'reputational damage' is more persuasive but still dubious. Arguably, Myanmar's international political and economic reputation had already hit rock bottom by 2001. The scant Western investments made in the early 1990s had largely been withdrawn by then amidst dissatisfaction at the military's economic mismanagement, and was subsequently locked out by economic sanctions. Asian investment also collapsed following the 1997 Asian financial crisis. The timing of events also problematises the constructivist explanation. The CMLL was introduced in 2002, following the 2001 blacklisting. However, Myanmar's domestic banking crisis – which is said to have been a reaction to FATF 'sanctions' and their effect on Myanmar's reputation – did not occur until February 2003, and FATF countermeasures were not imposed until November. The initial crisis was apparently precipitated not by FATF blacklisting but rather by the introduction of the CMLL, which prompted withdrawals by alarmed customers: it was induced by the threat of compliance with, not defiance of, FATF rules (Turnell 2009: 299). Moreover, although about fifteen per cent of total deposits were removed, the panic soon subsided (US Embassy 2005). A secondary crisis then hit the banking system in March, but this was caused by the collapse of financial 'Ponzi' schemes designed to offset Myanmar's rampant domestic inflation, said to involve the finance minister (who was forced to resign), and by rumoured heavy losses by Asia Wealth Bank on Chinese investments – *not* FATF blacklisting or foreign sanctions (Turnell 2006: 88–91). There is, therefore, scant evidence of any direct effect of 'reputational damage' from blacklisting. Contrarily, according to a former government banker, the domestically induced crisis 'essentially killed motivation in the Finance Ministry to push forward' on AML (US Embassy 2003b).

However, Myanmar was not entirely immune from reputational damage, reflecting how even relatively isolated economies are vulnerable to changes in global financial markets today. The domestic banking crisis caused Myanmar's GDP to contract by seven per cent in 2003–4 and cost the government 165 billion kyats (Turnell 2006: 81–5).[1] Courting further disruption would obviously be unwise. The regime's continued pursuit of Chinese, Thai and Indian investments, particularly in agribusiness, hydropower and extractive industries, also demonstrated a persistent thirst for foreign capital. Although Asian investors and governments have historically been far less concerned with Myanmar's political situation than Western ones, FATF countermeasures could deter them on economic grounds. Furthermore, the 2003 US sanctions, imposed to promote regime change, banned transactions with Myanmar in US dollars. As the then economic minister recalls, this was 'very difficult... we couldn't deal in the major currency we held... we suffered a lot, we couldn't do normal business' (Abel 2012). Myanmar's international businesses, including state-owned firms, were forced to use Euros, switch to cash-based border trade, use the informal *hundi* money-transmittance system,[2] or transact business through Singapore-based brokers or proxy companies. These methods increased transactions costs by five to ten per cent, reducing or even eliminating profit margins (Tha Than Oo 2012; Thiha Saw 2012), while tightening access to foreign exchange in Myanmar's highly dollarised economy. Singapore was already the Myanmar elite's favoured financial centre and its banks were vital to the evasion of sanctions on goods ranging from weapons to timber (Selth 2000; Milieudefensie 2009). Myanmar's vulnerability to the attitude of Singaporean banks consequently increased. Any fears the regime might have had were apparently borne out later, in 2008, when some regime-linked businessmen's proxy firms began experiencing difficulty

---

[1] Myanmar's then dual exchange rate system renders conversions to foreign currencies unhelpful. 165 billion kyats was equivalent to four per cent of Myanmar's GDP or 15.6 per cent of total government revenues in 2004 (Economy Watch 2013).

[2] *Hundi*, a trust-based banking system, operates as follows. Someone in country X pays a dealer US$100 (or its equivalent in goods and services). A chit is then provided, which another person in country Y then 'cashes' at a dealer for US$100 (or equivalent), minus a commission. This informal system is widespread in developing countries; in the Middle East, for example, it is called *hawala*. Many in Myanmar prefer *hundi* because it is cheaper and faster than the government banks, which monopolised international transactions from 1997 to 2012.

transacting through Singaporean banks (US Embassy 2008). Thus, even in Myanmar, the political economy of global financial markets created difficulties for local forces wishing to keep AML governance entirely local.

It is nonetheless vital to note that the CMLL was enacted in 2002, after the 2001 NCCT blacklisting but before all of these other events. David Abel (2012), then economic minister in the junta chairman's office, explains that the blacklisting was only a 'supporting reason' to pursue a policy already adopted in 2000 and announced that year at the UN: to crack down on opium cultivation. This policy – and the harnessing of AML regulation to it – should be understood primarily as part of a lengthy struggle to strengthen centralising forces at the expense of the borderlands' ethnic-minority resistance groups.

The first step, as noted, was to co-opt the groups' leaders through 'ceasefire capitalism' (Woods 2011), which initially gave them wide latitude to pursue illicit activities, including drug trafficking and money laundering, alongside involvement in 'legitimate' extractive and infrastructure investments in the borderlands. However, by facilitating their 'return to the legal fold', the military regime gradually enhanced its leverage. Ceasefire groups were now part of a military-controlled 'limited access order' (Meehan 2011), whereby government contracts, business permits and other lucrative opportunities were dispensed, and non-prosecution for illegal activities assured, on the basis of loyalty to the government (Meehan 2011; Woods 2011; Jones 2014a, 2014b). The regime also sought to weaken the ceasefire groups relative to Myanmar's military, doubling the army's size to around 400,000, importing over US$2 billion-worth of Chinese arms, and exploiting splits in ceasefire groups to co-opt some while attacking others. Economically, the regime became less dependent on drug-fuelled money laundering as oil and gas pipelines came on-stream in the early 2000s, yielding some US$2 billion annually, and it gradually took over more border checkpoints and/or re-routed trade via state-controlled Yangon ports and bazaars rather than ceasefire-group-controlled border crossings, depriving the erstwhile rebels of the revenues that had long sustained them (Jones 2014b: 153–4, 13; see Snyder 2006; Meehan 2011; Woods 2011).

An important component of this strategy to ensure the ceasefire groups' permanent subordination was an opium eradication campaign. The regime selectively pressed its ceasefire partners to end poppy cultivation in their areas and held public burning ceremonies of captured opium, the goal again being to sever the independent revenue streams sustaining resistance groups, thereby increasing their dependency on economic activities mediated by the regime and foreign investors (TNI 2011). Forceful crackdowns on poppy farming were concentrated either in areas of international scrutiny – to win foreign approval and aid – or in areas not controlled by strong, regime-aligned ceasefire groups, the net effect being to concentrate the trade in the hands of groups loyal to the state (SHAN 2003). Similarly, a post-2009 crackdown was selectively used to pressure militias resisting incorporation into Myanmar's army as part of the country's transition to 'democracy' (Meehan 2011). These crackdowns were not necessarily effective in reducing net drug trafficking and money laundering; drug production often either shifted location or moved from opium into methamphetamines. But that was not their purpose. Rather, the goal was to force Myanmar's ethnic minorities to accept the regime's hegemony.

The decision to rescale AML governance by adopting FATF's Recommendations in 2001 was primarily driven and shaped by this strategy. Adopting tougher regulations gave the government an additional weapon in the drive to sever revenue streams to rebel groups, and a means of coercing the recalcitrant with selective threats of prosecution. This was based on the logic of using AML to counter predicate crimes. As Abel (2012) explains, 'to reduce the poppy production, a crackdown on money laundering was essential'; without the CMLL, ceasefire groups 'would continue the cultivation of poppies...on a larger scale'. The law is officially regarded as a success. 'The business has not flourished, so poppy cultivation has dropped drastically in the border regions. Insurgencies directly related to them have completely been demolished' (Abel 2012). This is a serious overstatement, given that, as of late 2014, the government was still struggling to conclude a national ceasefire with ethnic-minority rebel groups, and opium cultivation was actually increasing (Democratic Voice of Burma, 8 October 2014). Nonetheless, that tackling the rebels was the principal goal of rescaling AML governance is further underscored by a more detailed examination.

The form and operation of Myanmar's AML regime
The form of Myanmar's AML governance has clearly been substantially transformed and rescaled along international guidelines. The 2002 CMLL was developed based on FATF Recommendations, UN

Conventions, UN model law and legislation in other ASEAN states (Joyce 2002: 80). Sharman (2011a: 121) says the regulatory standards in this 'state of the art AML legislation, largely written by the FATF . . . exceeded those of many FATF members'. The FATF (2008: 75) concurs that regulators now enjoy 'a wide variety of powers in line with those of similar bodies in other nations'. Praising Myanmar's progress, it lifted its countermeasures in 2006. With the embedding of internationally designed regulations, the creation of an FIU networked into transnational regulatory circuits and ongoing peer review processes, AML governance thus appears to have been internationalised in Myanmar, in line with FATF stipulations. However, in practice, both the form and operation of this system are shaped by the basic patterns of conflict and power described above. The CMLL regime was clearly constructed so as to protect dominant interests and create a tool, powerful but firmly under political control, that could be used selectively against enemies of the state, rather than functioning as a neutral, problem-solving, technical agency. This again demonstrates how the implementation of global governance regimes is shaped by local power relations.

This is readily apparent from the APG's review of Myanmar (FATF 2008). Notable are the particular FATF Recommendations that are not enshrined in the CMLL. The predicate crimes it identifies are very limited, excluding terrorist financing, market manipulation, trafficking in illicit goods, and much environmental crime. Corporations are protected, due to a lack of legal enforcement mechanisms against legal persons and no requirements to identify the beneficial ownership of shell companies. 'Politically Exposed Persons' – political and state officials and their close associates, whom FATF recommends should come under closer scrutiny – are entirely neglected. Thus, vast swathes of the political economy are essentially excluded from AML regulation – notably those connected with the corrupt businesses and patronage networks of the regime and its allies. For example, a minister who received bribes from a front company engaged in environmentally destructive extractive activities in the borderlands, a joint venture with ceasefire group elites, and/or Chinese investors, could not be investigated using the CMLL. Also neglected is any effort to regulate *hundi*, the informal banking system through which most money is remitted to Myanmar from overseas. This exclusion – a gaping hole in any effort to tackle money laundering – seems partly to reflect recognition that the cash-strapped, heavily dollarised economy would be profoundly disrupted by any effort to tackle *hundi*.

Finally, the FIU is subjected to heavy political control. All investigations must be pre-approved by the chief of police and a newly established Central Control Board, chaired by the Minister of Home Affairs with political representatives from the ministries of finance, home affairs and agriculture, plus officials from the justice ministry, the police and central bank. This gives key ministers *de facto* control over whom the FIU investigates. Furthermore, even if the FIU is permitted to form an Investigation Board to pursue a specific case, concerned ministry officials are included, such that, for example, money laundering allegedly linked to illegal logging would be investigated by a panel including a Forestry Ministry official (FATF 2008: 58–60, 71). This potentially allows ministers to shield their clients, or any other well-connected figures, from thorough investigation. By process of elimination, therefore, Myanmar's AML regime seems overwhelmingly directed at money laundering by groups *outside* the state's protection, whose proceeds come from drug trafficking. It offers little practical advance over Myanmar's existing 1993 law. The rescaling of governance has been harnessed and directed by centralising, progovernment forces for their own political ends.

This analysis is reinforced by the practical operation of AML governance. The main mechanism by which the FATF's AML approach is intended to operate is through financial institutions submitting STRs for any transaction exceeding 100 million kyats or US$10,000 to the FIU, which then investigates. However, although private banks account for forty-five per cent of the banking sector, they filed fewer than one per cent of the 1,073 STRs submitted from 2004 to 2008; two state-owned banks account for virtually all of the rest (FATF 2008: 65, 116). This is largely because, until 2012, state banks monopolised international transactions, which comprise most STRs. In practice, this means that the domestic private banking system, which was in substantial part founded to launder money, is non-compliant with the AML regime, yet apparently protected from scrutiny. Those borderlands elites who 'returned to the legal fold' by laundering money through regime-approved channels, and who remain loyal to the central state, thus have nothing to fear from the new regulations. This is underscored by economic minister Abel (2012), who reveals that the 'banks were pre-warned about money laundering ... after giving them the time to

clean their accounts, we cracked down on the banks'. That loyal elements are excluded from regulation is also suggested by a former
government banker's comment that 'state-owned banks would probably report any large deposit, unless the customer is well-known to the
bank – or to senior government officials' (US Embassy 2003b). That is,
the KYC principle works in the exact *opposite* way to FATF's intentions: relationships between individuals engaged in suspicious transactions and government officials, which should arouse concern, are
precisely the ones that are not scrutinised. This is because, one senior
economist suggests, bankers 'fear the repercussions of informing on
relatives of senior GOB [Government of Burma] leadership more than
any legal penalties' (US Embassy 2003b). Unsurprisingly, therefore,
from 2004 to 2008, the FIU's Investigation Board was only directed to
investigate twenty-three cases of money laundering, and it secured just
one conviction. By contrast, STRs generated many more investigations
for predicate crimes, with fifty-four convictions in 2006–7, the vast
majority for drug offences (FATF 2008: 66, 16).

Myanmar's AML regime was thus *designed* to be ineffective in actually tackling money laundering whilst achieving 'mock compliance'
with international standards (Walter 2008). This is difficult to explain
for realists, who depict international standards as being imposed by
powerful states, or constructivists, who emphasise the threat of reputational damage and the socialisation of officials. However, our perspective shows that this efficacy was functional for the interests involved in
the rescaling of governance in Myanmar. For the military regime, creating expert agencies empowered to actually tackle money laundering
was never the intention. Instead, the goal was to augment the government's capacity to extract loyalty from borderlands group leaders.
The regime thus promoted sufficient rescaling of AML governance to
concentrate greater power in its hands, but constrained it to a level
at which favoured interests would not be harmed. The new arrangements are seen as successful in meeting the regime's own goals by
merely enhancing the threat of potential prosecution, such that few
actual prosecutions were required, or even intended to occur. Abel
(2012) recalls: 'for their surrender and for their promise not to continue
poppy plantations, opium trade, production of heroin and all that, we
promised that there would only be confiscation [of illicit assets], we
wouldn't press charges against them. So, no legal charges were brought
against them, only confiscation, and they all surrendered'.

This underlying motivation is further illustrated by considering the sole prosecution actually secured. Tin Sein, the chairman of Myanmar Universal Bank, was convicted in 2007 for using drug trafficking proceeds to found the bank (FATF 2008: 43). The government closed the bank in August 2005 and, following the conviction, absorbed it into the state-owned Myanmar Economic Bank. Tin Sein's assets were seized and he was jailed indefinitely. Tin Sein was hardly unique in using drug money to found a bank – so why was he singled out? Details are understandably murky. However, the key seems to have been Tin Sein's links to ethnic-Shan opposition groups and Chinese tycoons (Turnell 2009: 308). In particular he was said to be linked to Htun Oo, the leader of the Shan Nationalities League for Democracy, who was arrested in February 2005 for crimes against the state (Kazmin 2005). Tin Sein's offence was apparently not money laundering, but rather consorting with anti-regime forces.

He may also have fallen victim to strife within the regime itself, which was apparently a further powerful influence on AML governance. The year 2003 saw the beginning of an internal struggle between the regime's two main factions, headed, respectively, by infantry commander General Maung Aye, the junta's deputy chairman, and intelligence chief General Khin Nyunt, the third-ranking member. Although Khin Nyunt had spearheaded the regime's ceasefire strategy and enjoyed close relations with many borderlands elites, both men had built substantial patronage networks and business interests, including among drug lords. Maung Aye, for example, was said to enjoy close relations with Khun Sa, whilst Khin Nyunt dealt with Lo Hsing Han (Bearnstein and Kean 1996; Geopolitical Drug Watch 1997). In 2003, Maung Aye's faction moved against Khin Nyunt and his network. Demoted from his post of Secretary-1 to Prime Minister, Khin Nyunt was later sacked altogether in October 2004 and, in July 2005, was imprisoned for corruption alongside his sons. The years 2004–5 saw a grand purge of Khin Nyunt's followers in the state apparatus and a reshuffling of the cronies and assets formerly in his network (ICFTU 2005: 7–8; Charney 2009: 181–2; Jagan 2006: 32). Myanmar's business elites were reportedly summoned and threatened with potential prosecution if they did not accommodate themselves to the new dispensation (US Embassy 2004). Notably, Tin Sein was reportedly close to Khin Nyunt (Turnell 2009: 309), and his own demise followed the fall of his powerful patron.

This interpretation is further strengthened by the closure of two other banks in 2005: Asia Wealth Bank and Myanmar Universal Bank. Both had apparently been investigated for money laundering in December 2003 and their licences were suspended, but no charges were ever brought. Both institutions had been rendered defunct by the earlier domestic banking crisis, so their eventual closure was largely a formality. According to Myanmar's police chief, it was not due to money laundering allegations, for which no evidence was found. However, Asia Wealth's owner, Eike Htun, was another tycoon said to be close to ethnic-Kokang drug traffickers and to Khin Nyunt (Turnell 2009: 261–2; *Irrawaddy* June 2000). He complained that his treatment reflected the post-purge reshuffling of patronage towards a rival crony capitalist, Tay Za (US Embassy 2007). Conversely, the main beneficiaries of the purge appear to have been interests linked to Maung Aye. With the demise of three of Myanmar's 'big five' banks, the primary winner was Kanbawza Bank, which assumed first place in terms of market share. Kanbawza is owned by Maung Aye's 'adopted son', Aung Ko Win. It was followed by Myawaddy Bank, which is linked to military-owned companies, the Cooperative Bank and First Private Bank, all of which belonged to a consortium headed by Kanbawza (Turnell 2009: 310–11, 264). Again, it appears that regulation was selectively used to consolidate economic power in the hands of favoured groups whilst picking off undesirable elements.

Thus, the net result of the constrained rescaling of AML governance in Myanmar has been to strengthen the power of central socio-political forces over peripheral ones and extend the state's reach, rather than to actually tackle the problem of money laundering or even its predicate crimes. There is little evidence that drug trafficking or money laundering has actually declined. In 2008, the US Embassy reported that there 'Remains . . . [a] significant risk of drug money being funnelled into commercial enterprises and infrastructure investment . . . Collusion between traffickers and Burma's ruling military junta . . . allows organized crime groups to function with virtual impunity . . . the criminal underground faces little risk of enforcement and prosecution' (US Embassy 2008). Furthermore, in 2010, four new private banks were licensed, all of which were part of leading conglomerates which, along with their owners, were on US sanctions lists for alleged links to narcotics (Turnell 2011: 144). However, eliminating drug trafficking and money laundering was not the CMLL's intended purpose. As with

Vanuatu, fending off the economic threats associated with 'reputational damage' was part of the regime's goal – though to a much lesser extent. More importantly, as in the case of Indonesia in relation to both transboundary pollution and avian influenza, state agencies selectively harnessed an international agenda to extend the functional reach of their authority, for their own domestic purposes. The security threat really addressed through this rescaling is not drug trafficking or transnational crime *per se*, but the threat posed by economically independent ethnic-minority resistance groups to the Bamar-dominated unitary state and the military's quest to assert its authority countrywide. Like the associated crackdown on opium cultivation, the CMLL was used not to eliminate drugs but rather to concentrate power and wealth in the hands of groups supportive of the military regime, whilst helping to eliminate those considered disloyal.[3] All this suggests that the 2014 Anti-Terrorism Bill, currently being considered by Myanmar legislators, is less an attempt to comply with FATF strictures than to further strengthen the government's hand against peripheral forces as the country moves sluggishly towards a national ceasefire and negotiations for a constitutional settlement that will settle Myanmar's long-running ethnic conflicts.

Conclusion

This chapter explored an apparent 'success story' of global governance as applied to NTS: the effort to tackle money laundering and terrorist financing and, through this, the predicate offences associated with transnational organised crime and terrorism. As with the other NTS cases examined in this book, in order to be implemented, the FATF's Recommendations require the deep transformation and rescaling of state apparatuses, including the creation of an internationally integrated regulatory focal point – the FIU – responsible for enforcing AML regulations on the private sector and other parts of the state. Against realist, constructivist, and poststructuralist explanations of the FATF Recommendations' near-universal adoption, which emphasise states' power to coerce or international organisations' capacity to

---

[3] The AML system was also used to tighten the 'coordination' of NGOs operating in the borderlands and impose new reporting requirements on international NGOs, again enhancing the state's power vis-à-vis politically dubious entities (FATF 2008: 149–51).

inflict reputational damage and socialise officials, we emphasised the specific political economy context of this issue-area. It is the highly integrated and fluid nature of global financial markets, and the crucial willingness of private-sector entities to use FATF rankings as proxy measures of risk, that explains the unusually broad uptake of the FATF regime. In our case studies, the concern to avoid isolation from global capital flows was an important factor, particularly for Vanuatu but even for a relatively isolated economy like Myanmar's. However, we also showed that, even under such unusual conditions – not replicated in any other NTS issue-area – the form and operation of the AML regime is heavily conditioned by local power relations: the defence of OFC interests in Vanuatu and state-building strategies in Myanmar. The specific dynamics around governance rescaling explain the substantial divergence between FATF's ideal vision of AML governance and actual practice, in a way that other approaches cannot. Having thus concluded our final case study, we now turn to compare our findings and their implications.

Conclusion

In recent decades, non-traditional security (NTS) issues have become core concerns for many governments, international organisations, businesses, NGOs and ordinary citizens. As we have shown, the diversity of NTS governance is striking, with forms, functions and outcomes sometimes varying even within a single country. We argued that existing approaches in security studies, while making an important contribution in describing how NTS issues have been added to the security agenda, cannot explain this diversity. Merely focusing on the discursive presentation of threats, as the Copenhagen School does, cannot explain how NTS issues are addressed – which often does not involve war-like 'extraordinary measures' but the banal instruments of security governance. Nor did the Paris School's narrow focus on formal security bureaucracies capture the 'whole-of-government' and multilevel governance approaches visible in security governance, or how these are shaped by broader socio-political contestation. Moreover, these approaches do not sufficiently recognise how the qualitative distinction between traditional and NTS threats – the latter's transboundary character, which renders them unmanageable by nation-state-based approaches – generates demands for novel, border-spanning forms of governance that cannot be explained through traditional, statist models of security politics.

These new modes of governance typically do not take the form of supranational, sovereignty-usurping institutions, which many IR scholars look for in vain, but rather the internal transformation of state apparatuses to contain and manage NTS threats. Our new framework for analysis – the State Transformation Approach (STA) – consequently foregrounded this dynamic. As we demonstrated in our case studies, NTS governance programmes seek to *rescale* relevant parts of state apparatuses in territories where transboundary threats and risks are seen to emanate. This means that ostensibly domestic institutions and agencies: (i) are no longer confined to a national or subnational

governance context, pursuing solely local goals and priorities; but
(ii) become embedded within regional or global regulatory regimes for
managing transboundary NTS problems, which typically involve agencies from other states and international organisations, and often NGOs
and private sector actors; and (iii) serve as mechanisms for enforcing
international regulatory disciplines upon other parts of their states
and societies. Foregrounding this rescaling dynamic as a general phenomenon showed how quite similar governance transformations are
occurring around security threats emerging in seemingly very different
issue-areas – health, the environment and organised crime – which are
usually treated as distinct and unique by their respective specialist literatures (e.g. Elbe 2010a; Oels 2012; Sharman 2011a). This underscores
our argument that the rise of NTS and associated governance systems
reflects the emergence of, and further promotes, 'non-traditional' forms
of disaggregated statehood across the world in recent decades.

   Of course, we did not claim that governance rescaling *always* happens as part of the securitisation of NTS issues. Rather, the STA was
geared towards explaining how far it occurs in particular contexts and
why rescaled institutions operate the way they do. Below, we compare
our key findings to offer some tentative conclusions, as well as equally
important normative considerations that flow from them, which we
believe should guide future efforts to manage NTS issues. Some may
question the generalisability of findings derived from a small number
of geographically concentrated cases. But one inescapable conclusion
of our study is that large-*n*, multiple country studies simply would
not produce meaningful findings. Our cases clearly show that understanding NTS governance rescaling is not a simple matter of measur-
ing compliance/non-compliance or governance efficacy using binary
or scalar variables. Understanding the outcome of rescaling attempts,
and how rescaled apparatuses work in practice, requires comprehensive analysis of dynamic and historically evolving socio-political power
relations and struggles, which cannot be captured using the tools of
macro-political analysis. Moreover, and related to this, the normative
assessment of such outcomes cannot meaningfully be confined to grad-
ing effectiveness. More significant questions include: whose interests
are privileged by different governance regimes and outcomes? And
what would have to change, politically, for us to alter these outcomes,
rather than merely lament them and make feeble recommendations for
technocratic tweaks or the application of more 'political will'?

Our empirical findings: comparisons and implications

Our three comparative case studies – of the transboundary 'haze' in Southeast Asia (chapter three), avian influenza in Indonesia and Thailand (chapter four), and anti-money laundering (AML) regulation in Myanmar and Vanuatu (chapter five) – all clearly exhibit significant state transformation and rescaling of domestic governance apparatuses associated with attempts to manage NTS problems.

Chapter three identified the emergence of a subregional regime that has promoted significant transformations in Indonesian land and forest governance, ostensibly linking the most local administrative tiers of government to an international ministerial steering committee. Extensive international capacity-building – in some cases, bypassing the national government altogether – has sought to embed ASEAN action plans and global scientific best practice in reducing the risks of fire and transboundary haze, encouraging domestic institutions to impose international disciplines on other parts of Indonesia's state and society. There were also tentative efforts to empower technical experts to guide the deployment of international fire-fighters to Indonesian territory.

Chapter four showed how international efforts to manage H5N1 avian influenza in Indonesia fostered large-scale programmes of surveillance and response at the district level in both animal and human health. These were linked to heavily internationalised H5N1 governance mechanisms at the provincial and national levels, funded by donors and directly involving experts from the World Health Organization (WHO) and the Food and Agriculture Organization (FAO). Indonesian domestic health governance, particularly those aspects relating to the management of infectious disease in general and H5N1 specifically, thereby became part of a broader international disease control regime, coordinated by the WHO and FAO. In nearby Thailand, although the national government exercised its 'scale management' function to block international intervention, it nonetheless applied the strictest 'best practice' disease eradication guidelines when managing infections in poultry, as advocated by the FAO and the World Organisation for Animal Health (OIE).

Chapter five showed how the Financial Action Task Force's (FATF) 40 Recommendations for combating money laundering and the financing of terrorism have been mostly adopted by Myanmar and Vanuatu. This has led to significant rescaling of the domestic AML apparatuses of these countries involving: the criminalisation of money laundering, the creation of domestic Financial Intelligence Units responsible for collating information and investigating money laundering reports, the networking of AML institutions with peers regionally and globally and the periodic monitoring and evaluation of the implementation and performance of AML apparatuses by the Asia/Pacific Group on Money Laundering (APG).

Although state transformation and governance rescaling are clearly happening in all of our cases, the extent of rescaling and the functioning of rescaled institutions vary greatly, with uneven consequences for different societal groups, even in the same issue-area within a single country. Following the STA, we traced this variation in security governance and its functioning to the specific political economy of the issue-area and socio-political struggles between those seeking to rescale governance and those wishing to prevent or limit rescaling, or frustrate the operations of rescaled institutions. For example, FATF has been very successful in compelling almost all states and territories to at least formally comply with its 40 Recommendations, leading to considerable state transformation and rescaling. On the other hand, efforts to manage climate change or infectious disease have been far less successful in inducing implementation. This discrepancy, we argued, reflects the particular nature of global financial markets, where investors are both concerned about financial losses and capable of rapidly shifting their portfolio investments from one jurisdiction to another. Their acceptance of the FATF's warnings as a proxy for jurisdictions' investment risk has meant that outright recalcitrance by non-cooperative countries or territories is severely punished by isolation from global financial flows. Meanwhile, as chapter three shows, because the market context is very different, a similar 'naming and shaming' approach, vis-à-vis palm oil, has yielded limited results. Yet, despite its superficial success, the extent of rescaling and actual functioning of AML apparatuses have – like all other NTS governance systems – been heavily shaped by local power relations. In Myanmar, AML regulations were used as a tool by the ruling regime to subdue its rivals, particularly those linked with ethnic minority rebel groups. In Vanuatu, AML regulations are clearly a case of 'mock compliance' (Walter 2008), designed to assuage nervy investors of Vanuatu's regulatory bona fides, but without making a single conviction to date.

In reality, then, AML governance outcomes are driven as much by local power struggles as those in our other cases. In the case study on haze, not only was governance rescaling resisted at the national and local scales by those benefiting from the use of fire and their allies, but so was the operation of transformed state apparatuses. In particular, agricultural interests embedded at the district level effectively deflected the haze regime away from the powerful oil palm plantation sector – the predominant source of fires and haze – onto politically marginal slash-and-burn farmers. Local socio-political power relations and political economy factors therefore rendered the regime ineffective, perpetuating threats to local livelihoods, regional health and the global climate. A similar pattern occurred in the governance of H5N1 in Indonesia, with the internationalised surveillance and response system directed away from politically protected commercial poultry interests towards 'backyard' farmers. Accordingly, H5N1 was not effectively suppressed. In Thailand, conversely, local power relations favoured measures that benefited large-scale poultry conglomerates, eliminating the smallholder sector. International best practices were adopted – and the NTS threat thereby effectively tackled – because they went with, rather than against, the grain of powerful local interests.

This discussion leads us to our *first* conclusion: *local power relations matter enormously for the form and content of global governance.* Global governance necessarily involves local implementation, whether at the national, subnational or even village level in some cases. The rescaling of state institutions and their integration into regional or global regulatory regimes is intended to circumvent politics, by empowering technocrats and experts and isolating parts of the state from political and popular pressures. In reality, however, our cases demonstrate that there is simply no possibility of evading the broader struggles shaping the use of state power. As Davis et al. (2012: 88) argue, irrespective of whether 'experts' see their knowledge production as apolitical, they are inevitably 'drawn into highly political conflicts'.

A *second* conclusion is that *governments, and states more broadly, retain a crucial role as 'scale managers', enabling them to reject or modify international interventions, even where they appear powerless.* Attempts to manage transboundary problems through state transformation are also efforts to circumvent state sovereignty. Governments are often reluctant to formally cede sovereignty to external actors or international bodies, particularly in postcolonial states, where elites are typically very conscious of the fragility of 'nation-building'. Engaging bureaucrats or regulators directly is thus often seen as a way of 'getting things done' without undermining countries' formal sovereignty,

dampening resistance (Slaughter 2004). But since governments thereby
retain their formal legal sovereignty, and also remain the largest presence in terms of governing capacities, interveners typically need their
cooperation with, or at least tacit acceptance of, activities to manage transboundary threats within their jurisdictions. Thus, the Thai
government flatly rejected international intervention to manage H5N1
outbreaks in poultry, focusing on a national-scale response. Meanwhile
in Indonesia, Health Minister Siti Fadilah Supari made world head-
lines when refusing to share specimens of the H5N1 virus harvested
in Indonesia with the WHO, claiming 'viral sovereignty' (Hameiri
2014). Yet, the Indonesian national government did back FAO and
WHO efforts to strengthen surveillance at the district level, in order
to claw back power over that tier of government that it had lost during decentralisation. The very same government can therefore simultaneously flex its sovereignty to selectively admit or exclude external rescaling programmes, according to the balance of local interests
(Jones 2012). Moreover, we found that central government agencies
often did this in order to extend the functional and territorial reach
of their own authority vis-à-vis political opponents and/or interests
entrenched within subnational institutions. Thus, governance rescaling can actually be used strategically to re-empower state-based interest
groups, as has been observed in relation to other forms of international
cooperation (Valverde and Mopas 2004: 236; Sending and Neumann
2006; Rajkovic 2012). This suggests that rescaling is neither objectively 'good' nor 'bad' but is simply used to advance different interests
and agendas – a point we explore further in our section on normative
implications, below.

   That states remain important 'scale managers' (Peck 2002) does not
imply, however, that NTS governance is 'state-centric', if this is taken
to mean that not much has changed. That control over governance has
not shifted wholesale into international organisations or into the hands
of non-governmental actors in no way contradicts our argument. The
STA rejects simplistic approaches seeking a zero-sum transference of
authority; the focus is not whether states are 'more' or 'less' powerful
with regard to other actors, but how their functions, institutions and
powers have transformed, and the implications of this. Our three case
studies all demonstrate significant transformations in response to NTS
concerns: in the location of state power, out of established institutions
of national government towards functional, internationally networked

agencies; in the kinds of actors exercising authority and state power, now increasingly technocrats and experts who are not politically or popularly accountable; and in how the exercise of state power is justified, from objectives like 'national development' towards an emphasis on protecting a country's reputation in an interconnected world. This is why we locate contestations over state transformation and rescaling at the heart of our analysis. Furthermore, states are not monolithic actors. Our cases revealed that many instances of struggles over rescaling and its functioning involved conflicts between different parts of states, linked with different non-state actors. In the case of the haze, for example, the relatively weak Ministry of the Environment, backed by environmentalist NGOs, sought to use international intervention and funding to assert itself against the more powerful Ministry of Forestry and Ministry of Agriculture (MoA), which enjoy close relationships with the powerful oil palm and forestry industries. Likewise, in Vanuatu, the manager of the effectively toothless FIU told us that he and his colleagues saw international inspections as opportunities to increase their clout within the state and improve their capacity to execute their regulatory duties (Mera 2012).

Finally, the inclination of different parts of the state to support or frustrate international regulatory efforts is not simply a matter of 'political will'. It is profoundly influenced by the broader, historically specific, political economy context shaping state–society relations, as well as by the political economy of the sector to be affected by rescaling, a point on which we elaborate below. This is what Jessop (2008) calls 'strategic selectivity': different parts of the state systematically privilege particular societal interests and strategies over others. In Thailand, for example, the devastating Asian financial crisis, followed by a widely despised IMF-imposed structural adjustment programme, contributed to the rise of the Thaksin-led *Thai Rak Thai* government in 2001, which was supported by a broad coalition of the Thai domestic bourgeoisie. Following the H5N1 outbreaks in 2004, unsurprisingly, this administration acted swiftly to protect the interests of industrialised poultry conglomerates, but showed scant regard for the effects on smallholder farms and other groups. Conversely, in Indonesia, the marginalisation of veterinary authority at all levels of government reflects the close relationship between government and livestock industries established under Suharto. The MoA's willingness to support international interventions extends only insofar as it can reassert authority over district governments. Technocratic suggestions to improve institutional design or apply greater political will – the predominant response of much of the NTS literature (e.g. Caballero-Anthony and Cook 2013) – simply ignore these structural determinants of how state power is used and are therefore 'pie-in-the-sky' recommendations with little chance of ever being accepted.

A *third* conclusion is that, notwithstanding their 'scale management' function, *national governments rarely reject governance rescaling entirely*, even in pariah states like Myanmar. This finding supports Chayes and Chayes' (1995) suggestion that the legitimacy of states has been recast in terms of their willingness and capacity to engage in transboundary regulation – to show that they are 'responsible' members of the so-called 'international community'. Rather than resisting outright, sceptical governments are more likely to formally accept rescaling, but warp outcomes to suit preferred interests. The only case of outright refusal we identified was the Indonesian parliament's refusal (until 2014) to ratify the ASEAN Agreement on Transboundary Haze Pollution, but even this was not decisive in preventing considerable governance rescaling. Another example, not in our case studies, was China's refusal to cooperate on SARS in 2003 (Fidler 2003a); but even this was temporary, with subsequent changes that 'eroded the boundary between . . . domestic and global health governance' (Chan et al. 2009).

Governments seem most likely to oppose governance rescaling – partially, if not outright – when one, or more, of four conditions apply. First, relevant industries face minimal penalties for (or would even gain from) non-compliance with international regulatory efforts – as in the case of oil palm, where agribusiness interests benefit from the use of fire to clear land. Second, no other powerful domestic groups favour rescaling. Again this was visible in the haze case, where only relatively weak environmental NGOs supported the ASEAN regime, and initially in the case of AML in Vanuatu, before the material effects of the reputational damage to the offshore financial centre were felt. Third, it is compatible with dominant political ideology. The protection of business interests and rejection of external 'interference', while clearly partial, had particular resonance in post-crisis Thailand, and in Indonesia where populist nationalism is a strong political tendency. Fourth, external diplomatic pressure is weak. Indonesia has clearly been more susceptible to pressure over H5N1 from powerful Western donor governments, for example, than the pleas of its ASEAN neighbours to tackle the haze.

A *fourth* conclusion is that, as mentioned above, *the political economy of the particular industry that rescaling is likely to impact will greatly affect the outcomes of governance transformations.* NTS issues are often viewed either as undesirable 'externalities' of rapid economic development and/or as enabled by technological advances in communication and transportation. Indeed, as our case studies show, NTS concerns typically have important economic dimensions and, thus, attempts to manage them inevitably engage the interests of particular industries. Two important questions arise: first, are business interests likely to want to frustrate or support rescaling, and to what extent? And, second, what is their capacity to do so by linking up with the state or other powerful groups in society? On the first question, we find that business groups do not always seek to block rescaling and increased regulation. Their response depends on the perceived effects of proposed governance systems on their profitability. Following the H5N1 outbreaks in Thailand, poultry conglomerates were at the forefront of a campaign to implement stringent, internationally agreed biosecurity standards because this was essential to regain lost export markets in Europe and Japan. In Indonesia, where production is for domestic consumption, poultry companies – including a subsidiary of a major Thai conglomerate – were at best indifferent to international efforts to improve biosecurity, while smaller farmers resisted it as a threat to their slender profit margins. But business interests' capacity to get the governance outcomes they want is clearly uneven. In Vanuatu, initial attempts by offshore financial centre operators to completely stymie the implementation of AML regulations turned to grudging acceptance or active support following the demise of Nauru's financial centre and limited sanctions imposed on Vanuatu in the late 1990s.

These uneven responses and outcomes reinforce the importance of a political economy analysis that is fine-grained, places equal weight on 'political' and 'economic' aspects and is sensitive to their interrelations. Contrary to realist approaches (Drezner 2007), one cannot simply assume that governments' international positions are directly determined by the aggregate 'adjustment costs' faced by entire 'national' sectors. First, our cases show that the costs of transboundary regulation fall unevenly on different segments of a single sector, and dynamic, ongoing struggles ensue over who should bear these burdens, shaping the degree and type of governance rescaling and the practical operation of rescaled institutions. In this sense the STA accords with, and could be further developed by, insights from 'business conflict' approaches which, rather than treating business as a homogenous group, elucidate how struggles among *fractions* of national and international capital shape global governance (see Roemer-Mahler 2013). Second, however, the distribution of adjustment costs cannot tell us whether affected businesses can achieve their desired outcomes. This depends on the strategies and alliances they are able to construct, and the context-specific, historically constituted relationship between certain fractions of capital and important state apparatuses relevant to particular issue-areas. Many so-called 'political economy' analyses, particularly in the liberal tradition, neglect this 'political' side of political economy, or reduce political conflict to unhelpful categories like 'rent-seekers' and 'the public' (Mattli and Woods 2009). In reality, those resisting regulation are not necessarily 'bad' or 'rent-seekers' – another point developed in our normative evaluation below.

A further point to emphasise is that the importance of business interests is not context specific, even though their specific weight and influence is. It may be tempting to ascribe the constrained outcomes of governance rescaling discovered here to the nature of developing countries, where governments are often thought to be 'weak' or 'captured' by predatory economic interests. However, Southeast Asia is traditionally understood in IR as a region of 'strong' states, where ministers have ruled with minimal reference to societal interests, at least until very recently (Dosch 2007). More importantly, insofar as this perspective is mistaken (see Jones 2012), the influence of business interests over NTS governance is still not unique to developing countries and cannot, therefore, be dismissed by simplistic references to corruption or weak governance institutions. Consider, for instance, the EU's Emissions Trading System, which seeks to tackle the NTS threat of climate change by creating a market in carbon permits. The design and operation of this palpably failing regime is clearly traceable to the interests of financial and industrial capital, 'whose bias is towards creating novel sources of profit rather than halting the flow of fossil fuels out of the ground'. Their influence ensures that 'emissions caps will be set, at best, just strictly enough to create scarcity for a new market, but not strictly enough to threaten the role of coal and oil in capital accumulation'. Consequently, far from tackling climate change, the regime 'has ended up subsidising carbon-profligate practices' (Lohmann 2013: 78, 82). We maintain that, rather than evaluating non-Western governance approaches as deficient when compared to European ones, as in the mainstream 'security governance' literature, *all* NTS governance should be subjected to the analysis conducted here.

A *fifth* conclusion is that, in every case of NTS governance we studied, *governments and dominant societal interests combined to attempt to deflect the costs of rescaling governance onto weaker groups in society, while the powerful were protected.* In relation to the 'haze', small and subsistence farmers bore the brunt of law enforcement, not plantation companies; in H5N1 governance, Thai smallholders and Indonesian backyard farmers were victimised, not the major conglomerates or their 'plasma' farms; and in Myanmar, AML institutions were used against official enemies, but not regime allies. The discourse of securitisation is used in such cases to rationalise the actions taken and present the distribution of costs as inevitable and beyond legitimate political contestation. Where this is unpersuasive, the victimised groups often lack the means to resist. Thai smallholders, for example, openly opposed their government's approach to H5N1, but found no allies within a regime dominated by the big bourgeoisie. Again, such outcomes are hardly confined to developing countries. For instance, the costs of climate change mitigation in developed countries are rarely if ever allocated to large-scale industrial polluters; firms often profit substantially from the allocation of tradeable carbon permits. Instead, the costs are passed onto individual consumers – the social group whose size and heterogeneity renders it least amenable to collective action – through taxation or increased utility bills, rationalised as necessary to 'save the planet'. Such uneven outcomes – which often carry consequences for NTS governance regimes' efficacy – were aided in our case studies by the depoliticised nature of the interventions promoting governance rescaling. External agencies often sought to mask the inherently political nature of their governance projects by presenting them merely as technical, problem-solving initiatives. They also followed a path of least resistance to score apparent 'successes', enabling their interventions to be deflected towards weaker groups. As in the case of H5N1 in Indonesia, this deflection was permitted even when scientific evidence did not support the direction taken. This behaviour reflects tendencies observed more widely in the field of international development assistance (Carothers and de Gramont 2013).

A *sixth* conclusion is that, *where governments cannot resist and costs cannot be deflected onto weaker groups, 'mock compliance' is the most likely outcome* (Walter 2008). We saw this in Vanuatu, where the government, following initial outright rejection, realised that resisting the FATF would destroy the island-state's offshore financial centre, but where the only entity capable of being targeted by AML governance was the offshore financial centre itself. Political elites linked to these interests therefore had to accept FATF-style governance rescaling, but work to isolate and undermine it in practice.

A *seventh* and final conclusion is that *avoiding mere 'mock compliance' and achieving the full implementation of global governance standards is extraordinarily difficult*, requiring a remarkable coincidence of local, political and economic interests and power relations with the substance of international regulations. In Thailand, there was a clear alignment between the Thaksin government's interests in protecting big business, the powerful poultry conglomerates' desire to regain export markets, and the implementation of stringent biosecurity measures as a pathway to achieving these goals, thus permitting the rigorous application of international 'best practice'. Notably, however, this was achieved with scant international involvement. Where international donors and agencies were involved, but powerful interests were misaligned with transnational regulations, no amount of funding, institutional capacity-building or even internationals' direct involvement in governance systems could fully achieve the desired outcome. 'Success' thus requires a confluence of factors that are simply beyond the capacity of international donors and regulators to influence, as studies of international development assistance have also discovered (see Hutchison et al. 2014). This again underscores the importance of local context for global governance. It also emphasises the importance of considering the fine detail of governance transformation. To mainstream IR scholars, Thailand's refusal of international involvement may smack of ASEAN's traditional attachment to sovereignty and 'non-interference', but this emphasis on rhetoric would miss the underlying reality of governance transformation to exhibit compliance with global regulatory standards.

Normative implications

This book has been primarily concerned with explaining real-world outcomes, not making normative judgements about them. Nonetheless, we now offer some suggestions about the normative implications of our findings, which scholars more inclined towards normative theory may find interest in challenging or developing further. The modes of governance being developed to manage NTS issues have much in common with other transnational regulatory regimes, and consequently raise similar normative concerns. Chief among these are the shift from democratic governance to unaccountable governance by experts, the attempt to prioritise 'global' concerns over local ones and the baleful effects of security governance on local people. Surveying these issues suggests that more security governance is not necessarily a good thing; rescaling can only be evaluated normatively in relation to the costs and benefits imposed on particular social groups, and external interveners should pay heed to this when designing their projects.

First, our cases show that NTS, like other transboundary issues, is subject to attempts to shift the locus of policymaking and authority into the hands of technical experts, possibly beyond the national scale, who are insulated from political pressures. In the haze case, there were attempts to empower experts in land governance and forest fire management to override local resistance to global 'best practices' and national government objections to the deployment of international fire-fighters. Bird flu governance interventions, pioneered by technical agencies like the WHO and FAO, sought to empower veterinarians to inspect, quarantine and cull livestock according to OIE guidelines, over the objections of local development officials. In AML governance, FATF, an unaccountable group of OECD technocrats, was empowered to dictate domestic governance systems worldwide, with authority concentrated in the hands of technical experts staffing local FIUs.

This immediately raises questions of the accountability and legitimacy of NTS governance. The attempt to empower experts is common to all of our cases because technical expertise is often required to identify and measure the extent of NTS threats, and because there is a wider tendency to outsource authority in this manner, associated with the rise of regulatory statehood. However, these experts are not democratically accountable, and the institutions created for them to lead are not amenable to popular participation or control. Indeed, part of the very purpose of these governance innovations is to circumvent mass politics and insulate technocrats from political 'interference', and to impose international disciplines on local societies that would otherwise not be enacted. The rescaling of NTS governance is thus part of the wider erosion of democratic government in the name of global cooperation and problem-solving.

This leaves NTS governance susceptible to many of the criticisms made of the democratic deficit in traditional multilateral organisations like the IMF, WTO and World Bank (Woods and Narlikar 2001; Dahl 2003), and particularly to the shift from territorially bounded, democratically accountable *government* to multilevel, networked *governance* regimes like the EU (Papadopoulos 2007). Zürn (2004: 260) thus points out that international institutions are now expressions of 'political denationalization' rather than complementary to 'a dominant national paradigm'. As Kennedy (2005: 5) puts it, as 'we are increasingly governed by experts' implementing laws 'far beyond their nominal territorial jurisdiction'; there is now 'law at every turn – and only the most marginal opportunities for engaged political contestation', at least through formal democratic institutions. This reinforces Ehrhart et al.'s (2014b) recent insistence that security governance ought not to simply be evaluated in terms of its functional efficacy, as if it were an unproblematic, consensual, non-hierarchical, problem-solving phenomenon; in fact, it is frequently the opposite. NTS governance requires critical analysis in terms of its attempt to overwhelm local priorities with 'global' ones, and its negative consequences for local people, which are typically exacerbated by struggles over rescaling.

In a nutshell, the purpose of NTS governance is to transform governance in risky spaces so that threats seen to originate there are managed, or at least contained, such that they do not spread to other jurisdictions. This often involves efforts to change the priorities of local institutions to reflect those of the forces behind governance interventions, whether this is the governments of advanced Western states dominating the WHO in the case of H5N1, or the FATF in the case of AML, or those of Malaysia and Singapore in the case of the haze. The functional, problem-solving orientation of the institutional innovations being proposed may appear unobjectionable, but in reality they involve advancing a particular agenda at the expense of others favoured by local people. In H5N1, for instance, the fact is that, from an Indonesian perspective, avian influenza is just one among many communicable diseases with which the overstretched domestic health system must grapple. Western governments' panic about zoonotic diseases killing hundreds of millions of people worldwide and disrupting global economic flows is simply not strongly shared in Jakarta, let alone in the villages subjected to intensive internationalised surveillance and the enforced culling of livestock, detrimentally affecting poor people's livelihoods. Indeed, there is considerable resentment of the Western insistence on urgent action on avian influenza, backed by dedicated resources, compared to a lack of support for improving healthcare in Indonesia more broadly. Western donors appear less concerned with the suffering of local people in these relatively impoverished societies than with containing NTS threats. This criticism mirrors wider critiques of global governance as reflecting not truly 'global' but rather 'Northern' priorities. This is particularly the case in global health governance, where the resources dedicated to infectious diseases capable of spreading across state boundaries to affect Northern interests vastly outweigh those devoted to those which remain largely *in situ* (Rushton 2011).

This overriding of local priorities is often masked in mainstream treatments of global governance. As noted above, it may be tempting to paint all those resisting attempts to tackle NTS concerns as wicked 'rent-seekers' or even dangerous lunatics, conspiring against the global 'public good'. The virulent reaction to Indonesian Health Minister Siti's refusal to share avian influenza samples with the WHO is an excellent case in point. Public health experts were simply outraged that this idiosyncratic Indonesian woman would selfishly dare to endanger the global influenza surveillance system and, by extension, millions of lives worldwide (e.g. Holbrooke and Garrett 2008). There was virtually no sympathy for her stated reason: to protest the WHO's practice of disseminating influenza samples to pharmaceutical companies, who made expensive vaccines that were then stockpiled by Western governments and unaffordable to developing countries like Indonesia where the samples originated. To unthinkingly condemn Siti, or to brand those resisting NTS governance rescaling more generally as corrupt rent-seekers, reflects the problematic ethos of technical expertise surrounding this approach to security. This ethos assumes that the 'public good' is readily identifiable and uncontested, that the tools to solve problems are readily at hand, and that their deployment could therefore only be resisted by pernicious individuals. In reality, what counts as the 'public good' is always contested, and legitimately so. For instance, European governments may believe that it is in everyone's interests to reduce deforestation in the name of global environmental security; but in developing countries, many people's livelihoods depend on exploiting and converting forests to agriculture. For them, basic human security may actually be imperilled by EU programmes. Certainly, the primary beneficiaries of deforestation are typically not ordinary, low-income people, but well-connected business interests; but this does not mean that conservation efforts are necessarily in the interests of the poor. At the very least, there is a legitimate debate to be had about the balance between environmental protection and economic development, particularly in less developed countries. However, securitisation discourses often seek to short-circuit such debates as inimical to tackling threats and risks to humanity as a whole.

Indeed, the interests of low-income groups are often damaged even further by the contestations over NTS governance rescaling. As noted above, these struggles tend to shunt the costs of transboundary regulation onto relatively weak and marginal groups. Meanwhile, dominant forces, potentially of an extremely authoritarian character, can often harness governance rescaling to bolster their own authority, as we saw in Myanmar and Indonesia. While Southeast Asian outcomes reflect local specificities, similar patterns are visible in Western NTS governance. For instance, the extension of Western states' border controls beyond their territorial boundaries to tackle irregular migration and terrorism has extremely pernicious effects for migrants, who are typically poor and vulnerable, while bolstering authoritarian regimes willing to cooperate with Western governments (Joffé 2007). Similarly, the main victims of the US 'war on drugs' are indigent African-Americans, who are subject to increasingly militarised forms of urban policing, and Latin American subsistence farmers whose crops are often destroyed in US-driven chemical defoliation campaigns. And yet, drugs are more widely available than ever and drugs barons are thriving (Carpenter 2003; Provine 2007).

Although other scholars have drawn attention to the negative 'unintended consequences' of security governance (Daase and Friesendorf 2010), the fact that poor and marginal groups bore the brunt of rescaling in *all* of our cases suggests that it is an intrinsic aspect of the politics of NTS. As a general rule, all regulation imposes costs; rational individuals and groups will generally seek to avoid higher costs, pushing them onto others; the most powerful and well connected will typically succeed; therefore, the burden will tend to fall most heavily onto weaker groups. To believe otherwise is to ignore the influence of local power struggles on the outcome of attempts to reshape governance. For this to change, local power relations would also need to change. In Southeast Asia, we would need to see something like a social democratic revolution, since only this would empower marginalised groups and entrench political regimes committed to protecting the poor and weak and capable of moving against the interests of big business. Such regimes are historically unprecedented in Southeast Asia, where serious structural constraints impede their emergence (Jayasuriya and Rodan 2007), and the remnants of such regimes elsewhere in the world are gradually being further eroded, as described in chapter one.

All this suggests that NTS governance is neither intrinsically 'good' nor 'bad', neither 'desirable' nor 'undesirable', but must instead be evaluated in terms of the agendas and interests it empowers and disempowers, helps or harms. This insight has already been employed to dispel the notion of 'bad' or 'good' domestic governance. For instance, a study of tobacco farming regulation in China shows how 'successful' regulation was achieved in one area, severely damaging the income and welfare of peasant farmers; conversely, in another area, where rent-seeking and corruption sabotaged effective implementation, peasants were far better off and local development ensued (Cheng and Ngo 2014). NTS governance, and arguably global governance more broadly, ought to be evaluated in a similar fashion. We should not merely evaluate whether a governance regime fulfils its stated goals, but who has benefited and suffered along the way. Here, the STA is extremely useful because it explicitly identifies the concrete interests at stake as part of the analysis. Ultimately, our attitude towards any given NTS regime will be determined by our sympathies towards these different interests.

What is to be done?

These conclusions suggest a new approach for policymakers seeking to construct new governance systems to tackle transboundary security problems. Most basically, they should recognise more explicitly the intrinsically political nature of their activity. A more clear-sighted identification of their objective – to transform state apparatuses and thereby reallocate power and change political outcomes – would both be more honest and more useful for planning purposes. A political economy analysis of a specific NTS issue-area in a given country would help identify the structural drivers generating the threat, the key interests to be reckoned with in trying to manage it, the forces available as partners in this goal, and the strategies that might be most useful in pursuing it.

Following Hutchison et al.'s (2014) study of development interventions, we would suggest conceptualising NTS governance projects as interventions in a situation of dynamic, ongoing social conflict. Accordingly, external agencies must eschew their preference for finding and aligning with committed ideological 'bedfellows' – typically, as in this case, likeminded experts and technocrats – to achieve international 'best practice' regulation. Instead, they need to focus on building tactical alliances with a variety of social groups capable of helping them attain limited and achievable outcomes. Some of these groups may not be donors and regulators' preferred partners, but they are necessary to create the political leverage required to enact meaningful change in specific domains, and/or to help find creative ways to secure the buy-in of sceptical or hostile groups capable of overwhelming local political economy barriers. As Linos (2007: 564) states, for attaining meaningful compliance, 'national agreements are less important than mobilising partisan groups at different scaled levels of governance'. Furthermore, as the situations we are observing are dynamic, external agencies must continue to closely monitor developments and adjust their tactical alliances and objectives accordingly. If this sounds like a tall order, it is. As noted above, external interveners cannot dictate the outcome of security governance innovations, which are too powerfully conditioned by local power relations. Thus, outsiders will need to choose their battles carefully, identifying and targeting areas where potential coalitions exist to enact real change and avoiding areas where there is no realistic prospect of change to avoid wasting energies and resources.

Adopting this approach, however, would also require a sea-change in the way many of the agencies of multilateral agencies and Northern states operate (see Carothers and de Gramont 2013). Too often they are excessively focused on expending their budgets and scoring quantifiable but superficial 'quick wins' – number of officials trained, capacity-building workshops held, reports submitted and so on – than on engaging in the hard, long and often fruitless task of political coalition-building. The good news is that, given the perceived urgency of NTS threats relative to the problems of international development, the likelihood of creative experimentation is higher. Certainly, if we are to make the world more secure from transboundary threats, aligning global regulatory efforts with local interests and power relations remains an essential task.

Bibliography

Abbott, Kenneth W. and Snidal, Duncan 2009. 'The Governance Triangle: Regulatory Standards Institutions and the Shadow of the State', in Walter Mattli and Ngaire Woods (eds.) *The Politics of Global Regulation*, 44–88. Princeton: Princeton University Press.

Abdul, Rahim 2012. Deputy Secretary-General II (Environment Management), Ministry of Natural Resources and Environment, Malaysia. Interview by Lee Jones, 5 January, Putrajaya.

Abel, David 2012. Former Myanmar Finance Minister. Interview by Lee Jones, 6 July, Yangon.

Abraham, Thomas 2007. *Twenty-First Century Plague: The Story of SARS*. Baltimore: Johns Hopkins University Press.

Abrahamsen, Rita and Williams, Michael C. (eds.) 2007. 'The Privatisation and Globalisation of Security in Africa', *International Politics* (special issue) 21(2): 131–253.

2011. *Security Beyond the State: Private Security in International Politics*. Cambridge: Cambridge University Press.

Abuza, Zachary 2003. *Militant Islam in Southeast Asia: Crucible of Terror*. Boulder: Lynne Rienner.

Acharya, Amitav 2004. 'How Ideas Spread: Whose Norms Matter? Norm Localization and Institutional Change in Asian Regionalism', *International Organization* 58(2): 239–75.

2009a. *Constructing a Security Community in Southeast Asia: ASEAN and the Problem of Regional Order*. London and New York: Routledge.

2009b. *Whose Ideas Matter? Agency and Power in Asian Regionalism*. Ithaca and London: Cornell University Press.

Achmad, Nurhanudin and Sawit Watch 2010. *Independent Smallholders in the Indonesian Oil Palm Industry*. Gadjah Mada University Yogyakarta: Sawit Watch.

Adinugroho, Wahyu Catur, Suryadiputra, I.N.N., Saharjo, Bambang Hero and Siboro, Labueni 2005. *Manual for the Control of Fire in Peatlands and Peatland Forest*. Bogor: Wetlands International.

Adler, Emanuel 1992. 'The Emergence of Cooperation: National Epistemic Communities and the International Evolution of the Idea of Nuclear Arms Control', *International Organization* 46(1): 101–45.

1997. 'Imagined (Security) Communities: Cognitive Regions in International Relations', *Millennium – Journal of International Studies* 26(2): 249–77.

Adler, Emanuel and Greve, Patricia 2009. 'When Security Community Meets Balance of Power: Overlapping Regional Mechanisms of Security Governance', *Review of International Studies* 35(S1): 59–84.

Adler-Nissen, Rebecca and Gammeltoft-Hansen, Thomas (eds.) 2008. *Sovereignty Games: Instrumentalising State Sovereignty in Europe and Beyond*. Basingstoke: Palgrave Macmillan.

Afrizal, Jon 2012. 'Jambi Rolls out Welcome Mat for Domestic, Foreign Investors', *Jakarta Post*, 23 November.

Agnew, John 1994. 'The Territorial Trap: The Geographical Assumptions of International Relations Theory', *Review of International Political Economy* 1(1): 53–80.

Alcabes, Philip 2009. *Dread: How Fear and Fantasy Have Fuelled Epidemics from the Black Death to Avian Flu*. New York: Public Affairs.

Ali, S. Harris and Keil, Roger 2009. 'Public Health and the Political Economy of Scale: Implications for Understanding the Response to the 2003 Sever Acute Respiratory Syndrome (SARS) outbreak in Toronto', in Roger Keil and Rianne Mahon (eds.) *Leviathan Undone? Towards a Political Economy of Scale*, 195–208. Vancouver: University of British Columbia Press.

Amoore, Louise 2006. 'Biometric Borders: Governing Mobilities in the War on Terror', *Political Geography* 25(3): 336–51.

Andreas, Peter 2013. 'Gangster's Paradise: The Untold History of the United States and International Crime', *Foreign Affairs* 92(2): 22–8.

Andri Jatikusumah and Riana Arief 2011. Center for Indonesian Veterinary Analytical Studies. Interview by Shahar Hameiri, 7 September, Bogor, West Java.

Anonymous 2011a. Palm oil conglomerate representative. Interview by Lee Jones, 2 December, Singapore.

Anonymous 2011b. Individuals familiar with the Singapore–Jambi Cooperation Project. Interview by Lee Jones, 1 December, Singapore.

Anonymous 2011c. Senior Official in the Ministry of Health, Republic of Indonesia. Interview by Shahar Hameiri, 6 September, Jakarta.

Anonymous 2011d. Indonesian poultry market expert. Interview by Shahar Hameiri, 19 July, Jakarta.

APFP [ASEAN Peatland Forestry Program] 2010. 'Technical Workshop on the Development of the ASEAN Peatland Fire Prediction and Warning System: Workshop Report', 13–14 July. Kuala Lumpur.

Aradau, Claudia and van Munster, Rens 2007. 'Governing Terrorism Through Risk: Taking Precautions, (Un)knowing the Future', *European Journal of International Relations* 13(1): 89–115.

2011. *Politics of Catastrophe: Genealogies of the Unknown*. London: Routledge.

Ardiansyah, Fitrian and Putri, Desak Putu Adhityani 2011. 'Risk and Resilience in Three Southeast Asian Cross-Border Areas: the Greater Mekong Subregion, the Heart of Borneo, and the Coral Triangle', Asia Security Initiative Policy Series no. 11, February. Singapore: RSIS Centre for Non-Traditional Security Studies.

ASEAN [Association of Southeast Asian Nations] n.d. 'Panel of Experts', http://haze.asean.org/?page_id=201.

1995. *ASEAN Cooperation Plan on Transboundary Pollution*, Jakarta: ASEAN Secretariat. http://www.aseansec.org/8938.htm.

1997. 'Regional Haze Action Plan', http://haze.asean.org/?page_id=213.

1998. 'Manila Declaration on the Prevention and Control of Transnational Crime', Adopted by the Asian Regional Ministerial Meeting on Transnational Crime, 25 March. Manila. http://cil.nus.edu.sg/rp/pdf/1998%20Manila%20Dec%20on%20the%20Prevention%20and%20Control%20of%20Tnatl%20Crime-pdf.pdf.

2002. 'ASEAN Agreement on Transboundary Haze Pollution', 10 June. Kuala Lumpur. http://haze.asean.org/?wpfb_dl=32.

2003. *Guidelines for the Implementation of the ASEAN Policy on Zero Burning*. Jakarta: ASEAN Secretariat.

2004a. *Guidelines for the Implementation of Controlled Burning Practices*. Jakarta: ASEAN Secretariat.

2004b. 'Chairman's Statement of the 10th ASEAN Summit', 29 November. Vientiane. www.asean.org/news/item/chairman-s-statement-of-the-10th-asean-summit-vientiane-29-november-2004.

2005a. 'Joint Communique', of the Fifth ASEAN Ministerial Meeting on Transnational Crime (AMMTC), 29 November. Hanoi. http://www.asean.org/communities/asean-political-security-community/item/joint-communique-of-the-fifth-asean-ministerial-meeting-on-transnational-crime-ammtc-ha-noi-29-november-2005.

2005b. *ASEAN Peatland Management Initiative*. Jakarta: ASEAN Secretariat.

2006a. 'ASEAN Regional Security: The Threats Facing it and the Way Forward', 10 April 2006. Jakarta: ASEAN Secretariat. http://www.asean.org/resources/item/asean-regional-security-the-threats-facing-it-and-the-way-forward-by-asean-secretariat.

2006b. 'Ha Noi Statement on Promoting Partnerships for the Implementation of the ASEAN Agreement on Transboundary Haze Pollution', 13 May. Hanoi. http://www.fire.uni-freiburg.de/GlobalNetworks/SouthEastAsia/ASEAN_CONFERENCE%20STATEMENT-FINAL_Hanoi_2006.pdf.

2007a. *ASEAN Peatland Management Strategy*. Jakarta: ASEAN Secretariat.

2007b. 'One Caring and Sharing Community', Chairperson's Statement of the 12th ASEAN Summit, 13 January. Cebu. www.asean.org/news/item/chairperson-s-statement-of-the-12th-asean-summit-he-the-president-gloria-macapagal-arroyo-one-caring-and-sharing-community.

2011. 'Joint Statement', Eighth ASEAN Ministerial Meeting on Transnational Crime (8th AMMTC), 11 October. Bali. http://www.asean.org/communities/asean-political-security-community/item/joint-statement-of-the-eighth-asean-ministerial-meeting-on-transnational-crime-8th-ammtc-bali-indonesia-11-october-2011.

ASEAN Secretariat Official 2011. ASEAN Environment Division Official. Interview by Lee Jones, Jakarta, 5 December.

Australian Government PMC [Department of the Prime Minister and the Cabinet] 2013. 'Strong and Secure: A Strategy for Australia's National Security', 23 January. Canberra: Australian Commonwealth Government, Department of the Prime Minister and Cabinet. http://apo.org.au/files/Resource/dpmc_nationalsecuritystrategy_jan2013.pdf.

Avant, Deborah D., Finnemore, Martha and Sell, Susan K. (eds.) 2010. *Who Governs the Globe?* New York: Cambridge University Press.

Aydinli, Ersel (ed.) 2010a. *Emerging Transnational (In)security Governance: A Statist-Transnationalist Approach*. Abingdon: Routledge.

Aydinli, Ersel 2010b. 'Statist-Transnationalism for a Security Cooperation Regime', in Ersel Aydinli (ed.) *Emerging Transnational (In)Security Governance: A Statist-Transnationalist Approach*, 1–22. Abingdon and New York: Routledge.

Azhar Muhammad and Noeri Widowati 2011. Campaign Management Unit, Indonesian Ministry of Agriculture. Interview by Shahar Hameiri, 9 September, Jakarta.

Bach, David, Newman, Abraham L. and Weber, Steve 2006. 'The International Implications of China's Fledgling Regulatory State: From Product Maker to Rule Maker', *New Political Economy* 11(4): 499–518.

Baker, Raymond W. 2005. *Capitalism's Achilles Heel: Dirty Money and How to Renew the Free-Market System*. Hoboken: Wiley.

Balzacq, Thierry 2005. 'The Three Faces of Securitization: Political Agency, Audience, and Context', *European Journal of International Relations* 11(2): 171–201.

2008. 'The Policy Tools of Securitization: Information Exchange, EU Foreign and Interior Policies', *Journal of Common Market Studies* 46(1): 75–100.

Banimataku, Allanrow 2012. Team Leader, Transnational Crime Unit, Vanuatu Police Force. Interview by Shahar Hameiri, 21 November, Port Vila.

Barkin, J. Samuel and Cronin, Bruce 1994. 'The State and the Nation: Changing Rules and the Norms of Sovereignty in International Relations', *International Organization* 48(1): 107–30.

Barkin, J. Samuel and Shambaugh, George E. (eds.) 1999. *Anarchy and the Environment: The International Relations of Common Pool Resources.* Albany: State University Press of New York.

Barnett, Michael and Finnemore, Martha 2004. *Rules for the World: International Organizations in Global Politics.* Ithaca and London: Cornell University Press.

Barr, Christopher, Resosudarmo, Ida A.P., Dermawan, Ahmad, McCarthy, John F., Moeliono, Moira and Setiono, Bambang (ed.) 2006. *Decentralization of Forest Administration in Indonesia: Implications for Forest Sustainability, Economic Development and Community Livelihoods.* Bogor: Center for International Forestry Research (CIFOR).

Bayer, Thomas M. 2012. Chairman, Pacific International Trust Company Ltd. Interview by Shahar Hameiri, 23 November, Port Vila.

Bearnstein, David and Kean, Leslie 1996. 'People of the Opiate: Burma's Dictatorship of Drugs', *The Nation*, 16 December. http://www.ainfos.ca/A-Infos96/8/0206.html.

Beck, Ulrich 1992. *Risk Society: Towards a New Modernity.* London: Sage Publications.

1999. *World Risk Society.* Cambridge: Polity Press.

Bettini, Giovanni 2013. '(In)convenient Convergences: "Climate Refugees", Apocalyptic Discourses and the Depoliticization of Climate-Induced Migration', in Chris Methmann, Delf Rothe and Benjamin Stephan (eds.) *Interpretive Approaches to Global Governance: (De)constructing the Greenhouse*, 122–36. Abingdon: Routledge.

Betts, Alexander and Orchard, Phil (eds) 2014. *Implementation and World Politics: How International Norms Change Practice.* Oxford: Oxford University Press.

Bevir, Mark and Hall, Ian 2014. 'The Rise of Security Governance', in Mark Bevir, Oliver Daddow and Ian Hall (eds.) *Interpreting Global Security*, 17–34. Abingdon and New York: Routledge.

Bhattacharya, Dhrubajyoti 2007. 'An Exploration of Conceptual and Temporal Fallacies in International Health Law and Promotion of Global Public Health Preparedness', *The Journal of Law, Medicine & Ethics* 35(4): 588–98.

Bieler, Andreas 2001. 'Questioning Cognitivism and Constructivism in IR Theory: Reflections on the Material Structure of Ideas', *Politics* 21(2): 93–100.

2005. 'Class Struggle over the EU Model of Capitalism: Neo-Gramscian Perspectives and the Analysis of European Integration', *Critical Review of International Social and Political Philosophy* 8(4): 513–26.

Bieler, Andreas and Morton, Adam David (eds.) 2001. *Social Forces in the Making of the 'New Europe': The Restructuring of European Social Relations in the Global Political Economy*. Basingstoke: Palgrave.

Bieler, Andreas and Morton, Adam David 2008. 'The Deficits of Discourse in IPE: Turning Base Metal into Gold?', *International Studies Quarterly* 52(1): 103–28.

Bigo, Didier 2001. 'The Möbius Ribbon of Internal and External Security(ies)', in Mathias Albert, David Jacobson and Yosef Lapid (eds.) *Identities, Borders, Orders: Rethinking International Relations Theory*, 91–116. Minneapolis and London: University of Minnesota Press.

2002. 'Security and Immigration: Toward a Critique of the Governmentality of Unease', *Alternatives* 27(1): 63–92.

Bingham, Nick and Hinchliffe, Steve 2008. 'Mapping the Multiplicities of Biosecurity', in A. Lakoff and S.J. Collier (eds.) *Biosecurity Interventions: Global Health and Security in Question*, 173–93. New York: Columbia University Press.

Bob, Clifford 2012. *The Global Right Wing and the Clash of World Politics*. Cambridge: Cambridge University Press.

Boehmer, Charles, Gartzke, Erik and Nordstrom, Timothy 2004. 'Do Intergovernmental Organizations Promote Peace?', *World Politics* 57(1): 1–38.

Booth, Ken 1991. 'Security and Emancipation', *Review of International Studies* 17(4): 313–26.

Brandt, Daniel 1995. 'Organized Crime Threatens the New World Order', *NameBase NewsLine*, No. 8, January–March. www.namebase.org/news08.html.

Brauch, Hans Gunter 2005. 'Threats, Challenges, Vulnerabilities and Risks in Environmental and Human Security', *Studies Of the University: Research, Counsel, Education*, No. 1/2005. Bonn: UNU Institute for Environment and Human Security.

Brauch, Hans Günter, Spring, Úrsula O., Mesjasz, Czeslaw, Grin, John, Kameri-Mbote, Patricia, Chourou, Béchir, Dunay, Pál and Birkmann, Jörn (eds.) 2011. *Coping with Global Environmental Change, Disasters and Security: Threats, Challenges, Vulnerabilities and Risks*. Berlin: Springer.

Brenner, Neil and Elden, Stuart 2009. 'Henri Lefebvre on State, Space, Territory', *International Political Sociology* 3(4): 353–77.

Brenner, Neil, Peck, Jamie and Theodore, Nik 2010. 'Variegated Neoliberalization: Geographies, Modalities, Pathways', *Global Networks* 10(2): 1–41.

Breslin, Shaun 2007. *China and the Global Political Economy*. Basingstoke: Palgrave Macmillan.

Breslin, Shaun and Croft, Stuart (eds.) 2012. *Comparative Regional Security Governance*. Abingdon: Routledge.

Brock, Lothar 1997. 'The Environment and Security: Conceptual and Theoretical Issues', in Nils-Petter Gleditsch (ed.) *Conflict and the Environment*, 17–34. Dordrecht: Kluwer.

Brower, Jennifer and Chalk, Peter 2003. *The Global Threat of New and Reemerging Infectious Diseases: Reconciling U.S. National Security and Public Health Policy*. Santa Monica: RAND Corporation.

Brown Weiss, Edith and Jacobson, Harold K. (eds.) 2000. *Engaging Countries: Strengthening Compliance with International Environmental Accords*. Cambridge: Massachusetts Institute of Technology Press.

Brown, Catherine 1999. 'Burma: The Political Economy of Violence', *Disasters* 23(3): 234–56.

Brown, Michael E. (ed.) 2003a. *Grave New World: Security Challenges in the 21st Century*. Washington, D.C.: Georgetown University Press.

2003b. 'Introduction: Security Challenges in the Twenty-First Century', in *Grave New World: Security Challenges in the 21st Century*, 1–13. Washington, D.C.: Georgetown University Press.

Brum, Eric 2011. FAO Officer in Indonesia. Interview by Shahar Hameiri, 5 September, Jakarta.

Bulkeley, Harriet 2001. 'No Regrets? Economy and Environment in Australia's Domestic Climate Change Policy Process', *Global Environmental Change* 11(2): 155–69.

Bulkeley, Harriet and Newell, Peter 2010. *Governing Climate Change*. Abingdon, Oxon: Routledge.

Bullinger, Cathrin and Haug, Michaela 2012. 'In and Out of the Forest: Decentralisation and Recentralisation of Forest Governance in East Kalimantan, Indonesia', *Austrian Journal of South-East Asian Studies* 5(2): 243–62.

Burgos, Sigfrido, Otte, Joachim, Pfeiffer, Dirk, Metras, Raphaelle, Kasemsuwan, Suwicha, Chanachai, Karoon, Heft-Neal, Samuel and Roland-Holst, David 2008. 'Poultry, HPAI and Livelihoods in Thailand – A Review', Mekong Team Working Paper No. 4, October. Rome: Food and Agriculture Organization. http://r4d.dfid.gov.uk/PDF/Outputs/HPAI/wp04_2008.pdf.

Busby, Joshua W. 2007. *Climate Change and National Security: An Agenda for Action*. New York: Council on Foreign Relations.

Büthe, Tim and Mattli, Walter 2011. *The New Global Rulers: The Privatization of Regulation in the World Economy*. Princeton and Oxford: Princeton University Press.

Butler, Declan 2007. 'Q&A: Siti Fadilah Supari', *Nature* 450(1137): 19.
  2013. 'Agency Gets a Grip on Budget', *Nature* 498(7452): 18–19.
Buzan, Barry and Hansen, Lene 2009. *The Evolution of International Security Studies*. Cambridge: Cambridge University Press.
Buzan, Barry and Wæver, Ole 2003. *Regions and Powers: The Structure of International Security*, Cambridge: Cambridge University Press.
  2009. 'Macrosecuritisation and Security Constellations: Reconsidering Scale in Securitisation Theory', *Review of International Studies* 35(2): 253–76.
Buzan, Barry, Wæver, Ole and de Wilde, Jaap 1998. *Security: A New Framework for Analysis*. Boulder: Lynne Rienner.
Caballero-Anthony, Mely 2008. 'Non-traditional Security and Infectious Diseases in ASEAN: Going Beyond the Rhetoric of Securitization to Deeper Institutionalization', *The Pacific Review* 21(4): 507–25.
Caballero-Anthony, Mely and Cook, Alistair D.B. (eds.) 2013. *Non-traditional Security in Asia: Issues, Challenges, and Framework for Action*. Singapore: ISEAS.
Caballero-Anthony, Mely, Emmers, Ralf and Acharya, Amitav (eds.) 2006. *Non-traditional Security in Asia: Dilemmas in Securitisation*. Aldershot: Ashgate.
Cabinet Office 2008. *The National Security Strategy of the United Kingdom: Security in an Interdependent World*. London: HMSO.
  2010. *A Strong Britain in an Age of Uncertainty: The National Security Strategy*. London: HMSO.
  2013. *National Risk Register of Civil Emergencies*. London: HMSO.
Calain, Philippe 2007. 'From the Field Side of the Binoculars: A Different View on Global Public Health Surveillance', *Health Policy and Planning* 22(1): 13–20.
Carothers, Thomas and de Gramont, Diane 2013. *Development Aid Confronts Politics: The Almost Revolution*. Washington, D.C.: Carnegie Endowment for International Peace.
Carpenter, Ted G. 2003. *Bad Neighbour Policy: Washington's Futile War on Drugs in Latin America*. New York: Palgrave Macmillan.
CASE Collective 2006. 'Critical Approaches to Security in Europe: A Networked Manifesto', *Security Dialogue* 37(4): 443–87.
Casson, Anne and Obidzinski, Krystof 2002. 'From New Order to Regional Autonomy: Shifting Dynamics of "Illegal" Logging in Kalimantan, Indonesia', *World Development* 30(12): 2133–51.
Center for Naval Analysis 2007. 'National Security and the Threat of Climate Change', April. Alexandria: Center for Naval Analysis. www.cna.org/sites/default/files/National%20Security%20and%20the%20Threat%20of%20Climate%20Change%20-%20Print.pdf.

Cerny, Philip G. 1997. 'Paradoxes of the Competition State: The Dynamics of Political Globalization', *Government and Opposition* 32(2): 251–74.
    2010. *Rethinking World Politics: A Theory of Transnational Pluralism.* Oxford: Oxford University Press.
Chan, L.H., Lee, P.K. and Chan, G. 2009. 'China Engages Global Health Governance: Processes and Dilemmas', *Global Public Health* 4(1): 1–30.
Chandra, Siddharth 2013. 'Mortality from the Influenza Pandemic of 1918–19 in Indonesia', *Population Studies* 67(2): 185–93.
Charney, Michael W. 2009. *A History of Modern Burma.* Cambridge: Cambridge University Press.
Charnoz, Olivier and Forster, Paul 2011. 'The Global Health Impact of Local Power Relations: Fragmented Governance, Big Business and Organisational Bias in Indonesian Animal Health Policies', LSE Global Governance Working Paper 02/2011. www.lse.ac.uk/globalgovernance/publications/workingpapers/indonesianhealthpolicies.pdf.
Chayes, Abram and Chayes, Antonia Handler 1995. *The New Sovereignty: Compliance with International Regulatory Agreements.* Cambridge and London: Harvard University Press.
Checkel, Jeffrey 1998. 'The Constructivist Turn in International Relations Theory', *World Politics* 50(2): 324–48.
Cheng, Yi-Wen and Ngo, Tak-Wing 2014. 'The Heterodoxy of Governance Under Decentralization: Rent-Seeking Politics in China's Tobacco Growing Areas', *Journal of Contemporary Asia* 44(2): 221–40.
Chorev, Nitsan 2012. *The World Health Organization Between North and South.* Ithaca and London: Cornell University Press.
Christou, George, Croft, Stuart, Ceccorulli, Michela and Lucarelli, Sonia 2010. 'European Union Security Governance: Putting the "Security" Back In', *European Security* 19(3): 341–59.
Ciută, Felix 2009. 'Security and the Problem of Context: A Hermeneutical Critique of Securitisation Theory', *Review of International Studies* 35(2): 301–26.
Clapp, Jenifer and Dauvergne, Peter 2003. 'Environment, Development, and Security in Southeast Asia: Exploring the Linkages', in David B. Dewitt and Carolina G. Hernandez (ed.) *Development and Security in Southeast Asia: The Environment*, 19–32. Aldershot: Ashgate.
Clapton, William 2009. 'Risk and Hierarchy in International Society', *Global Change, Peace, and Security* 21(1): 19–35.
Colás, Alejandro 2008. 'Open Doors and Closed Frontiers: The Limits of American Empire', *European Journal of International Relations* 14(4): 619–43.

Colchester, Marcus, Chao, Sophie, Jiwan, Norman, Andiko, Cinditiara, Intan, Hermawansyah and Kleden, Emilola 2013. 'PT Agrowiratama and the Melayu and Dayak Peoples of Sambas, West Kalimantan', in Marcus Colchester and Sophie Chao (eds.) *Conflict or Consent? The Oil Palm Sector at a Crossroads*, 28–53. Moreton-in-Marsh: Forest Peoples Programme.

Colchester, Marcus, Anderson, Patrick, Firdaus, Asep Yunan, Hasibuan, Fatilda and Chao, Sophie 2011. 'Report of an Independent Investigation into Land Disputes and Forced Evictions in a Palm Oil Estate', November. Forest Peoples Programme. http://www.forestpeoples.org/topics/palm-oil-rspo/publication/2011/human-rights-abuses-and-land-conflicts-pt-asiatic-persada-conc.

Coker, Richard J., Hunter, Benjamin M., Rudge, James W., Liverani, Marco and Hanvoravongchai, Piya 2011. 'Emerging Infectious Diseases in Southeast Asia: Regional Challenges to Control', *The Lancet* 377: 599–609.

Cooper, Robert 2000. *The Postmodern State and the World Order*. London: Demos.

Copeland, Brian 2008. 'The Pollution Haven Hypothesis', in Kevin Gallagher (ed.) *Handbook on Trade and the Environment*, 60–70. Cheltenham: Edward Elgar.

Cox, Robert W. 1981. 'Social Forces, States, and World Orders: Beyond International Relations Theory', *Millennium – Journal of International Studies* 10(2): 126–55.

Cox, Robert W. and Schechter, Michael G. 2002. *Critical Political Economy: New Reflections on Power, Equity, and Order*. Abingdon, Oxon: Routledge.

Cox, Robert W. and Sinclair, Timothy J. (eds.) 1996. *Approaches to World Order*. Cambridge: Cambridge University Press.

Credit Suisse Research Institute 2014. 'Global Wealth Report 2014', October. https://publications.credit-suisse.com/tasks/render/file/?fileID=60931FDE-A2D2-F568-B041B58C5EA591A4.

Crosby, Alfred 1986. *Ecological Imperialism: The Biological Expansion of Europe, 900–1900*. Cambridge: Cambridge University Press.

Crouch, Colin 2011. *The Strange Non-death of Neoliberalism*. Cambridge and Malden: Polity.

Curley, Melissa G. and Herington, Jonathan 2011. 'The Securitisation of Avian Influenza: International Discourses and Domestic Politics in Asia', *Review of International Studies* 37(1): 141–66.

Daase, Christopher and Friesendorf, Cornelius (eds.) 2010. *Rethinking Security Governance: The Problem of Unintended Consequences*. London: Routledge.

Dahl, Robert A. 2003. 'Can International Organizations Be Democratic? A Skeptic's View', in David Held and Andrew McGrew (eds.) *The Global Transformations Reader*, 530–41. Cambridge: Polity.

Dabelko, Geoff 2008. 'An Uncommon Peace: Environment, Development, and the Global Security Agenda', *Environment* 50(3): 32–45.

Dai, Xinyuan 2005. 'Why Comply? The Domestic Constituency Mechanism', *International Organization* 59(2): 363–98.

Dalby, Simon 2009. *Security and Environmental Change*. Cambridge: Polity.

Dale, Roger 2004. 'Forms of Governance, Governmentality, and the EU's Open Method of Coordination', in Wendy Larner and William Walters (eds.) *Global Governmentality: Governing International Spaces*, 174–94. London and New York: Routledge.

Dallinger, Jonas 2011. 'Oil Palm Development in Thailand: Economic, Social and Environmental Considerations', in Marcus Colchester and Sophie Chao (eds.) *Oil Palm Expansion in Southeast Asia: Trends and Implications for Local Communities and Indigenous Peoples*, 24–51. Forest Peoples Programme: Moreton-in-Marsh.

Dauvergne, Peter 1998. 'The Political Economy of Indonesia's 1997 Forest Fires', *Australian Journal of International Affairs* 52(1): 13–17.

Davies, Sara E. 2008. 'Securitizing Infectious Disease', *International Affairs* 84(2): 295–313.

2010. *Global Politics of Health*. Cambridge: Polity Press.

2012. 'The International Politics of Disease Reporting: Towards Post-Westphalianism?', *International Politics* 49(5): 591–613.

Davis, Kevin E., Kingsbury, Benedict and Merry, Sally E. 2012. 'Indicators as a Technology of Global Governance', *Law & Society Review* 46(1): 71–104.

Davis, Mike 2001. *Late Victorian Holocausts: El Niño Famines and the Making of the Third World*. London: Verso.

2005. *The Monster at Our Door: The Global Threat of Avian Flu*. New York: Owl Books.

Dean, Mitchell 1999. *Governmentality: Power and Rule in Modern Society*. London: Sage Publications.

Deere, Carolyn 2009. *The Implementation Game: The TRIPS Agreement and the Global Politics of Intellectual Property Reform in Developing Countries*. New York: Oxford University Press.

Deitelhoff, Nicole 2009. 'The Discursive Process of Legalization: Charting Islands of Persuasion in the ICC Case', *International Organization* 63(1): 33–65.

Delgado, Christopher, Narrod, Clare A. and Tiongco, Marites M. 2003. 'Policy, Technical and Environmental Determinants and Implications of the Scaling Up of Livestock Production in Four Fast-growing

Developing Countries: A Synthesis, Final Research Report of Phase II', 24 July. Rome: Food and Agriculture Organization.

Delima Azahari 2011. Ministerial Advisor for Agricultural Policy, Indonesian Ministry of Agriculture. Interview by Shahar Hameiri, 22 July, Jakarta.

Dennis, Rona 1999. *A Review of Fire Projects in Indonesia (1982–1998)*. Bogor: CIFOR.

Dennis, Rona A., Mayer, Judith, Applegate, Grahame, Chokkalingam, Unna, Pierce Colfer, Carol J., Kurniawan, Iwan, Lachowski, Henry, Maus, Paul, Permana, Rizki Pandu, Ruchiat, Yayat, Stolle, Fred, Suyanto and Tomich, Thomas P. 2005. 'Fire, People and Pixels: Linking Social Science and Remote Sensing to Understand Underlying Causes and Impacts of Fires in Indonesia', *Human Ecology* 33(4): 465–504.

Deudney, Daniel 1990. 'The Case Against Linking Environmental Degradation and National Security', *Millennium* 19: 461–76.

DFID [Department for International Development] 2004. 'African Conflict Prevention Pool: The UK Sub-Saharan Strategy for Conflict Prevention', London: Department for International Development.

DFID Asia Regional Team 2012. 'Operational Plan 2011–2015', June. London: Department for International Development.

DFID Caribbean 2012. 'Operational Plan 2011–2015', June. London: Department for International Development.

Diamond, Jared 2005. *Collapse: How Societies Choose to Fail or Survive*. London: Penguin.

Dingwerth, Klaus 2008. 'Private Transnational Governance and the Developing World: A Comparative Perspective', *International Studies Quarterly* 52(3): 607–34.

DoE [Department of Environment] 2009. 'Malaysia-Indonesia Collaboration in Preventive Measures to Deal with Land and Forest Fires in the Riau Province, Sumatra, Republic of Indonesia 2008–2009', Putrajaya: Department of Environment. http://haze.asean.org/wp-content/uploads/2013/06/ind-mal.pdf.

Dokken, Karin 2001. 'Environment, Security and Regionalism in the Asia-Pacific: is Evironmental Security a Useful Concept?', *Pacific Review* 14(4): 509–30.

Dosch, Jörn 2007. *The Changing Dynamics of Southeast Asian Politics*. Boulder: Lynne Rienner.

Drezner, Daniel W. 2007. *All Politics is Global: Explaining International Regulatory Regimes*. Princeton: Princeton University Press.

Dubash, Navroz K. and Morgan, Bronwen 2012. 'Understanding the Rise of the Regulatory State of the South', *Regulation and Governance* 6(3): 261–81.

Dubash, Navroz K. and Morgan, Bronwen (eds.) 2013. *The Rise of the Regulatory State of the South: Infrastructure and Development in Emerging Economies*. Oxford: Oxford University Press.

Duffield, Mark 2007. *Development, Security, and Unending War: Governing the World of Peoples*. Cambridge: Polity Press.

Dupont, Alan 1999. 'Transnational Crime, Drugs, and Security in East Asia', *Asian Survey* 39(3): 433–55.

  2001. *East Asia Imperilled: Transnational Challenges to Security*. Cambridge: Cambridge University Press.

Dupont, Alan and Pearman, Graeme 2006. *Heating up the Planet: Climate Change and Security*. Double Bay: Lowy Institute.

Durodié, Bill 2011. 'H1N1 – the Social Costs of Cultural Confusion', *Global Health Governance* 4(2): 1–19.

Dwazil Hidja 2011. *Dinas Kelautan Dan Pertanian* (Office of Fisheries and Agriculture), Jakarta Provincial Government. Interview by Shahar Hameiri, 8 September, Jakarta.

Eberlein, Burkard and Grande, Edgar 2005. 'Beyond Delegation: Transnational Regulatory Regimes and the EU Regulatory State', *Journal of European Public Policy* 12(1): 89–112.

Eckersley, Robin 2007. 'Ecological Intervention: Prospects and Limits', *Ethics and International Affairs* 21(3): 293–316.

Economy Watch 2013. 'Myanmar (Burma) Economic Statistics and Indicators', 6 May. www.economywatch.com/economic-statistics/country/Myanmar.

Ehrhart, Hans-Georg, Hegemann, Hendrik and Kahl, Martin 2014a. 'Editorial: Putting Security Governance to the Test: Conceptual, Empirical, and Normative Challenges', *European Security* 23(2): 119–25.

  2014b. 'Towards Security Governance as a Critical Tool: A Conceptual Outline', *European Security* 23(2): 145–62.

Elbe, Stefan 2006. 'Should HIV/AIDS Be Securitized? The Ethical Dilemmas of Linking HIV/AIDS and Security', *International Studies Quarterly* 50(1): 119–44.

  2008. 'Our Epidemiological Footprint: The Circulation of Avian Flu, SARS, and HIV/AIDS in the World Economy', *Review of International Political Economy* 15(1): 116–30.

  2009. *Virus Alert: Security, Governmentality and the AIDS Pandemic*. New York: Columbia University Press.

  2010a. *Security and Global Health: Towards the Medicalization of Insecurity*. Cambridge: Polity Press.

  2010b. 'Haggling Over Viruses: The Downside Risks of Securitizing Infectious Disease', *Health Policy and Planning* 25(6): 476–85.

Elliot, Lorraine 2007. 'Transnational Environmental Crime in the Asia Pacific: An Un(der)-Securitised Security Problem?', *The Pacific Review* 20(4): 499–522.

Ellis, Eric 2013. 'Out of the Haze, a Singaporean Spring?', *The Global Mail*, 25 June.

Emil Agustiono 2011. Deputy Minister Coordinator in Health, Population and Family Planning, Indonesian Government Coordinating Ministry for People's Welfare. Interview by Shahar Hameiri, 20 July, Jakarta.

Enemark, Christian 2009. 'Is Pandemic Flu a Security Threat?', *Survival* 51(1): 191–214.

2010. 'The role of the Biological Weapons Convention in Disease Surveillance and Response', *Health Policy and Planning* 25(6): 486–94.

Eriksson, Johan and Rhinard, Mark 2009. 'The Internal-External Security Nexus: Notes on an Emerging Research Agenda', *Cooperation and Conflict* 44(3): 243–67.

Esty, Daniel C. 1999. 'Pivotal States and the Environment', in Robert Chase, Emily Hill and Paul Kennedy (eds.) *Pivotal States: A New Framework for US Policy in the Developing World*, 290–314. New York: Norton.

EU [European Union] 2003. 'A Secure Europe in a Better World: European Security Strategy', 12 December. Paris: The European Union Institute for Security Studies. www.consilium.europa.eu/uedocs/cmsUpload/78367.pdf.

2006. 'Avian Influenza: Expectations Surpassed as International Community Pledges USD 1.9 bn in Beijing', *Europa Press Releases*, 18 January. http://europa.eu/rapid/press-release_IP-06-49_en.htm.

European Commission 2003. *Forest Law Enforcement, Governance and Trade (FLEGT): Proposal for an EU Action Plan*. Brussels: EU Commission. http://eur-lex.europa.eu/legal-content/EN/TXT/?uri=CELEX:52003DC0251.

2010a. 'The EU Internal Security Strategy in Action: Five Steps Towards a More Secure Europe', 22 November. Brussels: European Commission, Directorate General for Home Affairs. http://europa.eu/rapid/press-release_MEMO-10-598_en.htm?locale=en.

2010b. 'Statistical Annex of European Economy', Spring. Brussels: European Commission, Directorate General Economic and Financial Affairs. http://ec.europa.eu/economy_finance/publications/european_economy/2010/pdf/statistical_annex_spring2010_en.pdf.

Ewing, J. Jackson 2014. 'Cutting Through the Haze: Will Singapore's New Legislation Be Effective?', *RSIS Commentary* 166, 19 August. www.rsis.edu.sg/wp-content/uploads/2014/08/CO14166.pdf.

FAO, OIE, WHO, UN System Influenza Coordination, Unicef, and World Bank 2008. 'Contributing to One World, One Health: A Strategic

Framework Fore Reducing Risks of Infectious Diseases at the Animal-Human-Ecosystems Interface', United Nations, 14 October.

FATF [Financial Action Task Force] 2008. 'APG Mutual Evaluation Report on Myanmar Against the FATF 40 Recommendations (2003) and 9 Special Recommendations', 10 July. Paris: Financial Action Task Force. www.fatf-gafi.org/media/fatf/documents/recommendations/pdfs/FATF_Recommendations.pdf.

2012. 'International Standards on Combating Money Laundering and the Financing of Terrorism & Proliferation – the FATF Recommendations', 16 February. Paris: FATF. www.fatf-gafi.org/topics/fatfrecom mendations/documents/internationalstandardsoncombatingmoney launderingandthefinancingofterrorismproliferation-thefatfrecommen dations.html.

Federal Reserve Bank of St. Louis 2013. 'Graph: Compensation of Employees: Wages & Salary Accruals (WASCUR)/Gross Domestic Product', Economic Research. St Louis: FRED. http://research.stlouisfed.org/fred2/graph/?g=2Xa.

Ferraro, Gianluca 2014. *International Regimes in China: Domestic Implementation of the International Fisheries Agreement*. London: Routledge.

Fidler, David P. 2003a. 'SARS: Political Pathology of the First Post-Westphalian Pathogen', *Journal of Law, Medicine, and Ethics* 31(4): 485–505.

2003b. 'Public Health and National Security in the Global Age: Infectious Diseases, Bioterrorism, and Realpolitik', *George Washington International Law Review* 35(4): 787–856.

2005. 'From International Sanitary Conventions to Global Health Security: The New International Health Regulations', *Chinese Journal of International Law* 4(2): 325–92.

2007. 'Architecture Amidst Anarchy: Global Health Governance's Quest for Governance', *Global Health Governance* 1(1): 1–17.

Finley-Brook, Mary 2007. 'Green Neoliberal Space: The Mesoamerican Biological Corridor', *Journal of Latin American Geography* 6(1): 101–24.

Finnemore, Martha and Sikkink, Kathryn 1998. 'International Norm Dynamics and Political Change', *International Organization* 52(4): 887–917.

Firth, Stewart 2008. 'The New Regionalism and Its Contradictions', in Greg Fry and Tarcisius Tara Kabutaulaka (eds.) *Intervention and State-Building in the Pacific: The Political Legitimacy of 'Cooperative Intervention'*, 119–34. Manchester: Manchester University Press.

Florini, Ann 1996. 'The Evolution of International Norms', *International Studies Quarterly* 40(3): 363–89.

FoE [Friends of the Earth] 2008. 'Malaysian Palm Oil: Green Gold or Green Wash? A Commentary on the Sustainability Claims of Malaysia's Palm Oil Lobby, with a Special Focus on the State of Sarawak', Executive Summary, October. Amsterdam: Friends of the Earth. https://milieu defensie.nl/publicaties/rapporten/malaysian-palm-oil-green-gold-or-green-wash-summary.

Foo, Alvin 2013. 'Sime Darby, KLK units Among Firms Blamed for Fires', *Straits Times*, 26 June.

Forster, Paul 2010. 'On a Wing and a Prayer: Avian Influenza in Indonesia', in Ian Scoones (ed.) *Avian Influenza: Science, Policy and Politics*, 131–68. London: Earthscan.

Forster, Paul and Charnoz, Olivier 2013. 'Producing Knowledge in Times of Health Crises: Insights from the International Response to Avian Influenza in Indonesia', *Revue D'anthropologie des Connaissances* 7(1): w-az.

Furedi, Frank 2005. *Politics of Fear: Beyond Left and Right*. London: Continuum.

G8 [Group of 8] 1999. 'Communiqué', Ministerial Conference of the G-8 Countries on Combating Transnational Organized Crime, 20 October. Moscow. www.justice.gov/ag/events/g82004/99MoscowCommunique.pdf.

Garrett, Jemima 2011. 'Foreign Land-Grab Leaves Ni-Vanuatu Out in Cold: Gated Communities, Blocked Beaches, Fallow Farmlands', Pacific Islands Report, 9 February. Radio Australia. http://archives.pireport.org/archive/2011/February/02-10-02.htm.

Garrett, Laurie 1995. *The Coming Plague: Newly Emerging Diseases in a World Out of Balance*. London: Penguin.

Gehring, Thomas 1994. *Dynamic International Regimes: Institutions for International Environmental Governance*. Frankfurt: Peter Lang.

Geopolitical Drug Watch 1997. 'Burma', 1 September. Lebanon: Voltaire Network International. www.voltairenet.org/Birmanie,7421.

German Advisory Council on Global Change 2008. *World in Transition: Climate Change as a Security Risk*. London: Earthscan.

Gibson, Edward L. 2012. *Boundary Control: Subnational Authoritarianism in Federal Democracies*. Cambridge: Cambridge University Press.

Giddens, Anthony 1991. *Modernity and Self-Identity: Self and Society in the Late Modern Age*. Stanford: Stanford University Press.

1994. *Beyond Left and Right: The Future of Radical Politics*. Stanford: Stanford University Press.

Gilbertson, Tamra and Reyes, Oscar 2009. *Carbon Trading: How it Works and Why it Fails*. Uppsala: Dag Hammerskjöld Foundation.

Gill, Stephen 1992. 'Economic Globalization and the Internationalization of Authority: Limits and Contradictions', *Geoforum* 23(3): 269–83.

1995. 'Globalisation, Market Civilisation, and Disciplinary Neoliberalism', *Millennium: Journal of International Studies* 24(3): 399–423.

2002. 'Constitutionalizing Inequality and the Clash of Globalizations', *International Studies Review* 4(2): 47–65.

2008. *Power and Resistance in the New World Order*, 2nd edn. Basingstoke and New York: Palgrave Macmillan.

Gill, Stephen and Bakker, Isabella (eds.) 2003. *Power, Production, and Social Reproduction: Human In/security in the Global Political Economy*. Basingstoke and New York: Palgrave Macmillan.

Gill, Stephen and Cutler, A. Claire (eds.) 2014a. *New Constitutionalism and World Order*. Cambridge: Cambridge University Press.

2014b. 'New Constitutionalism and World Order: General Introduction', in *New Constitutionalism and World Order*, 1–21. Cambridge: Cambridge University Press.

Gilmore, William 1995. *Dirty Money: The Evolution of Money Laundering Counter-Measures*. Strasbourg: Council of Europe.

Gough, Jamie 2004. 'Changing Scale as Changing Class Relations: Variety and Contradiction in the Politics of Scale', *Political Geography* 23(2): 185–211.

Greenpeace 2008. *Burning up Borneo*. Amsterdam: Greenpeace.

Grindle, Merilee S. (ed.) 1980. *Politics and Policy Implementation in the Third World*. Princeton: Princeton University Press.

Grindle, Merilee S. 2007. *Going Local: Decentralization, Democratization, and the Promise of Good Governance*. Princeton: Princeton University Press.

Guyon, Anne and Simorangkir, Dicky 2002. 'The Economics of Fire Use in Agriculture and Forestry – a Preliminary Review for Indonesia,' Project FireFight South East Asia. Jakarta: IUCN. http://cmsdata.iucn.org/downloads/ff_economic_indonesia.pdf.

Haacke, Jurgen and Williams, Paul D. 2008. 'Regional Arrangements, Securitization, and Transnational Security Challenges: The African Union and the Association of Southeast Asian Nations Compared', *Security Studies* 17(4): 775–809.

Haas, Peter M. 1989. 'Do Regimes Matter? Epistemic Communities and the Mediterranean Pollution Control', *International Organization* 43(3): 377–403.

1992. 'Introduction: Epistemic Communities and International Policy Coordination', *International Organization* 46(1): 1–35.

Hadiz, Vedi R. 2004. 'Decentralisation and Democracy in Indonesia: A Critique of Neo-institutionalist Perspectives', *Development and Change* 35(4): 697–718.

2010. *Localising Power in Post-Authoritarian Indonesia: A Southeast Asia Perspective*. Stanford: Stanford University Press.

Hall, Rodney Bruce and Biersteker, Thomas J. (eds.) 2002. 'The Emergence of Private Authority in the International System', in *The Emergence of Private Authority in Global Governance*, 3–22. Cambridge: Cambridge University Press.

Hameiri, Shahar 2009a. 'The Region Within: RAMSI, the Pacific Plan, and New Modes of Governance in the Southwest Pacific', *Australian Journal of International Affairs* 63(3): 348–60.

2009b. 'Governing Disorder: The Australian Federal Police and Australia's New Regional Frontier', *The Pacific Review* 22(5): 549–74.

2010. *Regulating Statehood: State Building and the Transformation of the Global Order*. Basingstoke: Palgrave Macmillan.

2013. 'Theorising Regions Through Changes in Statehood: Rethinking the Theory and Method of Comparative Regionalism', *Review of International Studies* 39(2): 313–35.

2014. 'Avian Influenza, "Viral Sovereignty", and the Politics of Health Security in Indonesia', *Pacific Review* 27(3): 333–56.

Hameiri, Shahar and Jayasuriya, Kanishka 2011. 'Regulatory Regionalism and the Dynamics of Territorial Politics: The Case of the Asia-Pacific Region', *Political Studies* 59(1): 20–37.

Handoyo, Dri 2011. Head of Forest Protection, Tanjung Jabung Barat District. Interview by Lee Jones, 17 December, Jambi.

Hanrieder, Tine 2011. 'The False Promise of the Better Argument', *International Theory* 3(3): 390–415.

Hansen, Hans Krause 2011. 'Corruption and Risks: Managing Corruption Risks', *Review of International Political Economy* 18(2): 251–75.

Hansen, Hans Krause and Salskov-Iversen, Dorte (eds.) 2008. *Critical Perspectives on Private Authority in Global Politics*. Basingstoke: Palgrave Macmillan.

Hanson, Fergus 2012. *Shattering Stereotypes: Public Opinion and Foreign Policy*. Sydney: Lowy Institute for International Policy.

Harahap, Rizal 2013. 'Malaysian Companies Burning Land: Ministry', *Jakarta Post*, 23 June. www.thejakartapost.com/news/2013/06/23/malaysian-companies-burning-land-ministry.html.

Harman, Sophie and Williams, David (eds.) 2013. *Governing the World? Cases in Global Governance*. Abingdon and New York: Routledge.

Harrabin, Roger 2013. 'Margaret Thatcher: How PM Legitimised Green Concerns', BBC News, 8 April. www.bbc.co.uk/news/science-environment-22069768.

Harris, Kate 2012. *Climate Change in UK Security Policy: Implications for Development Assistance?* London: Overseas Development Institute.

Harrison, Graham 2004. *The World Bank and Africa: The Construction of Governance States*. New York and London: Routledge.

2007. 'Debt, Development, and Intervention in Africa: The Contours of a Sovereign Frontier', *Journal of Intervention and Statebuilding* 1(2): 189–209.

Harsono, Dina J.E. 2011. 'Analysis on Indonesian Sustainable Palm Oil (ISPO): A Qualitative Assessment on the Success Factors for ISPO', MA thesis, Bogor Agricultural University.

Hartati, Desuna, Asropi and Nulaksana 2011. Technical Officers, Jambi Province Environmental Agency. Interview by Lee Jones, 16 December, Jambi.

Hartmann, Betsy 2013. 'Climate Chains: Neo-Malthusianism, Militarism and Migration', in Chris Methmann, Delf Rothe and Benjamin Stephan (eds.) *Interpretive Approaches to Global Governance: (De)constructing the Greenhouse*, 91–104. Abingdon: Routledge.

Hartono 2011. President of Pinsar Unggas Nasional. Interview by Shahar Hameiri, 20 July, Jakarta.

Harvey, David 2005. *A Brief History of Neoliberalism*. Oxford: Oxford University Press.

(1982) 2006. *The Limits to Capital*. London: Verso.

2010. *The Enigma of Capital and the Crisis of Capitalism*. Oxford: Oxford University Press.

Hasyim, M. Zainuri 2011. Director, Yayasan Mitra Insani (local environmental NGO); coordinator, Telapak in Riau. Interview by Lee Jones, 10 December, Pekanbaru.

Hay, Colin 1996. *Re-stating Social and Political Change*. Buckingham: Open University Press.

Heartfield, James 2008. *Green Capitalism: Manufacturing Scarcity in an Age of Abundance*. London: Lulu.

Held, David and Young, Kevin 2013. 'Global Governance in Crisis? Fragmentation, Risk and World Order', *International Politics* 50(3): 309–32.

Heng, Yee-Kuang and McDonagh, Ken 2008. 'The Other War on Terror Revealed: Global Governmentality and the Financial Action Task Force's Campaign Against Terrorist Financing', *Review of International Studies* 34(4): 553–73.

Henry, James S. 2012. 'The Price of the Offshore Revisited: New Estimates for "Missing" Global Private Wealth, Income, Inequality, and Lost Taxes', July. Tax Justice Network. www.taxjustice.net/cms/upload/pdf/Price_of_Offshore_Revisited_26072012.pdf.

Heru Setjanto 2011. Vice President of the Indonesian Veterinary Medicine Association. Interview by Shahar Hameiri, 7 September, Bogor, West Java.

Hettne, Bjorn 2010. 'Development and Security: Origins and Future', *Security Dialogue* 41(1): 41–52.

Hewison, Kevin, Rodan, Garry and Robison, Richard (eds.) 1993. 'Introduction: Changing Forms of State Power in Southeast Asia', in *Southeast Asia in the 1990s: Authoritarianism, Democracy, and Capitalism*, 2–8. Sydney: Allen and Unwin.

HHS [US Department of Health and Human Services] 2005. 'Pandemic Influenza Plan,' November. Washington, D.C.: US Department of Health and Human Services. www.flu.gov/planning-preparedness/federal/hhspandemicinfluenzaplan.pdf.

Hidayat, Noor 2011. Director of Forest Fire Control, Ministry of Forestry, Indonesia. Interview by Lee Jones, 21 December, Jakarta.

High Level Panel 2004. 'A More Secure World: Our Shared Responsibility', Report of the Secretary-General's High Level Panel on Threats, Challenges and Change, 2 December. New York: United Nations. http://www1.umn.edu/humanrts/instree/report.pdf.

Hobsbawm, Eric J. 1962. *The Age of Revolution: Europe 1789–1848*. New York: Praeger.

   1975. *The Age of Capital: 1848–1975*. London: Weidenfeld and Nicolson.

   1987. *The Age of Empire: 1875–1914*. London: Abacus.

Hoffmann, Matthew J. 2005. 'What's Global About Global Governance? A Constructivist Account', in Alice Ba and Matthew J. Hoffmann (eds.) *Contending Perspectives on Global Governance: Coherence, Contestation, and World Order*, 110–28. London and New York: Routledge.

Holbrooke, Richard and Garrett, Laurie 2008. '"Sovereignty" that Risks Global Health', *Washington Post*, 10 August.

Holst, Johan Jørgen 1989. 'Security and the Environment: A Preliminary Exploration', *Bulletin of Peace Proposals* 20(2): 123–8.

Homer-Dixon, Thomas F. 1991. 'On the Threshold: Environmental Changes as Causes of Acute Conflict', *International Security* 16(2): 76–116.

Hönke, Jana 2013. *Transnational Companies and Security Governance: Hybrid Practices in a Postcolonial World*. London: Routledge.

Hooghe, Liesbet and Marks, Gary 2003. 'Unraveling the Central State, but How? Types of Multi-Level Governance', *American Political Science Review* 97(2): 233–43.

Hughes, Caroline and Hutchison, Jane 2012. 'Development Effectiveness and the Politics of Commitment', *Third World Quarterly* 33(1): 17–36.

Hülsse, Rainer 2007. 'Creating Demand for Global Governance: The Making of a Global Money Laundering Problem', *Global Society* 21(2): 155–78.

Humphreys, Jasper and Smith, M.L.R. 2014. 'The "Rhinofication" of South African Security', *International Affairs* 90(4): 795–818.

Hutchison, Jane, Hout, Wil, Hughes, Caroline and Robison, Richard 2014. *Political Economy and the Aid Industry in Asia*. Basingstoke: Palgrave Macmillan.

Hyde-Price, Adrian 2006. '"Normative" Power Europe: A Realist Critique', *Journal of European Public Policy* 13(2): 217–34.

ICFTU [International Confederation of Free Trade Unions] 2005. 'Doing Business In or With Burma', ICFTU Report, January. Brussels: ICFTU. www.ibiblio.org/obl/docs3/Doing_Business_in_or_with_Burma.pdf.

ICG [International Crisis Group] 2001. *Indonesia: Natural Resources and Law Enforcement*. Brussels: ICG.

Ignatius, David 2014. 'Can the US Help Africa Avoid Going the Way of the Middle East?', *Washington Post*, 7 August.

IIGCC [Institutional Investors Group on Climate Change], Investor Network on Climate Risk, Investor Group on Climate Change and UNEP Finance Initiative 2009. '2009 Investor Statement on the Urgent Need for a Global Agreement on Climate Change', www.unepfi.org/fileadmin/documents/need_agreement.pdf.

IMF [International Monetary Fund] 2003. 'Vanuatu: Assessment of the Supervision and Regulation of the Financial Sector Volume I – Review of Financial Sector Regulation and Supervision', IMF Country Report no. 03/253, August. Washington, D.C.: IMF.

    2011. *Anti-Money Laundering and Combating the Financing of Terrorism (AML-CFT): Report on the Review of the Effectiveness of the Program*. Washington, D.C.: IMF.

Indrarto, G.B., Murharjanti, P., Khatarina, J., Pulungan, I., Ivalerina, F., Rahman, J., Prana, M.N., Resosudarmo, I.A.P. and Muharrom, E. 2012. 'The Context of REDD+ in Indonesia: Drivers, agents and institutions,' Working Paper No. 92. Bogor: Center for International Forestry Research.

Indriyono Tantoro 2011. Special Advisor to the Minister of Health for Acceleration of Health Development and Bureaucratic Reform, Indonesian Ministry of Health. Interview by Shahar Hameiri, 7 September, Jakarta.

Jackson, Robert H. 1990. *Quasi-states: Sovereignty, International Relations, and the Third World*. Cambridge: Cambridge University Press.

Jaeger, Hans-Martin 2007. '"Global Civil Society" and the Political Depoliticization of Global Governance', *International Political Sociology* 1(3): 257–77.

    2010. 'UN Reform, Biopolitics, and Global Governmentality', *International Theory* 2(1): 50–86.

Jagan, Larry 2006. 'Burma's Military: Purges and Coups Prevent Progress Towards Democracy', in Trevor Wilson (ed.) *Myanmar's Long Road to National Reconciliation*, 29–37. Singapore: ISEAS.

Jahn, Egbert, Lemaitre, Pierre and Wæver, Ole 1987. 'European Security: Problems of Research on Non-military Aspects,' Working Paper No. 1. Copenhagen: Center for Peace and Conflict Research.

Jasparro, C. and Taylor, J. 2008. 'Climate Change and Regional Vulnerability to Transnational Security Threats in Southeast Asia', *Geopolitics* 13(2): 232–56.

Jayasuriya, Kanishka 2001. 'Globalization and the Changing Architecture of the State: The Regulatory State and the Politics of Negative Co-ordination', *Journal of European Public Policy* 8(1): 101–23.

   2005. 'Beyond Institutional Fetishism: From the Developmental to the Regulatory State', *New Political Economy* 10(3): 381–7.

   2006. *Statecraft, Welfare, and the Politics of Inclusion.* Houndmills: Palgrave Macmillan.

   2009. 'Regulatory Regionalism in the Asia-Pacific: Drivers, Instruments, and Actors', *Australian Journal of International Affairs* 63(3): 335–47.

Jayasuriya, Kanishka and Rodan, Garry 2007. 'Beyond Hybrid Regimes: More Participation, Less Contestation in Southeast Asia', *Democratization*, 14(5): 773–94.

Jessop, Bob 1990. *State Theory: Putting the Capitalist State in its Place.* Cambridge: Polity Press.

   1993. 'Towards a Schumpeterian Workfare State? Preliminary Remarks on Post-Fordist Political Economy', *Studies in Political Economy* 40: 7–40.

   2002. *The Future of the Capitalist State.* Cambridge: Polity Press.

   2008. *State Power.* Cambridge: Polity Press.

   2009. 'Avoiding Traps, Rescaling States, Governing Europe', in Roger Keil and Rianne Mahon (eds.) *Leviathan Undone? Towards a Political Economy of Scale*, 87–104. Vancouver: University of British Columbia Press.

Jikalahari 2008. 'Kejahatan Kehutan [Forestry Crimes]', May 2. http://jikalahari.or.id/index.php?option=com_docman&task=doc_download&gid=4&Itemid=139&lang=en.

   2009. 'Analisa Tata Kelola Kehutanan di Provinsi Riau [Analysis of Forestry Governance in Riau Province]', 18 May. http://jikalahari .or.id/index.php?option=com_docman&task=doc_download&gid=6& Itemid=139&lang=en.

   2010. 'Community-Based Fire Prevention in Rokan Hilir, Riau Province', Presented at the Technical Workshop on the Development of the ASEAN Peatland Fire Prediction and Warning System, 13–14 July. Kuala Lumpur.

Jiwan, Norman 2013. 'The Political Ecology of the Indonesian Palm Oil Industry: A Critical Analysis', in Oliver Pye and Jayati Battacharya (eds.) *The Palm Oil Controversy in Southeast Asia: A Transnational Perspective*, 48–75. Singapore: ISEAS.

Joes, Berton 2012. Training Manager, National Bank of Vanuatu. Interview by Shahar Hameiri, 22 November, Port Vila.

Joffé, George 2007. 'The European Union, Democracy and Counter-Terrorism in the Maghreb', *Journal of Common Market Studies* 46(1): 147–71.

Jones, David S. 2006. 'ASEAN and Transboundary Haze Pollution in South-east Asia', *Asia Europe Journal* 4(3): 431–46.

Jones, Lee 2011. 'Beyond Securitization: Explaining the Scope of Security Policy in Southeast Asia', *International Relations of the Asia-Pacific*, 11(3): 403–32.

2012. *ASEAN, Sovereignty, and Intervention in Southeast Asia*. Basingstoke: Palgrave Macmillan.

2013. 'Sovereignty and Intervention in Revolutionary Times', *Review of International Studies* 39(5): 1149–67.

2014a. 'Explaining Myanmar's Democratisation: The Periphery is Central', *Democratization* 21(5): 780–802.

2014b. 'The Political Economy of Myanmar's Transition', *Journal of Contemporary Asia* 44(1): 144–70.

Joseph, Jonathan 2010. 'The Limits of Governmentality: Social Theory and the International', *European Journal of International Relations* 16(2): 223–46.

Joyce, Brian P. 2002. 'Dynamics and Deficiencies of Anti-Money Laundering Efforts in Myanmar', *Journal of Money Laundering Control* 6(1): 80–84.

Jung, Dietrich 2003. *Shadow Globalization, Ethnic Conflicts and New Wars: A Political Economy of Intra-State War*. London: Routledge.

Kahl, Colin 2006. *States, Scarcity and Civil Strife in the Developing World*. Princeton: Princeton University Press.

Kahler, Miles and Lake, David A. 2009. 'Economic Integration and Global Governance: Why So Little Supranationalism?', in Walter Mattli and Ngaire Woods (eds.) *The Politics of Global Regulation*, 242–75. Princeton: Princeton University Press.

Kaldor, Mary 2007. *New and Old Wars: Organized Violence in a Global Era*, 2nd edn. Stanford: Stanford University Press.

Kamradt-Scott, Adam 2011. 'The Evolving WHO: Implications for Global Health Security', *Global Public Health* 6(8): 801–13.

Kaplan, Robert D. 1994. 'The Coming Anarchy', *Atlantic Monthly* 273(2): 44–76.

Kazmin, Amy 2005. 'Burma's Junta Seizes Privately Owned Bank', *Financial Times*, 8 August. www.ft.com/cms/s/0/73e1cb22–081f–11da-97a6–00000e2511c8.html#axzz2b4jTGTPe.

Keating, Michael 2008. 'Thirty Years of Territorial Politics', *West European Politics* 31(1–2): 60–81.

    2009. 'Rescaling Europe', *Perspectives on European Politics and Society* 10(1): 34–50.

Keck, Margaret E. and Sikkink, Kathryn 1998. *Activists Beyond Borders: Advocacy Networks in International Politics*. Ithaca: Cornell University Press.

Kelle, Alexander 2007. 'Securitization of International Public Health: Implications for Global Health Governance and the Biological Weapons Prohibition Regime', *Global Governance* 13(2): 217–35.

Kennedy, David 2005. 'Challenging Expert Rule: The Politics of Global Governance', *Sydney Law Review* 27(5): 5–28.

Keohane, Robert O. and Martin, Lisa L. 1995. 'The Promise of Institutionalist Theory', *International Security* 20(1): 39–51.

Keohane, Robert O. and Nye, Joseph S. 1977. *Power and Interdependence: World Politics in Transition*. Boston: Little, Brown and Co.

Keyuan, Zou 2004. 'Transnational Cooperation for Managing the Control of Environmental Disputes in East Asia', *Journal of Environmental Law* 16 (3): 341–60.

Kirchner, Emil J. 2007. 'Regional and Global Security: Changing Threats and Institutional Responses', in Emil J. Kirchner and James Sperling (eds.) *Global Security Governance: Competing Perceptions of Security in the 21st Century*, 3–22. Abingdon and New York: Routledge.

Kirchner, Emil J. and Domínguez, Roberto R. (eds.) 2011a. *The Security Governance of Regional Organizations*. Abingdon: Routledge.

    2011b. 'Regional Organizations and Security Governance', in *The Security Governance of Regional Organizations*, 1–21. Abingdon: Routledge.

Kirchner, Emil J. and Sperling, James (eds.) 2010. *National Security Cultures: Patterns of Global Governance*. London: Routledge.

Koh, Lian Pin, Miettinen, Jukka, Liew, Soo Chin and Ghazoul, Jaboury 2011. 'Remotely Sensed Evidence of Tropical Peatland Conversion to Oil Palm', *Proceedings of the National Academy of Sciences of the United States of America* 108(12): 5127–32.

Krahmann, Elke 2003. 'Conceptualizing Security Governance', *Cooperation and Conflict* 38(1): 5–26.

Krasner, Stephen D. 2004. 'Sharing Sovereignty: Institutions for Collapsed and Failing States', *International Security* 29(2): 85–120.

Kurniawan, Diki 2011. Advocacy Program Manager, Warsi Jambi. Interview by Lee Jones, 17 December, Jambi.

Labay, Fadrizal 2011. Head of Riau Province Environmental Agency. Interview by Lee Jones, 9 December, Pekanbaru.

Lakoff, Andrew 2010. 'Two Regimes of Global Health', *Humanity* 1(1): 59–79.

Lakoff, Andrew and Collier, Stephen J. (eds.) 2008. *Biosecurity Interventions: Global Health and Security in Question*. New York: Columbia University Press.

Larmour, Peter 2007. 'Evaluating International Action Against Corruption in the Pacific Islands', State, Society, and Governance in Melanesia Series – Discussion Paper 2007/1. Canberra: Australian National University, Research School of Pacific and Asian Studies. https://digital collections.anu.edu.au/bitstream/1885/10109/1/Larmour_Evaluating International2007.pdf.

Larner, Wendy and Le Heron, Richard 2002. 'The Spaces and Subjects of a Globalising Economy: A Situated Exploration of Method', *Environment and Planning D: Society and Space* 20(6): 753–74.

Larner, Wendy and Walters, William 2004a. 'Globalization as Governmentality', *Alternatives: Global, Local, Political* 29(5): 495–514.

Larner, Wendy and Walters, William (eds.) 2004b. 'Introduction: Global Governmentality: Governing International Spaces', in *Global Governmentality: Governing International Spaces*, 1–20. London and New York: Routledge.

Lawson, Sam 2011. Environmental Investigation Agency campaigner. Interview by Lee Jones, 3 November, London.

Lean, Geoffrey 2005. 'Bird Flu "as Grave a Threat as Terrorism"', The Independent, 26 June. http://www.independent.co.uk/environment/bird-flu-as-grave-a-threat-as-terrorism-6143851.html.

LeBillon, Philippe 2005. *Fuelling War: Natural Resources and Armed Conflict*. Oxford: Routledge.

Leboeuf, Aline 2009. 'The Global Fight Against Avian Influenza Lessons for the Global Management of Health and Environmental Risks and Crises', Health and Environment Reports No. 2, February. Paris: Institut Françes des Relations Internationales.

Lee, Desmond 2011. Research Fellow, Department of Civil Engineering, National University of Singapore. Interview by Lee Jones, 28 November, Singapore.

Leitner, Helga and Sheppard, Eric 2009. 'The Spatiality of Contentious Politics: More than a Politics of Scale', in Roger Keil and Rianne Mahon (eds.) *Leviathan Undone? Towards a Political Economy of Scale*, 231–46. Vancouver: University of British Columbia Press.

Leonard, David W. (ed.) 2009. 'Piecing it Together: Post-conflict Security in an Africa of Networked, Multilevel Governance', *IDS Bulletin* (special issue) 44(1): iii–x, 1–99.

Levy, David L. and Newell, Peter J. (eds.) 2005. *The Business of Global Environmental Governance*. Cambridge: Massachusetts Institute of Technology Press.

Levy, Marc 1995. 'Is the Environment a National Security Issue?', *International Security* 20: 35–62.

Li, Tania Murray 2007. *The Will to Improve: Governmentality, Development, and the Practice of Politics*. Durham: Duke University Press.

Libicki, Martin C. 2001. 'Global Networks and Security: How Dark is the Dark Side?', in Richard L. Kugler and Ellen L. Frost (eds.) *The Global Century: Globalization and National Security*, 809–24. Washington, D.C.: National Defense University Press.

Lillie, Nathan A. 2010. 'Bringing the Offshore Ashore: Transnational Production, Industrial Relations, and the Reconfiguration of Sovereignty', *International Studies Quarterly* 54(3): 683–704.

Linos, Katerina 2007. 'How Can International Organizations Shape National Welfare States?: Evidence From Compliance With European Union Directives', *Comparative Political Studies* 40(5): 547–70.

Lintner, Bertil 1998. 'Drugs and Economic Growth: Ethnicity and Exports', in Robert I. Rotberg (ed.) *Burma: Prospects for a Democratic Future*, 165–83. Washington, D.C.: Brooking Institution Press.

Lipschutz, Ronnie D. with Rowe, James K. 2005. *Globalization, Governmentality, and Global Politics*. Abingdon, Oxon: Routledge.

Liss, Carolin (ed.) 2013. New Actors and Maritime Security Governance in Southeast Asia, *Contemporary Southeast Asia* (special issue) 35(2): 141–283.

Lohmann, Larry 2013. 'Interpretive Openness and Climate Action in an Age of Market Environmentalism', in Chris Methmann, Delf Rothe and Benjamin Stephan (eds.) *Interpretive Approaches to Global Governance: (De)constructing the Greenhouse*, 72–87. Abingdon: Routledge.

López, Alexander 2010. 'Environmental Transborder Cooperation in Latin America: Challenges to the Westphalian Order', in Richard Matthew, Jon Barnett, Bryan McDonald and Karen L. O' Brien (eds.) *Global Environmental Change and Human Security*, 291–304. Cambridge: Massachusetts Institute of Technology Press.

Lowe, Celia 2010. 'Preparing Indonesia: H5N1 Influenza Through the Lens of Global Health', *Indonesia* 90(1): 47–70.

Löwenheim, Oded 2008. 'Examining the State: A Foucauldian Perspective on International "Governance Indicators"', *Third World Quarterly* 29(2): 255–74.

Lunstrum, Elizabeth 2013. 'Articulated Sovereignty: Extending Mozambican State Power Through the Great Limpopo Transfrontier Park', *Political Geography* 36: 1–11.

Luttrell, Cecilia, Obidzinski, Krystof, Brockhaus, Maria, Muharrom, Efrian, Petkova, Elena, Wardell, Andrew and Halperin, James 2011. 'Lessons for REDD+ from Measures to Control Illegal Logging in Indonesia', CIFOR Working Paper No. 74. Bogor: CIFOR.

Mabey, Nick 2008. 'Delivering Climate Security: International Security Responses to a Climate Changed World – Edited Summary', April. London: E3G. www.e3g.org/docs/E3G_Delivering_Climate_Security_-Edited_Summary.pdf.

Macdonald, Roy 2012. 'Leading the Race to Minimal Bureaucracy', *Offshore Investment* 226(May): 30–31.

Magrath, William B. 2010. 'Assessing and Benchmarking National FLEG Systems', in Michael J. Pescott, Patrick B. Durst and Robin N. Leslie (eds.) *Forest Law Enforcement and Governance: Progress in Asia and the Pacific*, 17–40. Bangkok: FAO.

Mahon, Rianne and Keil, Roger (eds.) 2009. 'Introduction', in *Leviathan Undone? Towards a Political Economy of Scale*, 3–23. Vancouver: University of British Columbia Press.

Mahyuddin, Afdhal 2011. External Communications Director, WWF Indonesia-Riau. Interview by Lee Jones, 8 December, Pekanbaru.

Maier-Knapp, Naila 2011. 'Regional and Interregional Integrative Dynamics of ASEAN and EU in Response to the Avian Influenza', *Asia Europe Journal* 8(4): 541–54.

Majone, Giandomenico 1994. 'The Rise of the Regulatory State in Europe', *West European Politics* 17(3): 77–101.

Malaysian Environmental Official 2012. Senior Official, Ministry of Natural Resources and Environment, Malaysia. Interview by Lee Jones, 5 January, Putrajaya.

Martin, Randy, Rafferty, Michael and Bryan, Dick 2008. 'Financialization, Risk, and Labour', *Competition and Change* 12(2): 120–32.

Massey, Doreen 1992. 'Politics and Space/Time', *New Left Review* 196: 65–84.

Mathews, Jessica T. 1989. 'Redefining Security', *Foreign Affairs* 68(2): 162–77.

Matthew, Ed and van Gelder, Jan Willem 2002. 'Paper Tiger, Hidden Dragons 2: April Fools', February. London: Friends of the Earth. www.foe.co.uk/sites/default/files/downloads/april_fools.pdf.

Matthew, Richard, Barnett, Jon, McDonald, Bryan and O'Brien, Karen (eds.) 2010. *Global Environmental Change and Human Security*. Cambridge: Massachusetts Institute of Technology Press.

Mattli, Walter and Woods, Ngaire (eds.) 2009. 'In Whose Benefit? Explaining Regulatory Change in Global Politics', in *The Politics of Global Regulation*, 1–43. Princeton: Princeton University Press.

Mayer, Judith 2006. 'Transboundary Perspectives on Managing Indonesia's Fires', *Journal of Environment and Development* 15(2): 202–23.

McCarthy, John F. 2006. *The Fourth Circle: A Political Ecology of Sumatra's Rainforest Frontier.* Stanford: Stanford University Press.

McCarthy, John F., Gillespie, Piers and Zen, Zahari 2012. 'Swimming Upstream: Local Indonesian Production Networks in "Globalized" Palm Oil Production', *World Development* 40(3): 555–69.

McCarthy, John and Zen, Zahari 2010. 'Regulating the Oil Palm Boom: Assessing the Effectiveness of Environmental Governance Approaches to Agro-industrial Pollution in Indonesia', *Law & Policy* 32(1): 153–79.

McCoy, Alfred 1972. *The Politics of Heroin in Southeast Asia.* New York: Harper and Row.

McDonagh, Ken and Heng, Yee-Kuang, in press. 'Managing Risk, the State and Political Economy in Historical Perspective', *International Politics* 52(2).

McDonald, Matt 2008. 'Securitization and the Construction of Security', *European Journal of International Relations* 14(4): 563–87.

2013. 'Discourses of Climate Security', *Political Geography* 33(1): 42–51.

McGrane, James 2011. FAO Representative to Indonesia. Interview by Shahar Hameiri, 20 July, Jakarta.

McInnes, Colin and Lee, Kelley 2006. 'Health, Security and Foreign Policy', *Review of International Studies* 32(1): 5–23.

McLeod, Anni 2010. 'Economics of Avian Influenza Management and Control in a World with Competing Agendas', *Avian Diseases* 54(s1): 374–9.

McSherry, Rodrick and Preechajarn, Sakchai 2005. 'Thailand Poultry and Products Annual, 2005', GAIN Report No. TH5092, September. Washington, D.C.: US Department of Agriculture Foreign Agricultural Service. http://apps.fas.usda.gov/gainfiles/200509/146130917.pdf.

Mearsheimer, John J. 1994/95. 'The False Promise of International Institutions', *International Security* 19(3): 5–49.

Meehan, Patrick 2011. 'Drugs, Insurgency, and State-Building in Burma: Why the Drugs Trade is Central to Burma's Changing Political Order', *Journal of Southeast Asian Studies* 42(3): 376–404.

Mera, Floyd Ray 2012. Manager, Vanuatu Financial Intelligence Unit. Interview by Shahar Hameiri, 20 November, Port Vila.

Meridian, Abu 2011. Forest Campaigner, Telapak. Interview by Lee Jones, 7 December, Jakarta.

Merry, Sally E. 2006. 'Transnational Human Rights and Local Activism: Mapping the Middle', *American Anthropologist* 108(1): 38–51.

Mert, Ayşem 2013. 'Discursive Interplay and Co-Constitution: Carbonification of Environmental Discourses', in Chris Methmann, Delf Rothe and Benjamin Stephan (eds.) *Interpretive Approaches to Global Governance: (De)constructing the Greenhouse*, 23–39. Abingdon: Routledge.

Methmann, Chris and Rothe, Delf 2013. 'Apocalypse Now! From Exceptional Rhetoric to Risk Management in Global Climate Politics', in Chris Methmann, Delf Rothe and Benjamin Stephan (eds.) *Interpretive Approaches to Global Governance: (De)constructing the Greenhouse*, 105–21. Abingdon: Routledge.

Methmann, Chris, Rothe, Delf and Stephan, Benjamin (eds.) 2013a. *Interpretive Approaches to Global Governance: (De)constructing the Greenhouse*. Abingdon: Routledge.

Methmann, Chris, Rothe, Delf and Stephan, Benjamin 2013b. 'Introduction: Why and How to Deconstruct the Greenhouse', in Chris Methmann, Delf Rothe and Benjamin Stephan (eds.) *Interpretive Approaches to Global Governance: (De)constructing the Greenhouse*, 1–22. Abingdon: Routledge.

2013c. 'Reflections', in Chris Methmann, Delf Rothe and Benjamin Stephan (eds.) *Interpretive Approaches to Global Governance: (De)constructing the Greenhouse*, 248–56. Abingdon: Routledge.

Meyer, Gary and Preechajarn, Sakchai 2006. 'Thailand Poultry and Products Annual, 2006', GAIN Report No. TH6086, 1 September. Washington, D.C.: US Department of Agriculture Foreign Agricultural Service. http://apps.fas.usda.gov/gainfiles/200609/146208842.pdf.

Migdal, Joel S. 2001. *State in Society: Studying How States and Societies Transform and Constitute One Another*. New York: Cambridge University Press.

Milieudefensie 2009. *Sanctioned But Not Stopped*. Amsterdam: Friends of the Earth.

Miller, Byron 2009. 'Is Scale a Chaotic Concept? Notes on Processes of Scale Production', in Roger Keil and Rianne Mahon (eds.) *Leviathan Undone? Towards a Political Economy of Scale*, 51–66. Vancouver: University of British Columbia Press.

Minogue, Martin and Cariño, Ledivina (eds.) 2005. *Regulatory Governance in Developing Countries*. Cheltenham: Edward Elgar.

Mische, Patricia M. 1989. 'Ecological Security and the Need to Reconceptualize Sovereignty', *Alternatives* 19(4): 389–427.

Misryiah 2011. Director of the Zoonotic Diseases Division, Indonesian Ministry of Health. Interview by Shahar Hameiri, 9 September, Jakarta.

Mit, Mambang 2011. Vice-Governor of Riau. Interview by Lee Jones, 9 December, Pekanbaru.

Mittelman, James M. 2010. *Hyperconflict: Globalization and Insecurity*. Stanford: Stanford University Press.

MNRE Official 2012. Senior Official, Ministry of Natural Resources and Environment, Malaysia. Interview by Lee Jones, 5 January, Putrajaya.

MoE [Ministry of Environment] 2011. 'SOP Pencegahan Dan Penanggulangan Kebakaran Hutan Dan Lahan Di Indonesia [SOP to Prevent and Tackle Forest and Land Fires in Indonesia]', on file with authors. Jakarta: MoE.

MoF [Ministry of Forestry] n.d. 'Overview of Forest Fire Control Programs and Activities', on file with authors. Jakarta: MoF.

Moon, Chung-in and Chun, Chaesung 2003. 'Sovereignty: Dominance of the Westphalian Concept and Implications for Regional Security', in Muthia Alagappa (ed.) *Asian Security Order: Instrumental and Normative Features*, 106–37. Stanford: Stanford University Press.

Mubarok, Zainal and Rudiansyah 2011. Field Organiser and Deputy Director, WALHI Jambi. Interview by Lee Jones, 16 December, Jambi.

Mulyanto 2011. Secretary of the Agricultural Quarantine Unit, Indonesian Ministry of Agriculture. Interview by Shahar Hameiri, 22 July, Jakarta.

Murdiyarso, Daniel and Adiningsih, E.S. 2007. 'Climate Anomalies, Indonesian Vegetation Fires and Terrestrial Carbon Emissions', *Mitigation and Adaptation Strategies for Global Change* 12(1): 101–12.

Murphy, Craig N. 2000. 'Global Governance: Poorly Done and Poorly Understood', *International Affairs* 76(4): 789–804.

Muslim 2011. Coordinator, Jikalahari. Interview by Lee Jones, 8 December, Pekanbaru.

Mya Maung 1998. *The Burma Road to Capitalism: Economic Growth Versus Democracy*. Westport: Praeger.

Nagata, Junji and Arai, Sachicho W. 2013. 'Evolutionary Change in the Oil Palm Plantation Sector in Riau Province, Sumatra', in Oliver Pye and Jayati Battacharya (eds.) *The Palm Oil Controversy in Southeast Asia: A Transnational Perspective*, 76–96. Singapore: ISEAS.

Naiyaga, Inia 2012. Deputy Governor, Reserve Bank of Fiji. Interview by Shahar Hameiri, 9 May, Suva.

NaRanong, Viroj 2007. 'Structural Changes in Thailand's Poultry Sector and Its Social Implications', Presented at the Conference on Poultry in the 21st Century: Avian Influenza and Beyond, Food and Agriculture Organization, 5–7 November. Rome.

NATO [North Atlantic Treaty Organization] 2010. *Active Engagement, Modern Defence: Strategic Concept for the Defence and Security of the Members of the North Atlantic Treaty Organization*. Brussels: NATO Public Diplomacy Division, www.nato.int/strategic-concept/pdf/Strat_Concept_web_en.pdf.

Navias, Martin S. 2002. 'Financial Warfare as a Response to International Terrorism', *The Political Quarterly* 73(s1): 57–79.

Naylor, R.T. 2004. *Wages of Crime: Black Markets, Illegal Finance, and the Underworld Economy*, Revised edn. Ithaca and London: Cornell University Press.

NEA [National Environment Agency] 2009. *Indonesia-Singapore Collaboration to Deal with Land and Forest Fires in Jambi Province*. Singapore: NEA.

Neal, Andrew 2009. 'Securitization and Risk at the EU Border: The Origins of Frontex', *Journal of Common Market Studies* 47(2): 333–56.

Neumann, Ivor B. 2002. 'Returning Practice to the Linguistic Turn: The Case of Diplomacy', *Millennium* 31(3): 627–51.

Newell, Peter and Paterson, Matthew 2010. *Climate Capitalism: Global Warming and the Transformation of the Global Economy*. Cambridge: Cambridge University Press.

Normile, Dennis 2007. 'Indonesia Taps Village Wisdom to Fight Bird Flu', *Science* 315(5808): 30–33.

Oels, Angela 2012. 'From "Securitization" of Climate Change to "Climatization" of the Security Field: Comparing Three Theoretical Perspectives', in Jürgen Scheffran, Michael Brzoska, Peter M. Link and Janpeter Schilling (eds.) *Climate Change, Human Security, and Violent Conflict: Challenges to Societal Stability*, 185–205. Berlin: Springer.

Oktavia, Rita and Suryono 2011. Community Involvement and Empowerment Officers, Jambi Province Environmental Agency. Interview by Lee Jones, 16 December, Jambi.

Olbrei, Erik 2013. 'Indonesia Sets a Carbon Time Bomb', *The Conversation*, 25 September. http://theconversation.com/indonesia-sets-a-carbon-time-bomb-17216.

Ong, Aihwa 2006. *Neoliberalism as Exception: Mutations in Citizenship and Sovereignty*. Durham: Duke University Press.

Oon, Chiam Keng 2010. 'Role of ASEAN Specialised Meteorological Centre in Regional Haze Monitoring', Presented at Technical Workshop on the Development of the ASEAN Peatland Fire Prediction and Warning System, 13 July. Kuala Lumpur.

Overbeek, Henk 2005. 'Global Governance, Class, Hegemony: A Historical Materialist Perspective', in Alice Ba and Matthew J. Hoffmann (eds.) *Contending Perspectives on Global Governance: Coherence, Contestation, and World Order*, 39–56. Abingdon and New York: Routledge.

Page, Susan E., Siegert, Florian, Rieley, John O., Boehm, Hans-Dieter V., Jaya, Adi and Limin, Suwido 2002. 'The Amount of Carbon Released from Peat and Forest Fires in Indonesia During 1997', *Nature* 420: 61–5.

Palan, Ronen, Murphy, Richard and Chavagneux, Christian 2010. *Tax Havens: How Globalization Really Works*. Ithaca: Cornell University Press.

Panitch, Leo V. and Gindin, Sam 2012. *The Making of Global Capitalism: The Political Economy of American Empire*. London: Verso.

Paoli, Letizia, Greenfield, Victoria A. and Reuter, Peter 2009. *The World Heroin Market: Can Supply Be Cut?* Oxford: Oxford University Press.

Papadopoulos, Yannis 2007. 'Problems of Democratic Accountability in Network and Multilevel Governance', *European Law Journal* 13(4): 469–86.

Parish, Faizal 2012. Director, Global Environment Centre/ Senior Technical Advisor, ASEAN Peatland Forests Project. Interview by Lee Jones, 4 January, Kuala Lumpur.

Pasuk, Phongpaichit and Baker, Chris 2004. *Thaksin: The Business of Politics in Thailand*. Copenhagen: NIAS.

Paterson, Matthew and Grubb, Michael 1992. 'The International Politics of Climate Change', *International Affairs* 68(2): 293–313.

Peck, Jamie 2002. 'Political Economies of Scale: Fast Policy, Interscalar Relations and Neoliberal Workfare', *Economic Geography* 78(3): 331–60.

Pellerin, Cheryl 2006. 'Donors Pledge Nearly $500 million to Avian Flu Fight', 8 December, USINFO. http://iipdigital.usembassy.gov/st/english/article/2006/12/20061208145536lcnirellep2.494448e-02.html#axzz3GUkBiBJq.

Pennisi di Floristella, Angela 2013. 'Are Non-traditional Security Challenges Leading Regional Organizations Towards Greater Convergence? The EU and ASEAN Security Systems in Comparative Perspective', *Asia Europe Journal* 11(3): 21–38.

Perry, Brian, Isa, Kamarudin Md. and Tarazona, Carlos 2009. *Independent Evaluation of FAO's Participatory Disease Surveillance and Response Programme in Indonesia*. Rome: United Nations Food and Agriculture Organization.

Pew Research Center 2007. 'World Publics Welcome Global Trade – But Not Immigration', 47-Nation Pew Global Attitudes Survey, 4 October. Washington, D.C.: Pew Research Center. www.pewglobal.org/2007/10/04/world-publics-welcome-global-trade-but-not-immigration/.

    2010. 'Obama More Popular Abroad Than At Home, Global Image of U.S. Continues to Benefit', *22-Nation Pew Global Attitudes Survey*, 17 June. Washington, D.C.: Pew Research Center. www.pewglobal.org/2010/06/17/obama-more-popular-abroad-than-at-home/.

Pierre, Jon and Peters, B. Guy 2005. *Governing Complex Societies: Trajectories and Scenarios*. Basingstoke: Palgrave Macmillan.

Poulantzas, Nicos 1978. *State, Power, Socialism*. London and New York: Verso.

Price, Richard 1997. *The Chemical Weapons Taboo*. New York: Cornell University Press.

Prins, Gwyn (ed.) 1993. *Threats Without Enemies: Facing Environmental Security*. London: Earthscan.

Provine, Doris M. 2007. *Unequal Under the Law: Race in the War on Drugs*. Chicago: Chicago University Press.

Qadri, S. Tahir (ed.) 2001. *Fire, Smoke and Haze: The ASEAN Response Strategy*. Manila: Asian Development Bank.

Quantum Indonesia Translogistic 2011. 'Indonesian CPO Exports Value Reached US$ 16.4 Billion in 2010', http://quantumindonesia.blogspot.co.uk/2011/01/indonesian-cpo-exports-value-reached-us.html.

Rahardjo, Tri Siswo 2011. Head of Natural Resources Conservation Agency, Ministry of Forestry, Jambi Province. Interview by Lee Jones, 19 December, Jambi.

Rajkovic, Nikolas M. 2012. '"Global Law" and Governmentality: Reconceptualizing the "Rule of Law" as Rule "Through" Law', *European Journal of International Relations* 18(1): 29–52.

Ratananakorn, L. and Wilson, D. 2011. 'Zoning and Compartmentalisation as Risk Mitigation Measures: An Example from Poultry Production', *Revue Scientifique et Technique – Office International des Epizooties* 30(1): 297–307.

Rawlings, Gregory E. 1999. 'Villages, Islands, and Tax Havens: The Global/Local Implications of a Financial Entrepôt in Vanuatu', *Canberra Anthropology* 22(2): 37–50.

2005. 'English Laws and Global Money Markets: The Rise of the Vanuatu Tax Haven', Centre for Tax System Integrity Series, Working Paper No. 61, January. Canberra: Australian National University, Regulatory Institutions Network. http://regnet.anu.edu.au/sites/default/files/CTSI-WorkingPaper61-full.pdf.

2007. 'Taxes and Transnational Treaties: Responsive Regulation and the Reassertion of Offshore Sovereignty', *Law & Policy* 29(1): 51–66.

Reich, Simon and Lebow, Richard Ned 2014. *Good-Bye Hegemony!: Power and Influence in the Global System*. Princeton: Princeton University Press.

Rhee, Steve, Kitchener, Darrell, Brown, Tim, Merrill, Reed, Dilts, Russ and Tighe, Stacey 2004. 'Report on Biodiversity and Tropical Forests in Indonesia', 20 February. Jakarta: USAID.

Riau Forestry Official 2011. Provincial Forestry Official. Interview by Lee Jones, 9 December, Pekanbaru.

Rider, Barry A.K. 2004. 'Law: The War on Terror and Crime and the Offshore Centres: The "New" Perspective?', in Donato Masciandro (ed.) *Global Financial Crime*, 61–95. Aldershot: Ashgate.

Risse-Kappen, Thomas 1994. 'Ideas Do Not Float Freely: Transnational Coalitions, Domestic Politics, and the End of the Cold War', *International Organization* 48(2): 185–214.

Risse-Kappen, Thomas, Ropp, Stephen C. and Sikkink, Kathryn (eds.) 1999. *The Power of Human Rights: International Norms and Domestic Change*. New York: Cambridge University Press.

2013. *The Persistent Power of Human Rights: From Commitment to Compliance*. Cambridge: Cambridge University Press.

Rittberger, Volker and Mayer, Peter (eds.) 1995. *Regime Theory and International Relations*. Oxford: Oxford University Press.

Roemer-Mahler, Anne 2013. 'Business Conflict and Global Politics: The Pharmaceutical Industry and the Global Protection of Intellectual Property Rights', *Review of International Political Economy* 20(1): 121–52.

Rosenau, James N. 2007. 'Governing the Ungovernable: The Challenge of a Global Disaggregation of Authority', *Regulation & Governance* 1(1): 88–97.

Ross, Michael L. 2001. *Timber Booms and Institutional Breakdown in Southeast Asia*. Cambridge: Cambridge University Press.

Rothe, Delf 2011. 'Managing Climate Risks or Risking a Managerial Climate: State, Security, and Governance in the International Climate Regime', *International Relations* 25(3): 330–45.

Rudd, Kevin 2008. 'First National Security Statement to the Australian Parliament', Speech to the Parliament by the Prime Minister, 4 December. http://www.royalcommission.vic.gov.au/getdoc/596cc5ff-8a33-47eb-8d4a-9205131ebdd0/TEN.004.002.0437.pdf.

Rudolph, Lloyd and Rudolph, Susanne 2001. 'Redoing the Constitutional Design: From an Interventionist to a Regulatory State', in Atul Kohli (ed.) *The Success of India's Democracy*, 127–62. Cambridge: Cambridge University Press.

Rushton, Simon 2011. 'Global Health Security: Security for Whom? Security from What?', *Political Studies* 59(4): 779–96.

Safman, Rachel M. 2010. 'Avian Influenza Control in Thailand: Balancing the Interests of Different Poultry Producers', in Ian Scoones (ed.) *Avian Influenza: Science, Policy and Politics*, 169–206. London: Earthscan.

Saharjo, Bambang Hero 2011. Dean, Faculty of Forestry, Bogor Agricultural University. Interview by Lee Jones, 20 December, Bogor.

Sanders, Bradford 2012. Safety and Aviation Manager, Asia-Pacific Resources International Limited. Telephone Interview by Lee Jones, 5 January.

Sandor, Adam 2014. 'Border Security and Drug-Trafficking in West Africa: Global Security Assemblages and AIRCOP', Presented at the Convention for the International Studies Association, 26–29 March. Toronto.

Sarsito, Agus 2011. Director of International Cooperation, Ministry of Forestry, Indonesia. Interview by Lee Jones, 13 December, Jakarta.

Suwandono, Agus 2011. *National Institute for Health Research*. Interview by Shahar Hameiri, 18 July, Jakarta.

Sassen, Saskia 2014. 'When the Global Inhabits the National: Fuzzy Interactions', in Stephen Gill and A. Claire Cutler (eds.) *New Constitutionalism and World Order*, 115–25. Cambridge: Cambridge University Press.

Scheffran, Jürgen 2010. 'Security Risks of Climate Change: Vulnerabilities, Threats, Conflicts and Strategies', in Hans-Gunter Brauch, Úrsula Oswald-Spring, Czeslaw Mesjasz, John Grin, Patricia Kameri-Mbote, Béchir Chourou, Pál Dunay and Jörn Birkmann (eds.) *Coping with Global Environmental Change, Disasters and Security: Threats, Challenges, Vulnerabilities and Risks*, 735–56. Berlin: Springer.

Scoones, Ian 2010. 'The International Response to Avian Influenza: Science, Policy and Politics', in Ian Scoones (ed.) *Avian Influenza: Science, Policy and Politics*, 1–18. London: Earthscan.

Scoones, Ian and Forster, Paul 2010. 'Unpacking the International Response to Avian Influenza: Actors, Networks and Narratives', in Ian Scoones (ed.) *Avian Influenza: Science, Policy and Politics*, 19–64. London: Earthscan.

Selth, Andrew 2000. *Burma's Secret Military Partners*. Canberra: ANU.

Sending, Ole Jacob and Neumann, Iver B. 2006. 'Governance to Governmentality: Analyzing NGOs, States, and Power', *International Studies Quarterly* 50(3): 651–72.

SHAN [Shan Herald Agency for News] 2003. 'Show Business: Rangoon's "War on Drugs" in Shan State', December. Chang Mai. www.shanland .org/oldversion/index-3160.htm.

Sharman, Jason C. 2005. 'South Pacific Tax Havens: From Leaders in the Race to the Bottom to Laggards in the Race to the Top?', *Accounting Forum* 29(3): 311–23.

2009. 'Privacy as Roguery: Personal Financial Information in an Age of Transparency', *Public Administration* 87(4): 717–31.

2010. 'Offshore and the New International Political Economy', *Review of International Political Economy* 17(1): 1–19.

2011a. *The Money Laundry: Regulating Criminal Finance in the Global Economy*. Ithaca: Cornell University Press.

2011b. 'Testing the Global Financial Transparency Regime', *International Studies Quarterly* 55(4): 981–1001.

Sharman, Jason C. and Mistry, Percy S. 2008. *Considering the Consequences: The Development Implications of Initiatives on Taxation, Anti-money Laundering, and Combating the Financing of Terrorism.* London: Commonwealth Secretariat.

Sharman, Jason C. and Rawlings, Gregory E. 2006. 'National Tax Blacklists: A Comparative Analysis', *Journal of International Taxation* 17(9): 38–47, 64.

Shaw, Howard 2011. Former Executive Director, Singapore Environment Council. Interview by Lee Jones, 30 November, Singapore.

Shaxson, Nicholas 2011. *Treasure Islands: Tax Havens and the Men Who Stole the World.* London: Vintage Books.

Sheil, Douglas, Casson, Anne, Meijaard, Erik, Van Noordwjik, Meine, Gaskell, Joanne, Sunderland-Groves, Jacqui, Wertz, Karah and Kanninen, Markku 2009. 'The Impacts and Opportunities of Oil Palm in Southeast Asia: What Do We Know and What Do We Need to Know?', CIFOR Occasional Paper No. 51. Bogor: CIFOR.

Shields, Peter 2005. 'When the "Information Revolution" and the US Security State Collide', *New Media and Society* 7(4): 483–512.

Schröder, Ursula 2011. *The Organization of European Security Governance: Internal and External Security in Transition.* London: Routledge.

Sidel, John T. 2004. 'Bossism and Democracy in the Philippines, Thailand and Indonesia: Towards an Alternative Framework for the Study of "Local Strongmen"', in John Harriss, Kristian Stokke and Olle Tornquist (eds.) *Politicising Democracy: The New Local Politics of Democratization*, 51–74. New York: Palgrave Macmillan.

Sijabat, Ridwan M. 2006. 'Environment Minister Warns of Haze's Serious Effects', *Jakarta Post*, 10 October. www.thejakartapost.com/news/2006/10/10/environment-minister-warns-haze039s-serious-effects.html.

Simmons, Beth 2000. 'International Efforts Against Money Laundering', in Dinah Shelton (ed.) *Commitment and Compliance: The Role of Nonbinding Norms in the International Legal System*, 244–63. Oxford: Oxford University Press.

Sipress, Alan 2005. 'On Front Lines of Asian Battle Against Bird Flu', *The Washington Post*, 22 May. www.washingtonpost.com/wp-dyn/content/article/2005/05/21/AR2005052100908.html.

Siti Fadilah Supari 2011. Former Indonesian Health Minister. Interview by Shahar Hameiri, 25 July, Jakarta.

Sizer, Nigel, Stolle, Fred, Minnemeyer, Susan, Anderson, James, Alisjahbana, Ariana, Putraditama, Andika and Johnston, Lisa 2013. 'Peering

Through the Haze: What Data Can Tell Us About the Fires in Indonesia', 21 June, World Resources Institute. www.wri.org/blog/2013/06/peering-through-haze-what-data-can-tell-us-about-fires-indonesia.

Slaughter, Anne-Marie 1997. 'The Real New World Order', *Foreign Affairs* 76(5): 183–97.

2004. *A New World Order*. Princeton: Princeton University Press.

Smith, Paul J. 2001. 'East Asia's Transnational Challenges: The Dark Side of Globalization', in Julian Weiss (ed.) *Tigers' Roar: Asia's Recovery and Its Impact*, 11–22. Armonk: ME Sharpe.

2007. 'Climate Change, Mass Migration and the Military Response', *Orbis* 51(4): 617–33.

Snyder, Richard 2006. 'Does Lootable Wealth Breed Disorder? A Political Economy of Extraction Framework', *Comparative Political Studies* 39(8): 943–68.

Sørensen, Georg 2004. *The Transformation of the State: Beyond the Myth of Retreat*. Basingstoke and New York: Palgrave Macmillan.

Sperling, James and Webber, Mark 2014. 'Security Governance in Europe: A Return to System', *European Security* 23(2): 126–44.

Stafford, Mark 2012. Partner, Barrett and Partners Chartered Accountants and Business Advisors, and Chairman, Financial Centre Association of Vanuatu. Interview by Shahar Hameiri, 26 November, Port Vila.

State Department 2006. 'Avian Influenza: International Partnership to Meet a Global Threat', 4 April. Washington, D.C.: US Department of State.

Sterling-Folker, Jennifer 2005. 'Realist Global Governance: Revisiting "Cave! hic Dragones" and Beyond', in Alice Ba and Matthew J. Hoffmann (eds.) *Contending Perspectives on Global Governance: Coherence, Contestation, and World Order*, 17–38. Abingdon and New York: Routledge.

Stern, Nicholas 2007. *The Economics of Climate Change: The Stern Review*. Cambridge: Cambridge University Press.

Stevenson, Michael A. and Cooper, Andrew F. 2009. 'Overcoming Constraints of State Sovereignty: Global Health Governance in Asia', *Third World Quarterly* 30(7): 1379–94.

Stilwell, Frank and Jordan, Kirrily 2007. *Who Gets What? Analysing Economic Inequality in Australia*. Melbourne: Cambridge University Press.

Stritzel, Holger 2007. 'Towards a Theory of Securitization: Copenhagen and Beyond', *European Journal of International Relations* 13(3): 357–83.

Su, Xiaobo 2012. 'Rescaling the Chinese State and Regionalization in the Great Mekong Subregion', *Review of International Political Economy* 19(3): 501–27.

Sulistowati 2011. Director for Climate Change Mitigation and Ozone Layer Protection, Ministry of Environment. Interview by Lee Jones, 21 December, Jakarta.

Sumarjo 2011. Head of Tebo District Forestry Office. Interview by Lee Jones, 19 December, Jambi.

Sumiarto, Bambang and Arifin, Bustanul 2008. 'Overview on Poultry Sector and HPAI Situation for Indonesia with Special Emphasis on the Island of Java – Background Paper', DFID Africa/Indonesia Region Report No. 3, 6 October. Rome and Nairobi: DFID. www.ifpri.org/sites/default/ files/publications/hpairr03_indonesia.pdf

Swain, Ashok 2013. *Understanding Emerging Security Challenges: Threats and Opportunities*. Abingdon and New York: Routledge.

Swyngedouw, Erik 2005. 'Governance Innovation and the Citizen: The Janus Face of Governance-Beyond-the-State', *Urban Studies* 42(11): 1991–2006.

Tacconi, Luca 2003. 'Fires in Indonesia: Causes, Costs and Policy Implications', CIFOR Occasional Paper No. 38. Bogor: CIFOR. www.cifor .org/fire/pdf/pdf23.pdf

Tacconi, Luca, Moore, Peter F. and Kaimowitz, Damien 2007. 'Fires in Tropical Forests – What is Really the Problem? Lessons from Indonesia', *Mitigation and Adaptation Strategies for Global Change* 12(1): 55–66.

Tan, Alan Khee-Jin 2005. 'The ASEAN Agreement on Transboundary Haze Pollution: Prospects for Compliance and Effectiveness in Post-Suharto Indonesia', *New York University Environmental Law Journal* 13(3): 647–722.

Tannenwald, Nina 2005. *The Nuclear Taboo: The United States and the Non-use of Nuclear Weapons Since 1945*. Cambridge: Cambridge University Press.

Tanpidau, Frans 2011. Head of Forest Protection, Provincial Forestry Office, Jambi Province. Interview by Lee Jones, 19 December, Jambi.

Tarigan, Abetnego 2011. Executive Director, Sawit Watch. Interview by Lee Jones, 20 December, Bogor.

Taufa, Albert and Tamaru, Douglas 2012. Transparency Vanuatu. Interview by Shahar Hameiri, 22 November, Port Vila.

Tavares, Rodrigo 2010. *Regional Security: The Capacity of International Organizations*. New York and London: Routledge.

Tavoa, Kayleen 2012. Director, Vanuatu Department of Public Prosecutions. Interview by Shahar Hameiri, 21 November, Port Vila.

Tay, Simon S.C. 2002. 'Fires and Haze in Southeast Asia', in Pamela J. Noda (ed.) *Cross-Sectoral Partnerships in Enhancing Human Security*, 53–80. Tokyo: Japan Center for International Exchange.

Tebu, Smith 2012. Chief Executive Officer, Vanuatu Investment Promotion Authority. Interview by Shahar Hameiri, 21 November, Port Vila.

Teoh, Cheng Hai 2013. 'Malaysian Corporations as Strategic Players in Southeast Asia's Palm Oil Industry', in Oliver Pye and Jayati

Battacharya (eds.) 2013. *The Palm Oil Controversy in Southeast Asia: A Transnational Perspective*, 19–47. Singapore: ISEAS.

Tha Than Oo 2012. Executive Committee Member, Myanmar Federated Chambers of Commerce and Industry. Interview by Lee Jones, 20 July, Yangon.

Thamrin, Husni 2011. Director of PINSE. Interview by Lee Jones, 17 December, Jambi.

Thiha Saw 2012. Editor-in-Chief, *Open News* and *Myanma Dana*. Interview by Lee Jones, 24 July, Yangon.

Thomas, Nicholas 2006. 'The Regionalization of Avian Influenza in East Asia: Responding to the Next Pandemic(?)', *Asian Survey* 46(6): 917–36.

Thomson, James 2012. 'The ATO's Big New Target: Tax Havens', *Crikey*, 24 July. www.crikey.com.au/2012/07/24/the-atos-big-new-target-tax-havens/.

Tilly, Charles 1992. *Coercion, Capital, and European States AD 990–1992*. Malden: Blackwell.

Toka, Edmond Rengacki 2012. Liquidation and Legal Officer, Insolvency, Legal, Enforcement, and Compliance Department, Vanuatu Financial Services Commission. Interview by Shahar Hameiri, 27 November, Port Vila.

TNI [Transnational Institute] 2011. *Financing Dispossession: China's Opium Substitution Programme in Northern Burma*. Amsterdam: Transnational Institute.

Tun Myint 2012. *Governing International Rivers: Polycentric Politics in the Mekong and the Rhine*. Cheltenham: Edward Elgar.

Turnell, Sean 2003. 'Myanmar's Banking Crisis', *ASEAN Economic Bulletin* 20(3): 272–82.

2006. 'Burma's Economy 2004: Crisis Masking Stagnation', in Trevor Wilson (ed.) *Myanmar's Long Road to National Reconciliation*, 77–97. Singapore: ISEAS.

2009. *Fiery Dragons: Banks, Moneylenders, and Microfinance in Burma*. Copenhagen: Nordic Institute of Asian Studies Press.

2011. 'Fundamentals of Myanmar's Macroeconomy: A Political Economy Perspective', *Asian Economic Policy Review* 6(1): 136–53.

UK Government 2010. 'A Strong Britain in an Age of Uncertainty: The National Security Strategy', October. London: Prime Minister's Office. https://www.gov.uk/government/uploads/system/uploads/attachment_data/file/61936/national-security-strategy.pdf.

Ullman, Richard H. 1983. 'Redefining Security', *International Security* 8(1): 129–53.

UN [United Nations] 2004. *A More Secure World: Our Shared Responsibility*. New York: United Nations.

UNCTADstat 2013. http://unctadstat.unctad.org/EN/.

Underdal, Arild and Hanf, Kenneth (eds.) 2000. *International Environmental Agreements and Domestic Politics. The Case of Acid Rain.* Burlington: Ashgate.

UNDP [United Nations Development Programme] 1994. 'Human Development Report 1994', New York: Oxford University Press. http://hdr.undp.org/sites/default/files/reports/255/hdr_1994_en_complete_nostats.pdf.

Unger, Brigitte and Rawlings, Gregory E. 2008. 'Competing for Criminal Money', *Global Business and Economics Review* 10(3): 331–52.

US DoD [United States Department of Defense] 2010a. 'Nuclear Posture Review Report', April. Washington, D.C.: US Department of Defense. www.defense.gov/npr/docs/2010%20nuclear%20posture%20review%20report.pdf.

2010b. 'Quadrennial Defense Review Report 2010', February. Washington, D.C.: US Department of Defense. www.defense.gov/qdr/images/QDR_as_of_12Feb10_1000.pdf.

US Embassy 2003a. 'New Money Laundering Sanctions Could Be Useful', Reference ID 03Rangoon1317, 21 October, Yangon. Wikileaks. http://wikileaks.org/cable/2003/10/03RANGOON1317.html.

2003b. 'Burma: No Progress on Money Laundering Rules', Reference ID 03Rangoon1253, 1 October, Yangon. Wikileaks. http://wikileaks.org/cable/2003/10/03RANGOON1253.html.

2004. 'The Burmese Regime Airs its Dirty Laundry: Former PM "Corrupt and Insubordinate"', Reference ID 04Rangoon1482, 12 November, Yangon. Wikileaks. http://wikileaks.org/cable/2004/11/04RANGOON1462.html.

2005. 'The State Takes over another Private Bank in Burma', Reference ID 05Rangoon924, 10 August, Yangon. Wikileaks. http://wikileaks.org/cable/2005/08/05RANGOON924.html.

2007. 'Burma: How the Well Connected Make Money', Reference ID 07Rangoon114, 1 February, Yangon. Wikileaks. http://wikileaks.org/cable/2007/02/07RANGOON114.html.

2008. 'Top Cronies Feeling the Pinch of US Sanctions', Reference ID 08Rangoon222, 25 March, Yangon. Wikileaks. http://wikileaks.org/cable/2008/03/08RANGOON222.html.

USAID 2009. 'Commercial Poultry Private Sector Partnership Program, Year One', Community-based Avian Influenza Control Project, 11 November. United States Agency for International Development. Jakarta. https://www.k4health.org/sites/default/files/CBAIC_2009_PSPYr1_Report.pdf.

Usman, Hariansyah 2011. Executive Director, Walhi Riau. Interview by Lee Jones, 10 December, Penkanbaru.

Valverde, Mariana and Mopas, Michael 2004. 'Insecurity and the Dream of Targeted Governance', in Wendy Larner and William Walters (eds.) *Global Governmentality: Governing International Spaces*, 233–50. London and New York: Routledge.

van Apeldoorn, Bastiaan 2002. *Transnational Capitalism and the Struggle over European Integration*. London: Routledge.

van Apeldoorn, Bastiaan, Overbeek, Henk and Nölke, Andreas 2007. *The Transnational Politics of Corporate Governance Regulation*. London: Routledge.

van der Pijl, Kees 1998. *Transnational Classes and International Relations*. London: Routledge.

  2012. *The Making of an Atlantic Ruling Class*. London: Verso.

van der Pijl, Kees, Assassi, Libby and Wigan, Duncan (eds.) 2004. *Global Regulation: Managing Crises After the Imperial Turn*. Basingstoke: Palgrave Macmillan.

van Fossen, Anthony 2002. 'Offshore Financial Centres and Internal Development in the Pacific Islands', *Pacific Economic Bulletin* 17(1): 38–62.

  2003. 'Money Laundering, Global Financial Instability, and Tax Havens in the Pacific Islands', *The Contemporary Pacific* 15(2): 237–75.

  2012. *Tax Havens and Sovereignty in the Pacific Islands*. St Lucia: University of Queensland Press.

van Heeswijk, Laura 2010. 'Combating Illegal Logging: The EU-FLEGT Action Plan. A Discourse Analysis of the Development of a Legality-Definition Between and Within the European Union and Indonesia', MA Thesis, Wageningen University.

Vandeweerd, Veerle, Glemarec, Yannick and Caballero, Vivienne 2011. 'Climate Change and Development: UNDP's Approach to Helping Countries Build a New Paradigm', in Hans Günter Brauch, Úrsula Oswald Spring, Czeslaw Mesjasz, John Grin, Patricia Kameri-Mbote, Béchir Chourou, Pal Dunay and Jörn Birkmann (eds.) *Coping with Global Environmental Change, Disasters and Security: Threats, Challenges, Vulnerabilities and Risks*, 1303–18. Springer: Berlin.

Vari, Noel N. 2012. Director, Financial Institutions Supervision Department, Reserve Bank of Vanuatu. Interview by Shahar Hameiri, 28 November, Port Vila.

Varkkey, Helena 2012. 'Patronage Politics as a Driver of Economic Regionalisation: The Indonesian Oil Palm Sector and Transboundary Haze', *Asia Pacific Viewpoint* 53(3): 314–29.

  2013a. 'Patronage Politics, Plantation Fires and Transboundary Haze', *Environmental Hazards* 12(3–4): 200–217.

2013b. 'Malaysian Investors in the Indonesian Oil Palm Plantation Sector: Home State Facilitation and Transboundary Haze', *Asia Pacific Business Review* 19(3): 381–401.

2013c. 'Oil Palm Plantations and Transboundary Haze: Patronage Networks and Land Licensing in Indonesia's Peatlands', *Wetlands* 33(4): 679–90.

2014. 'Regional Cooperation, Patronage and the ASEAN Agreement on Transboundary Haze Pollution', *International Environmental Agreements* 14(1): 65–81.

Vibert, Frank 2007. *The Rise of the Unelected: Democracy and the New Separation of Powers*. Cambridge: Cambridge University Press.

Victor, D.G., Raustiala, K. and Skolnikoff, E.B. (eds.) 1998. *International Environmental Commitments. Theory and Practice*. Cambridge: Massachusetts Institute of Technology Press.

Vu, Tuong 2011. 'Epidemics as Politics with Case-Studies from Malaysia, Thailand, and Vietnam', *Global Health Governance* 4(2): 1–22.

Wæver, Ole 1995. 'Securitization and Desecuritization', in Ronnie D. Lipschutz (ed.) *On Security*, 46–86. New York: Columbia University Press.

2011. 'Politics, Security, Theory', *Security Dialogue* 42(5): 465–80.

Wagnsson, Charlotte, Sperling, James and Hallenberg, Jan (eds.) 2009. *European Security Governance: The European Union in a Westphalian World*. Abingdon and New York: Routledge.

Wahyu Santoso and Ritanugraini 2011. Banten Provincial Government Health *Dinas* officials. Interview by Shahar Hameiri, 8 September, Serang, Banten.

Wakker, Eric 2005. *Greasy Palms: The Social and Ecological Impacts of Large-scale Oil Palm Plantation Development in Southeast Asia*. London: Friends of the Earth. www.foe.co.uk/sites/default/files/downloads/greasy_palms_impacts.pdf.

Walt, Stephen M. 1991. 'The Renaissance of Security Studies', *International Studies Quarterly* 35(2): 211–39.

Walter, Andrew 2008. *Governing Finance: East Asia's Adoption of International Standards*. Ithaca and London: Cornell University Press.

Wapner, Paul 1996. *Environmental Activism and World Civic Politics*. Albany: State University of New York Press.

Webber, Mark, Croft, Stuart, Howorth, Jolyon, Terriff, Terry and Krahmann, Elke 2004. 'The Governance of European Security', *Review of International Studies* 30(1): 3–26.

Weber, Katja 2011. 'Lessons from the ASEAN Regional Forum: Transcending the Image of Paper Tiger?', in Emil J. Kirchner and Roberto Dominguez (eds.) *The Security Governance of Regional Organizations*, 219–42. Abingdon: Routledge.

Webersik, Christian 2010. *Climate Change and Security: A Gathering Storm of Global Challenges*. Santa Barbara: Praeger.

WEF [World Economic Forum] 2006. *Global Risks 2006*. A World Economic Forum Report. Geneva. www.weforum.org/pdf/CSI/Global_Risk_Report.pdf.

Weiss, Thomas G. 2013. *Global Governance: Why? What? Whither?* Cambridge: Polity.

Weiss, Thomas G. and Wilkinson, Rorden 2014. 'Rethinking Global Governance? Complexity, Authority, Power, Change', *International Studies Quarterly* 58(1): 207–15.

Wendt, Alexander 1999. *Social Theory of International Relations*. Cambridge: Cambridge University Press.

    2004. 'The State as Person in International Theory', *Review of International Studies* 30(2): 289–316.

Westing, Arthur H. 1986. *Global Resources and International Conflict: Environmental Factors in Strategic Policy and Action*. Oxford: Oxford University Press.

White House 1998. 'A National Security Strategy for a New Century', October. Washington, D.C.: The White House. www.fas.org/man/docs/nssr-98.pdf.

    2005. 'Fact Sheet: United States Leadership on Avian Influenza', 19 November. Washington, D.C.: State Department. http://2001-2009.state.gov/g/oes/rls/fs/57225.htm.

    2006. 'The National Security Strategy of the United States of America', March. Washington, D.C.: The White House. www.comw.org/qdr/fulltext/nss2006.pdf.

    2010. 'National Security Strategy of the United States', May. Washington, D.C.: The White House. www.whitehouse.gov/sites/default/files/rss_viewer/national_security_strategy.pdf.

WHO [World Health Organization] n.d.a. 'Cumulative Number of Confirmed Cases of Avian Influenza A(H5N1) Reported to the WHO'. Geneva: The World Health Organization. www.who.int/influenza/human_animal_interface/H5N1_cumulative_table_archives/en/.

    n.d.b. 'The WHO Department of Global Capacity: About', Geneva: World Health Organization. http://who.int/ihr/about/01_GCR_Department.pdf.

    2007. *The World Health Report 2007 – A Safer Future: Global Public Health Security in the 21st Century*. Geneva: World Health Organization.

WHO and Heymann, David L. 2007. *The World Health Report 2007: A Safer Future: Global Public Health Security in the 21st Century*. Geneva: World Health Organization.

Wiener, Antje 2008. *The Invisible Constitution of Politics. Contested Norms and International Encounters*. Cambridge: Cambridge University Press.

2009. 'Enacting Meaning in Use. Qualitative Research on Norms and International Relations', *Review of International Studies* 35(1): 175–93.

Wiku Adisasmito 2011. Director of Partnership and Business Incubator, University of Indonesia. Interview by Shahar Hameiri, 19 July, Depok, West Java.

Williams, David 2013. 'Development, Intervention, and International Order', *Review of International Studies* 39(5): 1213–31.

Williams, Michael C. 2003. 'Words, Images, Enemies: Securitization and International Politics', *International Studies Quarterly* 47(4): 511–31.

Wilson, Trevor 2010. 'The Use of Normative Processes in Achieving Behaviour Change in Myanmar', in Nick Cheesman, Monika Skidmore and Trevor Wilson (eds.) *Ruling Myanmar: From Cyclone Nargis to National Elections*, 294–318. Singapore: ISEAS.

Winer, Jonathan M. and Roule, Trifin J. 2002. 'Fighting Terrorist Finance', *Survival* 44(3): 87–104.

Wiwiek Bagja 2011. President of the Indonesian Veterinary Medicine Association. Interview by Shahar Hameiri, 21 July, Jakarta.

Wolf, Simon 2013. 'Climate Politics as Investment: Understanding Discourse Through Governmental Practice', in Chris Methmann, Delf Rothe and Benjamin Stephan (eds.) *Interpretive Approaches to Global Governance: (De)constructing the Greenhouse*, 43–56. Abingdon: Routledge.

Woods, Kevin 2011. 'Ceasefire Capitalism: Military-Private Partnerships, Resource Concessions, and Military-State Building in the Burma–China Borderlands', *Journal of Peasant Studies* 38(4): 747–70.

Woods, Ngaire and Narlikar, Amrita 2001. 'Governance and the Limits of Accountability: The WTO, the IMF and the World Bank', *International Social Science Journal* 53(170): 569–83.

World Bank 2008. *Responses to Avian Influenza and State of Pandemic Readiness Fourth Global Progress Report*. Washington, D.C.: World Bank.

World Growth 2011. 'The Economic Benefit of Palm Oil to Indonesia', February. http://worldgrowth.org/site/wp-content/uploads/2012/06/WG_Indonesian_Palm_Oil_Benefits_Report-2_11.pdf.

Wraith, Caroline and Stephenson, Niamh 2009. 'Risk, Insurance, Preparedness, and the Disappearance of the Population: The Case of Pandemic Influenza', *Health Sociology Review* 18(3): 220–33.

WWF [World Wildlife Fund] 2008. 'How Pulp & Paper and Palm Oil from Sumatra Increase Global Climate Change and Drive Tigers and

Elephants to Local Extinction', WWF Indonesia Technical Report, February. https://www.wwf.or.jp/activities/lib/pdf_forest/carbon/200 80227riau_co2_report_short.pdf.

Yacoob, Salahadin and Lee, Audrey 2012. Technical Director and Biodiversity and Conservation Manager, Round Table on Sustainable Palm Oil. Interview by Lee Jones, 6 January, Kuala Lumpur.

Yanga, Emmy A.B. 2013. 'Securitizing Climate Change in Southeast Asia', *Thamassat Review* 16(2): 81–97.

Yasmi, Yurdi, Anshari, Gusti Z., Komarudin, Heru and Alqadrie, Syarif 2006. 'Stakeholder Conflicts and Forest Decentralization Policies in West Kalimantan: Their Dynamics and Implications for Future Forest Management', *Forests, Trees and Livelihoods* 16: 167–80.

Yui, Michael 2010a. 'Transnational Organised Crime and the Threat to Strategic Stability: Part 2', *Asia Pacific Defence Reporter* 36(8): 26, 28–30.

2010b. 'Trends in Transnational Organised Crime in the Asia Pacific: Part 3', *Asia Pacific Defence Reporter* 36(9): 48–50.

Zheng, Yongnian 2004. *Globalization and State Transformation in China*. Cambridge: Cambridge University Press.

2007. *De Facto Federalism in China: Reforms and Dynamics of Central-Local Relations*. Singapore: World Scientific.

Zielonka, Jan 2007. *Europe as Empire: The Nature of the Enlarged European Union*. Oxford: Oxford University Press.

Zukarnian, Kassim 2012. Training Director, Malaysian Fire and Rescue Service. Interview by Lee Jones, 4 January, Kuala Lumpur.

Zulfahmi 2011. Forest Campaign Team Leader, Greenpeace Southeast Asia. Interview by Lee Jones, 13 December, Jakarta.

Zürn, Michael 2004. 'Global Governance and Legitimacy Problems', *Government and Opposition* 39(2): 260–87.

Index